SNAKE

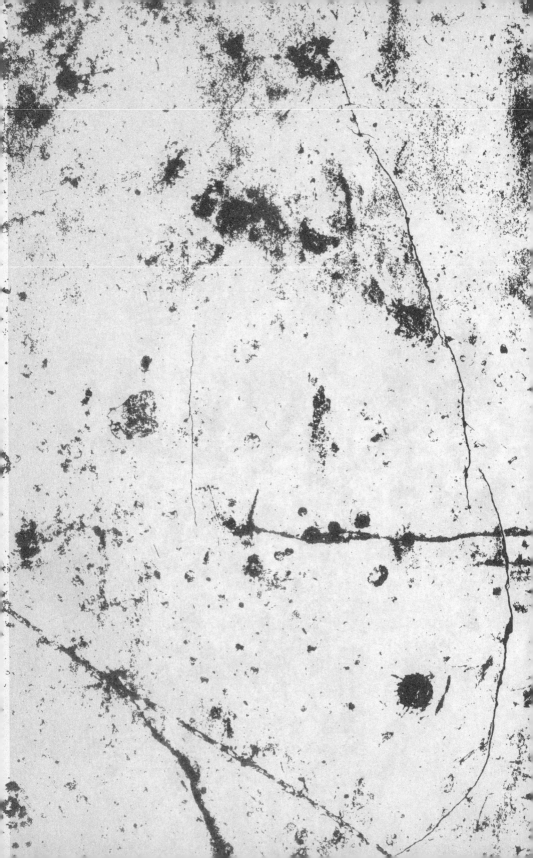

AKE

The Legendary Life of Ken Stabler

MIKE FREEMAN

DEY ST.

An Imprint of WILLIAM MORROW

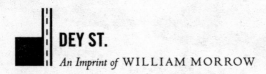

DEY ST.

An Imprint of WILLIAM MORROW

Photograph on title page courtesy Dave Randolph/*San Francisco Chronicle*/Polaris

HarperCollins books may be purchased for educational, business, or sales promotional use. For information, please email the Special Markets Department at SPsales@harpercollins.com.

FIRST EDITION

Designed by Paula Russell Szafranski

Library of Congress Cataloging-in-Publication Data has been applied for.

ISBN 978-0-06-248425-3

16 17 18 19 20 DIX/RRD 10 9 8 7 6 5 4 3 2 1

To Kelly...

I will never be able to thank you enough

for your kindness and care.

Contents

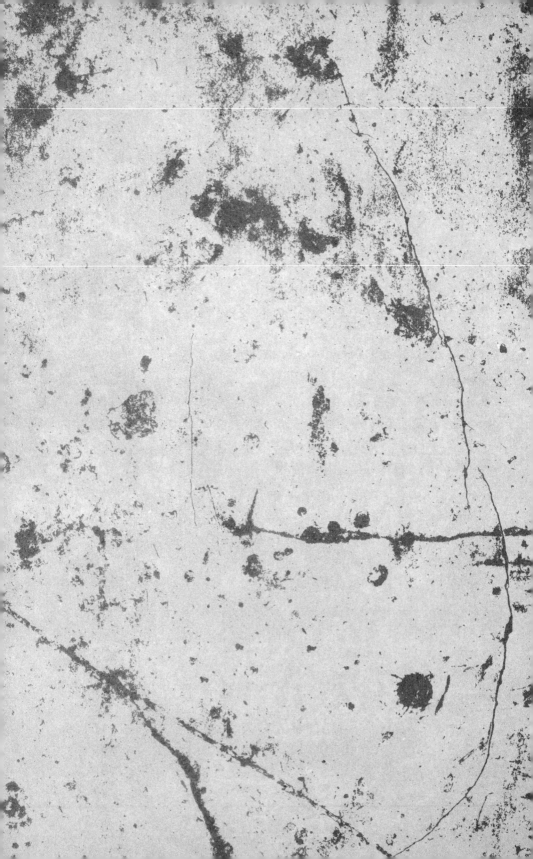

A Daughter Remembers Her Father

Kendra Stabler Moyes was asked to talk about her dad. Her words are beautiful, not solely because they show how strong the connection was between a quarterback dad and his girls, but also because they illustrate a man few people ever truly knew.

Everyone knows Snake. Few people know Ken Stabler the father.

"My parents divorced when I was very young," Kendra says. "I would spend summers with him in Gulf Shores, Alabama. My favorite memories are from those summers. He had a great home on Ono Island. A long pier led to his speedboat. We would catch crabs off the pier from the traps and cook them for dinner. We would fish, cruise in his boat. Long summer nights spent playing with my cousin Scott. Hanging with my Nana. My dad and his mom and his sister, Carolyn, were very close. We all just loved hanging out. It was simple.

"I was seven when he won the Super Bowl, and shortly after realized he was a much bigger deal than just being my dad. It was a very different upbringing because my parents were divorced and my dad was always gone playing football. He basically grew up while I did. He retired when I was a sophomore in high school. I would spend some Christmases with him wherever he was playing. Wake up, open gifts, go to a football game. Not your average Christmas. I do remember how nice he always was. After the game, families would wait outside the locker rooms and wait for their husband or dad to come out. Back then fans would also be waiting outside to meet their favorite player and get autographs. My dad would stop for every single person that asked. He always took so much time to meet his fans, get to know them, and he made them feel like they were a part of our family. He was always the *last* one to leave because of this.

"As a little girl I didn't appreciate it and didn't want to share my dad, because my time with him was so precious. As I got older I realized how amazing that was that he always took so much time with people. It didn't matter who you were. You could have been the president of the United States or the janitor and he treated you equally and that never changed throughout his life. I have so many great early memories of him. He was just my sweet, fun, goofy dad."

Then, Kendra probably gave the best description of her father I've ever heard:

"What I think made him special was his way of making people feel so important," she said. "Making them feel like they had been friends with him forever. I love that he stayed true to his southern roots. He was humble and a gentleman. He loved his mother and baby sister like no other. He protected them. My dad is fiercely loyal. He wasn't the best husband, I have to admit. Three marriages but I do think he found true love with his partner, Kim Bush, of sixteen and a half years. I love that he lived life on the edge and did it his way. He didn't conform. He was wild but responsible. He would get knocked down but kept getting up.

He was gracious. He was goofy and loved to laugh. His philan-
thropic work was the most important to him. He always said you
can always do more. Give back. Make a difference.

"He loved playing football and the joy he brought to his fans.
He loved animals, music, art, and people. He loved his coaches
and what each of them taught him. He had so much respect for
them. He loved his family more than anything. He was so proud
of each of his three daughters. Always bragging to each of us
about the other. His grandsons were his world. He was a *huge*
light in their lives. He is, and will always be, our hero. There will
never be another Ken Stabler."

SNAKE

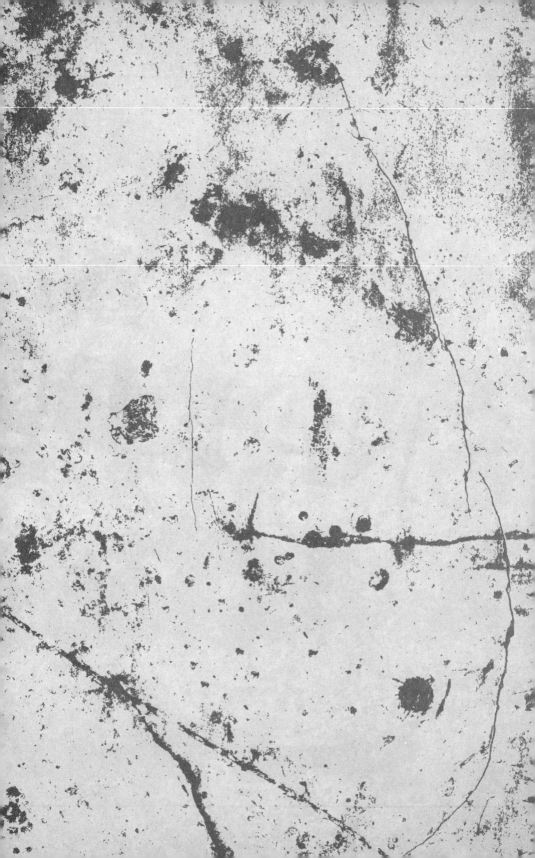

t was several days before Oakland's Super Bowl matchup against the Minnesota Vikings, and Oakland coach John Madden had seen enough. He called off practice.

Ken Stabler had thrown dozens of footballs in that practice and not a single one hit the ground. Deep passes landed gently into the hands of receivers. Short passes moved with great speed but with similar accuracy. Nothing went high or low. Each was thrown perfectly. "It was the damnedest thing I ever saw," said Madden.

The Raiders had seen Stabler sharp before. Most of the time, in fact. He was the most accurate passer of his time and, many decades later, he'd be known as one of the most accurate quarterbacks to ever play the sport.

But this was different. Stabler had reached a level that had shocked everyone. In fact, the entire Raiders team was nearly flawless that day. Practice lasted twenty minutes, some twenty-five shorter than usual. Madden barely had to explain it to the team. They all knew why. He'd approach Stabler later on: "I think you're ready." Stabler didn't disagree. "I'm ready," he said. "We're all ready."

That gorgeous passing demonstration continued what had been a trait of his, the best combination of flamboyance, skill, and coolness under pressure the sport had ever seen. No player was more comfortable in his own body (or chasing female ones) than Ken Stabler.

As Stabler honed his throwing skill, he paid a visit to the Playboy Mansion in Los Angeles the week of Super Bowl, which was being held at the Rose Bowl. "Just went to share a few thoughts about football with some of the librarians there," he'd say to me years later, the smile almost coming through the telephone.

That Super Bowl week, in some respects, would be a continuation of the Stabler way. Actually, on the Stabler scale, visiting a few Playboy bunnies was tame—the Stabler equivalent of sneaking a glance at a woman wearing a pretty dress when she's not looking. From the time he was a teenager wrecking a police car, to his Raiders days collecting the undergarments of the women he slept with, he was a destroyer of the myth that a man needed sleep and clean living to play quarterback. In fact, he thrived on obliterating the notion that a football player had to be a robot to be successful. This was a belief he'd embrace at a young age and would continue to hold throughout his career. Off the field, all that mattered were women, fast cars, and fast boats. And bourbon. As long as life moved quickly, Stabler was happy. The turmoil, the messiness of it all, attracted him. There was the time his second wife (or was it his first?) caught him cheating on her in the parking lot of a bar. Or there was the repeated drinking up until game time. Stabler needed to push the edge. It was his joy.

Even the way Stabler was covered in the media was different from any other NFL player at the time, different even from Joe Namath, one of the gold standards of high-profile, lady-chasing quarterbacks. This from the December 14, 1987, issue of *People* magazine: "Former football great Kenny Stabler, who wrote about his years of hard drinking and womanizing in his best-selling autobiography, *Snake*, finds himself between the covers again. This time around, he's the model for the boozing and babe-chasing exploits of the character called Billyjim (the Twister) Thibodeaux in *Between Pictures*. It's a new novel by Jane Loder, the writer-producer of the documentary 'Atomic Cafe.' Loder says she and Stabler had a romance when she was 15 and he was in his early 20s. 'In the book Billyjim overdoses, but in real life Kenny got married and settled down,' she says. 'Her name does not ring a bell with me,' says Stabler, but adds he plans on getting a copy of the book."

Off the field, in his years as a player, the messier the better; yet on it, there was a gorgeous meticulousness with how he played football. He cherished order and calmness, and these facets of his game would engender respect and even love for him in return from teammates and coaches.

The Super Bowl on January 9, 1977, was indicative of Stabler's talent but also his ability to morph into whatever the game plan needed. The game, initially at least, didn't go as well as that canceled practice, though. Stabler's offense was able to move the football but early drives ended with field goals instead of touchdowns. This caused John Madden to nearly go apoplectic on the sideline. Then Stabler approached him and would say something prophetic. "The offense came off [the field] and I was really pissed," Madden says in the book *Badasses*. "My thought process was immediate: 'Gotta get seven, goddamnit. Don't want too many threes.' I believed in finishing, and I'm thinking. 'Fuck it, we got to get that ball in the end zone, goddamnit!' So Stabler put his hand on my shoulder and said, 'John, don't worry. There's plenty more where that came from.' He was like a little kid. It kind of calmed me down. I thought, 'Shit, we *are* moving the ball, and he *is* right, and there *is* plenty more where that came from.'"

"One of (Stabler's) greatest strengths," the late Al Davis told me, "was his ability to remain the same person under great duress on the field as he was off the field. No one kept their composure like he did. He was very skilled but also very cool."

"When you're the quarterback," Stabler said, "everyone looks to you for leadership. If you look like you're panicking, the team is gonna look at you and say, 'Why the fuck should I follow that guy?'"

Stabler's coolness would sooth Madden and his accuracy would pick apart the Vikings. A 16–0 halftime lead grew to 26–7 in the fourth quarter and a 32–14 final. Defense won that game. The running game won the day. But that game illustrates one of the lesser-known aspects of Stabler's personality—his ability to adapt and not allow his ego to succumb to jealousy or insecurity. Stabler wouldn't be perfect in this endeavor, but he was damn close.

Stabler had entered that Super Bowl as the AFC's top passer, with 2,737 yards and 27 touchdowns. That season, his seventh in the NFL, Stabler completed 66.7 percent of his throws, and in the Super Bowl, though he would only pass 19 times, he averaged 15 yards a pass; his throws to the game's Most Valuable Player, Fred Biletnikoff, led to touchdowns on three of Biletnikoff's four catches.

After the game, the Raiders partied. This is to be expected. And while the drinking lasted most of the night, the alcohol didn't inhibit Stabler's ability to think deeply. The thoughtful and contemplative part of his personality was another facet few people outside of his Raiders and familial orbits knew.

"I remember how relieved we were to win," Stabler recalled. "There were a lot of people who thought the Raiders would never win a Super Bowl." There's a pause. "There were people who thought I'd never make it to a Super Bowl. Yet there I was, this guy from a small Alabama town, a Super Bowl winner . . . there I was. Unbelievable, isn't it?"

Flash back to the AFC divisional playoff game against the Miami Dolphins on December 21, 1974. The game is in Oakland. Two minutes and eight seconds left. The Dolphins have a five-point lead over the Raiders. Stabler has the football in his hands.

The completions came quick and sharp. Six yards. Twenty yards. Darts and lobs and strikes. It was vintage Stabler. The football eventually ended up at the Miami eight-yard line with 35 seconds left. Oakland took its final timeout. Madden remembers having to say little to Stabler during that pause. "He would get in such a rhythm sometimes," says Madden, "that it was best to just get out of his way." Smart coaches do that. For Stabler in that moment, like others, time would slow. Remember playing in the backyard? There was a casualness to it. No pressure. That is how he played, even at the most crucial, pressure-blasted moments.

Once the timeout ended and the play began, Stabler began to scramble, then Miami defensive lineman Vern Den Herder grabbed Stabler from behind. Stabler began to fall and as he did, he managed to get a modicum amount of power into the throw. Not much. Just enough. The football floated into the hands of Raiders running back Clarence Davis. The final score: Raiders 28, Miami 26.

This play would forever be known as the Sea of Hands—the irony being that Davis had notoriously bad hands. The Raiders would go on to play the Steelers in the AFC title game that year.

It was the Sea of Hands that would grow the Stabler legend exponentially. So many years later, Stabler refused to take credit. He called it a total Raiders effort. Giving credit, too, was also a Stabler trademark. Stabler had a saying: I'm always thinking and thanking. Thinking because he was analytical, and thanking because he knew his success relied on teammates, the way theirs relied on his.

"I cried after that play," says then–Dolphins coach Don Shula, mostly joking. Mostly. "I admit it. Stabler made me cry. But Stabler made a lot of people cry."

The Raiders were fun. They were impossible not to watch.

They were equal parts brilliant and carefree. Even when they weren't part of one of the most well-known plays in NFL history, they were doing the impossible. In many ways, this was the definition of them and their quarterback.

One of the most Raiders-like plays happened in September 1978. The Chargers were beating the Raiders, 20–14, with ten seconds left in the contest. Stabler dropped back to pass and was hit, and, in a move that would show both his skill and smarts, he pretended to fumble the football forward, toward a teammate. There was a scramble for the football, which was careening off bodies and the ground and finally ended up in the hands of tight end Dave Casper. He recovered it in the end zone for a touchdown. This series of "accidents" would lead to another nickname for a wild play: the Holy Roller.

The description from the Raiders' play-by-play man is fantastically Raiders: "The ball, flipped forward, is loose! A wild scramble, two seconds on the clock, Casper grabbing the ball—it is ruled a fumble! Casper has recovered in the end zone! The Oakland Raiders have scored on the most zany, unbelievable, absolutely impossible dream of a play. Madden is on the field. He wants to know if it's real. They said yes, get your big butt out of here! He does! There's nothing real in the world anymore! The Raiders have won the football game! The Chargers are standing, looking at each other! They don't believe it! Nobody believes it! I don't know if the Raiders believe it! It's not real! Fifty-two thousand people minus a few lonely Raider fans are stunned. A man would be a fool to have to write a drama and make you believe it! This one will be relived forever!"

"My thought when I went into the huddle," Stabler told me, "was, 'Do not take a sack under any circumstances.' Well, that thought was tested when Woodrow Lowe—fellow Alabama guy, by the way—got to me. That thought came back to me: 'Don't get sacked.' So I just rolled the ball out there and hoped something would happen. [Dave] Casper inadvertently kicked it three times. Total coincidence he kicked it." Stabler laughed knowing it was anything but a coincidence.

———————

Scenes from a life lived largely, and often, unapologetically . . .

Stabler used to say about the Pro Football Hall of Fame: "If I got inducted, it won't change how I put my socks on every day."

Then came February 2016. Stabler had died of colon cancer in July 2015. Hall of Fame voters, who had wrongly rejected his candidacy for decades, gathered in a large hotel ballroom in downtown San Francisco beginning around six thirty in the morning. The arguments were made, the votes were tallied, and some hours later, at a press conference, Justin and Jack Moyes, the grandkids of Ken Stabler, stood before the media and talked about one of the newest entrants into the Hall of Fame. It was Stabler's twenty-seventh year of eligibility.

Stabler's death rocked many people, including me. I think he died without many truly understanding just how impactful he was as a quarterback, but also as a father and human being. He lived a rock star's life, but deep underneath there was a different man who would later cherish just being around his daughters and grandkids. I wanted to make sure this part of his legacy was told as well. That is one of the main purposes of this work.

"My grandfather, he was just a really good man," Justin said. "I never saw him turn down an autograph. He was just special. He loved football, and that was life for him. He loved watching us play, came to every single one of our games, and we were superlucky to have him in our lives."

And such is the complicated persona of Ken Stabler: devoted family man meets devoted party boy. The story from *People* in November 1977 begins this way: "'I've got bad ways. Part of me wants the dog, TV, kids and fireplace, the other part wants to chase,' admits Oakland Raider quarterback Ken Stabler while sipping whiskey at Clancy's, a team hangout. After home games the Raiders often take over the mike and entertain the crowd. Alabama-born Stabler's contribution is to yodel Dixie. 'Drunk, you can do anything,' he reckons, then adds thoughtfully, 'Even when I've been bombed the night before a game I've played good.'"

To Stabler, life was a party.

He was a fan of firecrackers: big ones and small ones. He'd bring hundreds to camp, and then hide throughout different parts of the complex and toss them behind unsuspecting victims. He told me about this once and, after telling the story, laughed for several seconds, and then smiled. Decades later, it was still funny to him.

Stabler also recounted a story about a toy tank, those afore-mentioned firecrackers, "and how I scared the shit out of John Madden." One of Snake's teammates had crafted a small remote-controlled tank. Snake acquired it and after doing so left a note in the player's box: "Don't worry. The Snake will return."

In a remarkable piece of engineering, Snake had attached a number of his more powerful firecrackers to the tank, and equipped them with a longer fuse, just long enough so the firecrackers wouldn't detonate until they reached the coaches' offices. *Vroom, vroom, vroom* went the tank. Just as it rolled into the office, the fireworks went off. Madden came running out, screaming, and as he stood there, the tank rolled between his legs. Later, on occasion when sitting in his office, Madden would stuff cotton in his ears.

The Raiders were a team that knew how to have fun—like Snake. But they were also great professionals. Madden allowed the players to be themselves and never regretted extending that trust even when one or two (or three or four) of them busted curfew on occasion. In some ways, curfew busting was a Raiders tradition that began even before Snake. There was the night veteran tight end Ken Herock decided that a curfew wasn't for him. Herock developed a plan. He took two pillows and placed them in the bed, the pillows serving as his torso. Then Herock put a desk lamp in the bed as a substitute for his head. A blanket was pulled over the entire disguise. When a coach came into the room to check, he turned on the light switch by the wall, and the lamp lit up. Herock was busted.

In the 1970s, as sexual freedom and civil disobedience continued in earnest throughout American society, football was still a militaristic, bland apparatus. Personalities were crushed under the weight of uniformity. But Stabler was symbolic of something else. In many ways, he was the first NFL player who was publicly unrepentant about having sex, drinking beer—a lot of beer, and a lot of whiskey—and living life as he wanted, not as the NFL wanted. The entire Raiders team was this way.

Stabler was more than a partier, though, more than football's avatar for the unrepressed. He was a gorgeous marksman, the league's first cocky, swashbuckling pass thrower, his insides riddled by whiskey, concussions, and gall.

He was an accurate enough thrower to be a downfield threat in the passing game, and just enough of a scrambler to evade defenses and force them to pound turf. Stabler was one of the modern era's first dual-threat quarterbacks.

There's no question now that when football historians, football media, and fans of the sport looked back at Stabler's career, his genius was undervalued. It's clear that Stabler is a vital part of NFL history, an incomparable figure that should be put alongside such names as Unitas, Montana, Marino, Favre, Brady, and Manning.

Stabler's life traveled several different arcs. Only one or two other players (notably Jim Brown) were as comfortable in their skin and out of their clothes as Stabler. In 1981, the magazine *Partner* ran a special edition of its racy magazine, called "Sex Stars: Our Naked Celebrity Hall of Fame." On the cover, near the bottom of the magazine, was a picture of Stabler, his face neatly snuggled between the breasts of topless dancer Carol Doda. A newspaper account of Stabler's appearance in the magazine read:

"Harold's Bookstore reports it is sold out of the December issue of Partner magazine, which includes a picture spread of Oakland Raiders quarterback Ken Stabler and San Francisco topless queen Carol Doda cavorting in a hotel room. Spokesman Davey Rosenberg said Wednesday that 'Partner is a men's magazine, but in this case we have had almost as many women buying copies as men. They want to see Kenny.'"

Stabler played recklessly, and without fear, but there was also great skill. Even when he eventually left the Raiders for the Houston Oilers, and age was creeping in, Stabler was still scary. One year, after owner Al Davis made the controversial move to not re-sign Stabler, it was Madden who said: "Al always believed in getting rid of a guy before he has pissed the very last drop. But Kenny's like Bobby Lane or Bill Kilmer. Even if he has lost a little arm strength, he'll find other ways to piss on you."

It's because Stabler was adaptive and, perhaps more than anything, mentally and physically tough; he may even be the most mentally strong quarterback the league has ever seen. Stabler was hit hard and often by defenses. There was one sack where the top of a defender's helmet collided with Stabler's chin. A gash opened and as Stabler stood, wiping blood from his face, he was also dizzy. He'd been concussed. This was a different era. You only came out of a game if a limb had been severed. There were no concussion protocols.

A disoriented Stabler stayed in the contest. He looked at the scoreboard and saw nothing but haze. It was a familiar feeling. He staggered to the huddle, where the players were curious to see what would happen next.

"I think you know this about me," Stabler once told teammate Gene Upshaw. "I screw women. I drink. I drink all the time. I don't sleep much. I don't need it. Football keeps me going. I love football more than anything. When it's time to play, I'm ready. I won't be drunk. I'll be ready."

In the decades after football, a different Stabler would emerge. The partier would settle into a more calm life. This is as much of the Stabler story as his football prowess and off-field antics. There would be multiple marriages and in each, Stabler genuinely tried to be a good husband, but marriage wasn't in his genome. In 1984, he married Rose Molly Burch, who had an MBA; that marriage, Stabler's third, would last until 2002. "It wasn't an easy transition going from football player to civilian without any preparation," Stabler once said, "and I felt damn lucky that I had Molly. It seemed like I came to love her more and more each day. She was the only woman I didn't dominate in a relationship. . . . Molly was the only woman I've dealt with on an equal basis and made an effort to make the relationship work."

He would sell real estate, visit with family members he hadn't seen in years, and speak at charity events. There were the golf tournaments. Lots of golf tournaments. He became an agent, starting a firm called Stabler Sports Management, representing athletes in contract negotiations with teams. He was inducted into the Alabama Sports Hall of Fame. Eventually, his life became about spending as much time with his daughters and grandkids as he could.

Stabler's death in July 2015 was a major news story and had a big impact on the football world. It wasn't just because of his gorgeous and electric play on the field, or how he deeply affected people off it; it was because he was a symbol of a different era. Snake studied his playbook by the light of a jukebox; today's players study by the light of an iPad. Stabler was married three times and cheated on all of his wives. In the open and unabashedly. If that happened today, pictures of Stabler's infidelity would pop up across the Internet like gremlins. As *Sports Illustrated* writer Chris Burke put it, Stabler was a man made for social media, in a non–social media world.

But it is also true that as Stabler grew, and his kids from all of those marriages got older and had their own children, a more mature Stabler started to emerge. Stabler began thinking of his legacy and slowly wanted to distance himself from those stories of the past. To himself, that Stabler was a relic.

The football metrics alone show just how important he was in NFL lore. Stabler was voted the Associated Press MVP in 1974 and should have won the award in 1976 as well. That year, he led the NFL in passer rating, touchdown passes, yards per pass, and completion percentage. He also led the NFL in fourth-quarter comebacks, with four, and had five game-winning drives, both raw indicators of his mental sturdiness.

During a six-year stint, from 1973 to 1979, he ranked in the top ten in passing yards, completion percentage, and touchdown passes. In 1976, Stabler completed 66.7 percent of his passes, a stunning figure for that time. Stabler was the only quarterback in the pre-1980s NFL to complete 65 percent of his passes in a season in which he attempted at least 250. In 1976, when Stabler led the league with a passer rating of 103.4, the league average passer rating was 63.6.

He led the Raiders to a championship in Super Bowl XI. He threw two of the most famous passes of the 1970s, the "Sea of Hands" and "Ghost to the Post." He fumbled (purposely) his way to a Raiders touchdown with the infamous "Holy Roller."

There is, of course, more to Stabler than data. The remarkable impact he had on those around him, friends and fans alike, goes beyond even what happened on the football field. Today's game is at times soulless and shackled. Players fear being themselves. Much of what the NFL does now is solely about making money. Stabler reminds us of an NFL that was, yes, far more dangerous and raw, but also far more real.

This book is a biography and doesn't shy away from Stabler's unflattering facets, but frankly, the book is also part appreciation. It's been in the works for twenty years. Stabler, with me, was always informative, smart, prone to reminisce, and, well, extremely kind. I interviewed Stabler over that time span at various events and places, and the quotations here, unless indicated otherwise, are from those interviews. I've been fascinated with Stabler since I was a child and always appreciated him as one of the truly unique men in the dangerous, exhilarating, and joyous sport of football. Stabler was beautiful, brilliant, and flawed—just like the league he conquered. Just like many of us. Just like me. He was just better at it.

Stabler would influence a legion of quarterbacks. One was a player named Brett Favre. Favre and Stabler were inducted in the same 2016 Hall of Fame class. Favre remembered when he went to a Saints game at fourteen years old and saw the man who would become his idol.

"As we sat in our seats prior to the kickoff, the crowd stood and pointed in the direction of the Saints' tunnel," Favre said during his Hall of Fame induction speech, "and as I stood, I saw this long, gray haired, scruff-bearded player emerging from the tunnel. And I knew then and there, as goose bumps ran up my arm, and the hair on the back of my neck stood up, that *that* was what I was destined to be. I wanted to be that player. Well, that player happened to be none other than Kenny Stabler."

A friend of Stabler's once read him a quote from writer and social activist Jack London: "I would rather be a meteor, every atom of me in magnificent glow, than a sleepy and permanent planet. The proper function of man is to live, not to exist. I shall not waste my days in trying to prolong them. I shall use my time."

"What does that mean to you?" Stabler was asked.

He thought and contemplated. Seconds passed.

"Throw deep," he said.

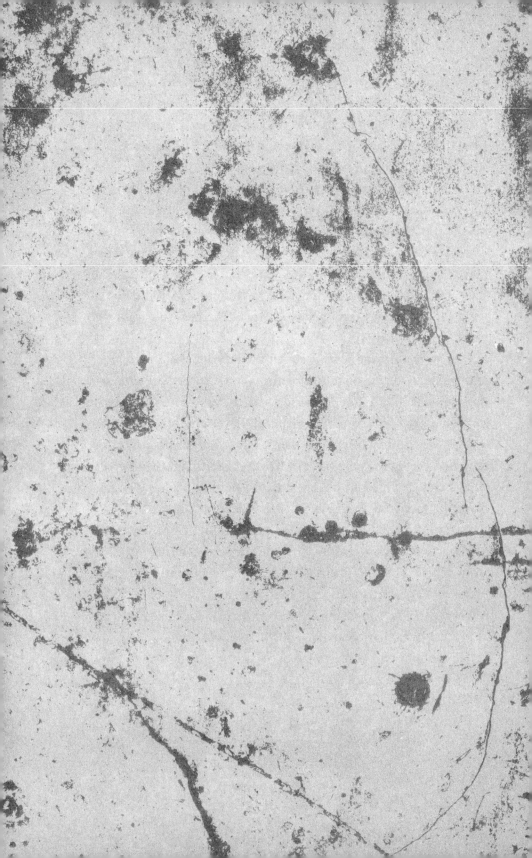

PART ONE

"I'm Not the Man You Think I Am"

CHAPTER ONE

The Italian Campaign

As with many stories, the duality and contradictions that would dot Ken Stabler's life, like spots on a sun, begin with his father, Slim Stabler. Slim was a God-fearing man but eventually stopped going to church in favor of spending Sundays at the American Legion, since that was the only place he could drink his bourbon on the holy day. If Slim wasn't drinking there, he was drinking the bourbon that was snuggled neatly in his wife Sally's purse. He was particular about his bourbon, often choosing the brands Ezra Brooks or Early Times. He smoked Lucky Strikes cigarettes, as many as five packs a day.

Slim was a fisherman and also skilled on the guitar. Hank Williams songs were among his favorites to play. He smiled and laughed with his friends, often showing no effects from his time serving during World War II.

But he was different when his friends weren't there. None of them knew of his cruelty. It was well hidden, usually remaining behind the walls of the Stabler home. Yet occasionally his harshness would leak outside them.

By the time Ken Stabler was thirteen, he was already a gangling six feet tall and weighed around 130 pounds. In baseball he was a skilled pitcher and hitter and because he was a lefty, he could throw a significant curveball. Even at that young age, a trend with Stabler was becoming clear: he would always be one of the best players on whatever team he was on. This was the case with his baseball team and when Stabler became a football and baseball star at Foley High School.

Despite that, Slim was at times the typical overbearing youth sports parent. In one game, Stabler made an error while playing first base, which cost his team the game. Slim had been watching, and he moved toward Stabler, got inches from his face, and screamed at him for missing the play. Then Slim pushed Stabler to the ground right in front of his teammates and demanded that Stabler apologize to them. A teary Stabler did.

Slim saw at an early age that Stabler was skilled in sports, and as Stabler began moving toward baseball (and even basketball), Slim had a different idea. One day, when Stabler was just in tenth grade, Slim gave him a 1954 Ford. This was, in effect, a bribe to get Stabler to focus on football. Slim did this because he saw the football talent in his son. Slim could see the beginnings of something special. Later, when that car died, Slim gave his son a 1963 Chevy Impala Super Sport 327. It was done. The bribe worked. Stabler dove into football.

This was the good Slim. He'd attend all of Stabler's games in high school and later at the University of Alabama. "My father was so much fun generally, he was never visited by demons when he was having fun," Stabler wrote in his autobiography. "Maybe that's why, from way back, going for the good times became such an important part of my life. Having fun, I could not be set upon by anything like Slim's demons."

The demons, however, were never far away. Several times

while Stabler was playing football at Alabama, crafting a legacy and battling the coach he'd later believe was one of the great influences on his life, Stabler would occasionally have to travel back to Foley and confront the violent Slim. In each instance, Stabler had to be a protector of his mother and sister. His sister Carolyn once called to say that Slim had beaten up Sally. One day later, Stabler was back in Foley, looking for Slim. At this point Stabler was tall and lanky, but still physically substantial. More important, he was ready, if needed, to fight his father.

Stabler found Slim in a bar drinking. As Stabler approached, Slim produced a small knife. It stunned Stabler for a moment, but Slim soon put the knife back in his pocket. They left the bar together and Stabler, as he had done before, and would do again, was able to prevent his father from harming his own family.

"Not something I want to talk about," Stabler said when asked about his father's dark side. "What I always believed was that he was messed up badly by the war. I think that would have happened to a lot of men."

———

In July 1943, two sprawling armies landed on the coast of Sicily. One was American and the other, British. They were there to fight 300,000 Axis troops. The Allies arrived using three thousand ships, carrying hundreds of thousands of soldiers. Once situated on the beach, at Anzio, the Allies prepared for a German counterattack. Hitler told one of his generals: "The battle must be waged with holy hatred."

Heavy shelling started. "Anzio was a fishbowl," one American soldier wrote; "We were the fish." Wrote another soldier, speaking of a small group of fighters from Iowa: "They had been at it so long they had become more soldier than civilian. Their life consisted wholly and solely of war. . . . They survived because the fates were kind to them, certainly—but also because they had become hard and immensely wise in the animal-like ways of self-preservation."

Across all of Italy, and in the totality of the 608-day campaign to liberate the country, there would be 312,000 Allied casualties. Three-quarters of a million Americans served in Italy, and those casualties would reach 120,000, with 23,501 killed.

The men who fought were ordinary people with exceptional abilities. According to Rick Atkinson in his book *The Day of the Battle: The War in Sicily and Italy, 1943–1944*, one navy lieutenant listed the occupations of the sailors on his ship headed to battle: "farm boys and college graduates . . . lawyers, brewery distributors, millworkers, tool designers, upholsterers, steel workers, aircraft mechanics, foresters, journalists, sheriffs, cooks and glass workers."

Some of the veterans who fought in the Italian Campaign, at Anzio and other battles, such as the Battle of Rapido River, returned as different men, their innards hollowed by seeing constant carnage and death. Leroy Slim Stabler was one of those men.

⸻

One of the first Stablers in America was Gottlieb Stabler, who was the fifth-great-grandfather of Kenny, born in Germany. During the summer of 1752, Gottlieb traveled from Germany to Rotterdam, Netherlands, where he boarded the ship *Upton*, captained by John Gardiner, and then sailed to England. There the ship took on provisions and water for the sixty-day trip across the Atlantic.

The *Upton* arrived in Charleston, South Carolina, on September 14, 1752, and anchored in the Ashley River. The next day, a strong hurricane hit the city. Scientists now estimate the storm was a Category 4. Hurricane Katrina, the storm that devastated New Orleans in 2005, was a Category 3 when it made landfall.

The storm prevented the passengers from unloading and Gottlieb, like the other passengers, rolled from side to side, the wind and waves crashing against the hull. The lucky ones on the ship only broke their arms and legs. Twenty passengers died. All the ships in the harbor except one were washed ashore. Some were carried as far as thirty miles inland. The *Upton* was shoved into the marsh around Wappoo Creek on James Island, and it took several months to get it out; it did not sail again till February 1753. In all, 103 people in Charleston lost their lives, and sixteen ships were destroyed. Small boats in the harbor were turned into debris. The storm surge—about seventeen feet high—covered almost the entire present-day downtown area of Charleston. When the wind shifted, the water fell five feet in ten minutes. Two hundred fifty years after the hurricane, the high-water marks were still visible.

In what would be a sign of toughness and survivability of the Stabler family to come, Gottlieb emerged from the storm, after so many perished.

He would later have a son, and sometime between 1818 and 1830, that son, John Jacob Stabler, moved his family of thirteen to Alabama, most likely after it was admitted as a state in 1819. The opening of land in the Mississippi Territory caused what was known as "Alabama fever." They probably traveled by wagons in a large group of adventurous pioneers along the old wagon road from Georgia, through central Alabama, and when they reached present Monroe County, decided to settle. After a few years, he applied for a land patent of forty acres close to the Alabama River. Cotton was the crop grown in that area and was transported to market on the river.

In 1840, John Jacob Stabler still had seven children living at home. He died in 1844 having seen three of his sons die first, one in the Creek Indian War of 1836, while serving in the local militia. John Jacob's oldest son, Samuel, also served in Smith's Volunteers during that same war. About that time he also got a land grant of eighty acres close to his father's land. By the time Samuel's oldest son, Benjamen Eleander—Kenny's great-grandfather—was in his thirties, he was a large landowner in the same area as his grandfather and father. Benjamen's third son, William Edgar Stabler, was born in 1894. He married his sixteen-year-old sweetheart, Marie Williamson, in 1915. They settled on a farm close to his father in Jeddo, also in Monroe County. In 1917, he was ordered to Georgia to train for World War I. Sometime between 1926 and 1930 he moved his family of two sons and three daughters to Foley, in Baldwin County. There the youngest son, Jimmy, was born. The land in Monroe county had probably given out and hearing of the long growing season and better weather, the family wanted to try their luck in Foley. Jimmy was Kenny's grandfather.

Kenny's mother's side of the family has been traced all the way back to Jamestown, Virginia. Thomas Osborne, who was born in England about 1580, was the founder of the Osborne family in America. He came to the colonies in 1619 on the two-hundred-ton *Bona Nova*, which sailed in August 1619, with 120 persons. No family members are known to have accompanied him at this time. Whether his wife had previously died in England is not known, but her name does not appear in any of the extant colonial Virginia records. Thomas was selected by the London Company to serve as the leader of the military contingent in the settlement of College Land, a large area near Henricus City. The latter was the second permanent settlement in Virginia, the first, of course, being Jamestown. He appears in the two early lists of inhabitants, dated February 1623–24 and January 1624–25, as a resident of "Colledge Land."

After an attack by Native Americans in 1622, when roughly one-third of the settlers between Jamestown and Henricus City were killed, Lieutenant Thomas Osborne led a retaliatory attack. Later he appears in records as Captain Thomas Osborne. From

1625 to 1633 he served in the Virginia House of Burgesses and, having been granted a large tract of land known as Coxendale, settled there around 1625. The first town in Coxendale, Gatesville, was later named Osbornes and became an important inspection, storage, and shipping center for tobacco, until well into the late nineteenth century. Thomas lived his entire life in Coxendale (that part which is now Chesterfield County), and the succeeding four generations also made Coxendale their home.

The family migrated through the years to North Carolina, South Carolina, and Georgia before ending up in Alabama, where this branch has for the most part stayed. During this time the men served in most major military conflicts involving the United States.

Francis Marion Osborne was born about 1824 in Georgia and served in the Fifty-Third Cavalry; his third wife, Sarah Jane, received his pension after his death in 1888. During the 1920s, William Cauthen Osborne, born in 1882, packed up his wife of forty years and their eight children and moved to southern Alabama, where he'd been told the soil was rich. The baby of the family was Myrtle Margaret, Kenny's mom, who was five at the time. So most of her memories were of growing up in Foley, where she lived the rest of her life.

All of this shows that Kenny comes from a long line of explorers and soldiers, each a fighter. Kenny wouldn't sail a vast ocean in wooden ships, or plow fields, or fight for a colony. He would, however, in his own way demonstrate the same courage and ability to persevere. To be unique and to lead.

It was courage his father demonstrated when he fought Nazis in Italy, and the same courage he displayed recovering from his wounds. What wasn't known about Slim's days fighting in Italy until now—not even by Kenny himself—was the extent of Slim's bravery. Like so many men who fought in World War II, he showed unparalleled courage.

Among Slim's military records, obtained from the National Personnel Records Center, one reads: "Battles, engagements, skirmishes, expeditions: Italian Campaign/Bronze Sv Star for Italian Campaign." So, according to the U.S. government, Slim won some of his country's highest honors for valor in battle. He was also awarded the European–African–Middle Eastern Theater Campaign Ribbon.

The records show that Slim left for Europe on November 2, 1943, arrived twenty-three days later, left on July 14, 1944, and arrived back in the United States on July 30. The records also show that on January 22, 1944, Slim was injured when an artillery shell exploded near his position during the Battle of Rapido River. That fight was one of the costliest undertaken by the U.S. Army during the war.

The explosion caused severe damage and pain to Slim's spine and hip, his records show. He spent six months in a military hospital.

From the *Foley Onlooker* newspaper, on November 1, 1944: "Pfc. Leroy Stabler, who formerly lived in Foley, has recently arrived at Welch Convalescent Hospital, the Army's new reconditioning center in Daytona Beach, Fla. The carefully-planned program of physical and educational reconditioning not only will keep him busy but will also return him to good physical condition. Pfc. Stabler, the son of Mrs. Marie Stabler, was formerly employed by the Double Cola Co. He entered the Army April, 1943 at Fort McClellan, Ala., and has since served ten months in Italy."

It's likely Slim suffered—and understandably so—some type of post-traumatic stress. It doesn't excuse the abuse but it provides more context. Thus Slim was a man who deserved understanding, pity, and scorn. He was a complicated mix, someone who both supported Stabler and held him back. He was a family man, and an abuser. Like many human beings, including Stabler himself, Slim was a man of many contradictions, beginning with his nickname. He stood at six feet, five inches and weighed almost 220 pounds. There was nothing slim about that.

Stabler's build and athleticism came from Slim, who was every bit as good an athlete as his son. Slim played basketball and baseball at Blacksher High School in Uriah, Alabama, in the late 1930s. He was perhaps headed to a career in professional baseball, but the death of his father led to his quitting high school in eleventh grade. He worked for a mechanic in Foley and eventually married Myrtle Margaret, whom everyone called Sally. She worked in a doctor's office. Slim was embarrassed, even angry, about Sally working, but she did it anyway. Stabler was born on Christmas Day 1945, and five years later his sister, Carolyn, was born. Sally went back to work just six weeks after the birth of each child.

There would come a time when Stabler would conquer the football world. He'd win a Super Bowl and be mentioned as one of the best in the league. He'd return to Foley a conquering hero, to a packed auditorium, with the mayor in attendance. He'd be so popular that his native residents would have a Stabler roast ($12.50 a plate) with Stabler seated in a chair shaped like a throne, his friends throwing sharp but vicious verbal darts, uncaring about political correctness—it didn't exist—with the quarterback hero laughing along.

"Eight beers and two hours' sleep a night," teammate Pete Banaszak would say at the roast; "that's the way to stardom as an NFL quarterback." Or this one: "He's a one-woman man—one woman a night."

"The other day," another roaster would say, "my son asked me, 'Daddy, when are they going to roast you?' 'When I get overweight and overpaid,' I told him."

The roast would end and Stabler would drive home with a *Sports Illustrated* writer and remark, speaking of Foley, "Yeah, I'll die here." *Yeah, I'll die here.*

But for now, before kinghood and the adulation, before pondering where he'd finally lay to rest, he would grow up under the roof of a father who alternated between kindness and cruelty. Slim was able to threaten his family without attracting much public attention. There are no records of any arrest by the Foley Police Department (a check of a dusty records room was made by officials there). Relatives of the sheriff at the time, who later became part of the Foley police themselves, don't remember any type of police investigation into Slim's violence in his home. There are no reports of neighbors hearing or seeing any of it.

What is certain is that the war changed Slim. He returned more sullen, and as a young Stabler grew, there would be few war stories, or any type of explanation for Slim's behavior toward the family. Most questions about the war went unanswered. Leroy didn't even talk to Sally about Anzio. The war would hang over the Stabler family like a thick film and would intensify Stabler's tumultuous relationship with Slim.

There was one time when Slim mentioned the war to Stabler. They were both watching the show *Gunsmoke*, which was Slim's favorite program. One of the reasons was the star, James Arness. Arness was at Anzio and upon landing on the beach, the water up to the waist of his six-foot-seven frame, he had been shot by a German machine gunner in the knee and lower leg. Arness earned a Bronze Star and Purple Heart for bravery under fire. He'd later use the GI Bill to get a college education that would springboard him into acting.

They were watching the show when Slim's eyes became bright and entranced. "You know, Bud," he told Stabler, using his favorite nickname for his son, "every fifth round in a machine gun belt was a tracer. There were times when we fought right through the night. So I took out all of the tracers and replaced them with regular bullets. Tracers help you spot your target. But if you can see where they're going, I figured the enemy could damn well see where they were coming from."

He never spoke about the war again to Stabler. Those words carried a deeper message for Stabler, who always believed that Slim was providing wisdom on how there are many ways to get the job done, and it doesn't always have to be what the majority dictates. It can be any way as long as the mission is completed.

Other than that moment, Slim never truly revealed who he was to anyone, not even to his wife, Sally, and his children. While it's likely, looking back on how Slim behaved after the war, that he was suffering from some type of post-traumatic stress disorder, the illness of course was not yet recognized. The American Psychological Association didn't list PTSD as a mental disorder until 1980.

The war must have scorched Slim's insides, and alcohol may well have accelerated the occasional release of those demons. There's no question that was the case in another frightening moment inside the Stabler home.

There is a picture of the Stabler family taken when Stabler was in high school. Slim is sitting in a comfortable chair, wearing tan pants and a plaid shirt. His hair is buzzed short, his larger ears protruding, his face expressionless. Stabler is to his left, seated on the arm of the chair, wearing a black shirt and tan pants as well. His hair is neatly trimmed and there is a tiny smile on his face. Sally is seated on the opposite arm of the chair, wearing a dark-colored dress and striped top. Carolyn is situated in front of them all, wearing a white dress. Her hair is longer, and flirts with her shoulders. She is expressionless. They look like a normal American family from that time—happy and close.

The picture was deceptive. Beneath the superficial calm was something else. In his college and NFL careers, on the field and in the huddle, Stabler was always the calming agent. As things became more intense and gut-wrenching, Stabler would get cooler. This aspect of his personality would come to be one of the most defining of his Raiders tenure. That same characteristic would be the reason that, one day, Stabler saved the life of himself and his entire family.

When Kenny was attending the University of Alabama, his college career beginning to blossom, he received a phone call in his dormitory. It was Carolyn. She was panicked. The words came fast. "Daddy's got his shotgun," she told Stabler. "He says he's gonna kill us and then kill himself."

Stabler was terrified. He had a Corvette that he raced home in, daring the police to stop him, and covered the more than two hundred miles faster than he ever had. Some three hours after Carolyn's call, around midnight, he arrived in Foley. When he entered the home, he saw a frightening scene. Sally was sitting on a large couch, her eyes red, hands in her lap. It was clear to Stabler that she had been crying. Close to Sally was Carolyn, who looked similarly shaken. Slim was sitting in a chair, holding a shotgun in his lap.

When I asked Stabler about this scene, he declined to talk about it. That cool January night, so long ago, was still fresh to him. It's understandable. The account Stabler gives in his autobiography isn't something anyone would ever forget—or want to recall: On Slim's lap was the shotgun, and next to him, on a table, was a bottle of Early Times bourbon. One of Slim's hands was on the pump of the shotgun, the other on the trigger. Stabler wasn't sure what to do or say, but his first instinct, as it was then, and always would be, was to protect his mother and sister. Stabler asked them to leave. They got up and began moving to the door.

"Dad, I'm gonna go, too," Stabler said, "as long as you're like this."

Slim stood from his chair and repositioned the shotgun, which was now pointed at the three of them. He wasn't letting them go. There was more pain to extract.

"I'm going to kill everybody and then kill myself," said Slim.

Stabler knew a day like this might come, even though he also knew there was nothing he could do to prevent it. He wasn't going to allow his mother and daughter to be killed, so he rushed his father. He was able to get both hands on the weapon and they fought for what Stabler thought was an eternity but was only a few seconds. Then, Slim simply stopped struggling and retreated to the bedroom. It was over.

There would be other threats from Slim and each time, after the drinking and handling of the shotgun, there would be silence. Sometimes that quiet would last for days. Stabler always figured that was Slim's mechanism for dealing with the trauma he inflicted on his own family.

Those moments would help form the structure of Stabler's life. They would dictate how he lived off the field and, in many ways, on it. Despite being terrorized by his father, Stabler was still dedicated to him. But he was also practical. He knew that his father's traits were somehow a part of him, and he tried everything to keep those potentially destructive, if not deadly, forces relegated to some distant realm of his genes or the recesses of his mind. Though he would be successful in never becoming his violent father, he was unsuccessful in totally eradicating all of his father's influences.

Five of the most important paragraphs ever written about Slim were made by Stabler. He explains how and why he conducted himself the way he did, particularly when he played in the NFL, and later when he was done with football.

"He was such a good man most of the time. His friends won't believe what I'm writing about Slim Stabler. But when he drank that bourbon hard, he got depressed—about his circumstances, the fact he couldn't give us more—and he felt miserable. Then he got mean, wanted to kill himself and his family, put us out of what he must have seen, somewhere near the bottom of the bourbon bottle, as *our* misery.

"Thank God he never did it. Thank God he never acted on the demonic thought that was buried in him and given expression only by the booze. I have thought about this through all the years since the incidents occurred. I know my father loved us all. And I believe that it was his love that prevailed against the demons.

"I also knew that I was basically made up of Slim Stabler's genes, that I had his temper, and that I had to guard against ever losing control the way he did. When he wasn't occupied, my father was always thinking, something grinding away in his mind that he never let loose. Every woman I've had a long relationship with has said the same thing about me. My [then] wife Molly tells me now, 'You're always preoccupied and I never know what you're thinking.'

"Still, my father was so much fun generally, and he was visited by his demons when he was having fun. Maybe that's why, from way back, going for the good times became such an important part of my life. Having fun, I could not be set upon by anything like Slim's demons.

"Football was fun. I was always higher on the field than any glow alcohol could ever produce. But off the field the party glow wasn't half bad either. Just stay in the fast lane and keep moving."

CHAPTER TWO

The Bribe That Changed Football

Stabler's philosophy of living life to its fullest, and enjoying the ride, out of fear of becoming his father, actually began when he was in his early teens, when he started drinking beer. Stabler occasionally slipped out of his home on weekend nights to join friends. (It's difficult to believe the controlling Slim didn't know his son was escaping the home to go drink. It's more likely Slim let Stabler go with them.) As Stabler became stronger and more athletic, his penchant for finding trouble also grew. On this night, Stabler and his friends went from Foley to Pensacola, Florida, a trip that took less than an hour to drive. They ran out of alcohol and money and had the idea to steal hubcaps off cars and sell them for cash. Stabler wasn't the ringleader but he also wasn't an innocent.

The police caught the group almost immediately. They were all too young to be arrested but not too young to be suspended from school for three days. The other hubcap pilferers weren't athletes like Stabler. It was Stabler who suffered the most since he wouldn't be allowed to play in a scheduled basketball tournament. Understandably, Stabler believed his father's punishment would be extreme, and he imagined a violent Slim angrily punishing him. Instead, something completely different happened. Slim made a calm and fatherly speech to his son. "You can have a good athletic career ahead of you," Slim said, "maybe even get yourself to college playing ball. But you get a reputation as a thief, you won't get no chance. You've seen good athletes in high school not get scholarships because they couldn't stay out of trouble. Colleges don't take troublemakers. Now, you keep that in mind."

That was the good and prescient Slim. He knew what his son was becoming. He also knew that Stabler, despite his infatuation with basketball and baseball, and the fact that Stabler still barely weighed 140 pounds as he entered high school (though he was over six feet), had a great chance of becoming a good football player. Slim began the earnest task of pushing Stabler toward that sport. The problem was, Stabler didn't like playing it, and hadn't played since he was eight years old. He hated the violence.

Stabler believed that nothing would change that view. It didn't change even when Slim took him to a preseason game between the New York Titans and Houston Oilers, played in Houston on October 9, 1960, at Jeppesen Stadium. The head coach of the Titans was Sammy Baugh, a longtime quarterback and Hall of Famer. It was interesting that Stabler's first game included Baugh, because eventually Stabler would become a more advanced version of him, an elusive and accurate passer. The other quarterback that game was George Blanda, who also had striking similarities to the Stabler to come. Blanda had retired in 1958 but two years later was back, joining the expansion Oilers and being ridiculed as a reject who couldn't make the real league, the NFL.

After that game, Stabler got Blanda's autograph. Stabler had no idea that just over a decade later, he would be holding for Blanda's field goal tries when both were with the Raiders. In Stabler's rookie year, 1970, he'd constantly and sincerely address Blanda as "sir." They'd become close friends and golf buddies.

Despite his fun and autographs, Stabler still wasn't sold on football. Slim changed that. He altered the destiny of Stabler and the NFL with a car—a black 1954 Ford. That car would change everything.

Stabler came home one night as his father was working on it. His father smiled when Stabler asked about it. The family didn't have great wealth. The cars were the fruit of Slim's hard work and his ability to rebuild the broken-down vehicles.

"It's yours if you play football, Bud," Slim said.

Stabler didn't hesitate: "I'm going to be a real good football player, Dad." And so it began.

———

How *exactly* he got the nickname is a slight mystery. Stabler always maintained that his coach Denzil Hollis exclaimed, "Damn, that boy runs like a snake," as he watched Stabler dodge and weave on the field.

Hollis's widow says what her husband actually said was more succinct. When Stabler came to the sideline after that run, Denzil, she says, simply remarked, "Good job, Snake."

What's not up for debate is how Hollis once described high school Snake: "Straight up from top to bottom, and when he turned sideways, he weren't no thicker than a airmail letter."

What also isn't up for debate is the run itself. The play that created the Snake legend came on a dizzying punt return. Snake ran some 60 yards for a score, evading tacklers by cutting back and forth, from sideline to sideline, four times.

"He'd run two hundred yards to score from twenty yards out," Hollis once recalled.

"Got the nickname from returning punts, of all things," said Snake.

———

Hollis coached football, basketball, baseball, golf, and track at Foley High School, so he knew every type of athlete, which also meant he knew a special one when he saw it. Snake was that, and it was Hollis's job to nurture that specialness. "I have tried to teach them to show class, to have pride, and to display character," he once said.

Once Snake made varsity, Ivan Jones, one of the legends of Alabama high school football, coached him. From 1960 to 1964, Jones's teams won 47 of 50 games. He never had a losing record, and Foley won despite being at a massive numbers disadvantage. Census records show the population of Foley in 1960 was just 2,889 people.

In high school, Snake threw the ball an average of just ten times a game. He was mostly a runner in a ground-and-pound offense, and he wasn't necessarily fast. His 40-yard dash would not dazzle but Stabler possessed what one NFL coach once described as "swivel hips." He was able to cut on a dime and that ability would only sharpen.

Snake also didn't look the part of a shake-and-bake runner. He was tall and awkward and there was a sort of hitch in his run as he approached full speed. But when watching tape of Snake in high school or at Alabama, he is constantly outrunning and outmaneuvering defenders. One minute, a linebacker is about to make the tackle, and in the next, he's gasping for air as Snake runs past. "When you're a guy who is smart and is quick," says Joe Namath, "that counts for a lot. He could make those quick cuts and fool guys."

It was in Snake's sophomore year in high school that his super-powers truly began to form. He was still playing baseball and basketball but football was where Snake was making his mark. There was also the rebellion. That sophomore season, Snake was fighting for the backup quarterback position. It was important because the one who captured the second-string position would most likely be the starter the following season. Snake decided he was going to get that backup job, even if he angered his coach in trying.

Snake's team, as it often did, had a large lead at the end of the game, so Jones allowed Snake to play quarterback, and the player Snake was fighting to get the starting job, Jimmy Paul, was in the backfield. Because football was so important in Foley, and the town was so small, the players in the town were semi-celebrities. The *Foley Onlooker*, on October 4, 1962, took a pic-ture of Snake and Paul after a game against the Alba Sharks, won by Foley, 37–0. Snake was wearing his number 12 jersey; his uniform was dirty and his ears protruded wildly because of a short haircut. "The unbeaten Lions traveled to Bayou La Batre to tangle with the Sharks of Alba on Friday," the story read. "Halfback Wayne Chisenhall scored on a 52-yard run on the second play of the game. For the second touchdown Kenny Snake threw an 18-yard pass to end Ronnie Helton. Still in the first quarter, sophomore Norman Moore scored from 18 yards out. Snake threw his second touchdown pass of the night by hitting Jimmy Paul in the end zone. Late in the first half, Otis Reed scored from the six-yard line. The Lions' last score was a seven-yard run from Reed in the third quarter. The Sharks never threatened."

This brief would read like many others during Snake's high school years. In one particular game, Snake had taken the offense into the red zone when Jones called for what was the core play for Foley and almost all of high school football then: the option play. The play was supposed to be Snake faking a handoff to Jimmy Paul but then keeping the football. Instead, Snake decided to change the play and hand the football off left to Paul. The problem for Snake in that play was that he turned the wrong way and the play blew up. The offense didn't score.

Jones was angry. Beyond angry. Jones believed that Snake changed the play so he could purposely blow the handoff to Paul and Paul wouldn't score. If Paul didn't score, then he wouldn't have a potential advantage over Snake in the fight for starting quarterback. The coach basically thought his quarterback was a saboteur. Snake wasn't, and later, Jones would recognize this and apologize to Snake, cementing a closeness that would last for decades.

That doesn't mean Snake didn't test every inch of Jones's patience. After the Ford given to Snake suffered engine failure, Slim gave his son another car: a 1963 Impala SuperSport. The car was gorgeous, one of the true pieces of automobile muscle at the time, sporting 250 horsepower, and new bumpers, hoods, rear deck contours, and accentuated side panels. It was gorgeous, as were some of the women Snake bedded in it. He describes one time taking "a girlfriend off for a little romancing before practice" and as a result of that encounter, Snake decided to skip practice. Snake thought Jones would be understanding.

The following day, Snake told his coach that he missed practice because he wasn't feeling well. Jones didn't believe him. The fact that Snake lied to Jones likely bothered Jones more than the missed practice. Snake should have known this. All the players knew that Jones was no-nonsense. Once, when Jones was upset with one of Snake's teammates, believing the player wasn't firing off his blocks with the necessary urgency, he stopped practice. The player was in full pads and Jones was wearing nothing but shorts and a shirt. Jones got down in a four-point stance. "Fire off. I want you to hit me like you would in a game!"

Jones was hit hard and knocked back about three feet. He calmly got up. "By God, that's what I mean," Jones said. "That's what I want you to do every time."

Jones told Snake they needed to talk in Jones's office. As soon as they got inside, Jones closed the door. He turned to Snake: "Bend over and grab your ankles."

Snake was momentarily stunned but the wannabe nonconformist complied. Jones hit Snake on the backside three times. *Whap, whap, whap.* "Next time," Jones told Snake, "you get ten."

The punishment didn't hold, because Snake would get in trouble. Again. With the cops.

One of Snake's close friends on the team was Otis Reed. Snake remembered Reed as one of the best pure athletes he ever played with. Reed remembers Snake as so talented that he didn't need to practice.

"We ran around together," Reed said. "His dad put us on restriction because we seemed to get in trouble a lot when we were together. Things would just happen."

Things always happened. Sometimes Snake was the ringleader; sometimes it was Reed or someone else. On this night, it was a drunken Snake. He wanted retribution against the police who occasionally harassed his friend Reed. "Let's get back at them for fucking with you," said Snake.

That wasn't just the alcohol talking. Even then, loyalty was part of Snake's core. The drinking was the spark, but it was Snake's desire to have the back of his friend and teammate that was the engine. This would be a Snake trait throughout his football life, and up until his death. It's why so many teammates and others always felt a great sense of closeness to him.

The revenge taken against the police was a simple act of childishness. Snake and Reed saw a random police car and jumped on its hood, denting it, and then Snake smashed the light on the top of the car as Reed kicked the windshield.

The next day, the police, knowing who may have been responsible, showed up at Snake's school, asking the two teenagers questions. Both denied the incident, but the police did not give up. They went to the station, and the police chief brought the two to the damaged cruiser. "Take your shoes off," the chief told them.

They complied and in a simple piece of police work, the shoes were matched to the dents on the police car's hood. They were busted.

The damage to the vehicle was about four hundred dollars. Again, as when Snake got into trouble before, he expected some type of beating from Slim. Slim again surprised him. "Bud, I'm working just as hard as I can to take care of this family," Slim told his son, "and you know it. I'm trying to pay off those cars, and now I have to pay for your foolishness, too. I sure ain't got any four hundred dollars laying around. I can't hardly believe you did such a dumb thing as bust up a police car. Damn, you disappoint me."

Snake was devastated to see how hurt his father was. He redoubled his efforts on the football field, the quiet result being one of the most impressive high school football careers in Alabama history.

○━━━━━━○

Reed remembers Snake being "as slow as poison." They'd run a play where Snake would roll right and Reed would block. Reed would look in one spot, expecting Snake to be there, only Snake was running so slowly, he'd be yards behind. But, Reed says, "Snake was so slithery."

The athleticism was there, all over the place. What many people either forget or do not know is that in high school, Snake also played safety. "Playing on defense really helped me understand what it took to fool defenders," Snake said.

The 1961 Foley team went unbeaten and untied by scores of 52–0, 34–0, 41–6, 31–0, 33–0, 41–0, 59–0, 52–0, 37–0, and 53–0. The 1962 team won games by 13–7, 20–14, 37–0, 32–6, 27–0, 34–0, 37–6, 52–6, 27–7, and 21–7. The 1963 team, Snake's last year, lost only its opening game, to Vigor High School, but went on to win the rest of its contests. "I remember we went to Escambia [Florida] in 1962," Jones said. "I think Kenny ran one in and threw for two more, and we were able to upset them 20–14. Then his senior year, we played UMS-Wright when they were coached by Doug Barfield." Barfield would go on to become the head coach at Auburn.

"Kenny had a great game against them," Jones said. "I think he threw for two in that game and maybe scored on a draw play or something, and we won [21–14]. I think he may have completed fifteen of eighteen or something close to that."

One play in that game demonstrated just how smooth Snake was. Right after dropping back to pass, there was immediate pressure in Snake's face. He dodged left and tried to spin, but the defender still had a handful of jersey. So Snake dipped closer to the ground, and that loosened the defender's grip, and as Snake ran for what would be a long score, his shoulder pad was exposed thanks to the linebacker who had tried to wrangle Snake but could only grab some of his shirt, causing it to come loose from the pad.

Snake's performance as shown on tape at Foley is uncanny. There would be a legion of running quarterbacks to come— Staubach, Tarkenton, Young, Vick, Newton. Snake was as talented a runner as almost any of them and it all began on a high school field in tiny Foley.

Of the hundreds of fans who came out weekly to watch Snake scamper and slither and throw, a man named Lawrence

Hennessey—whom everyone called "Dude"—watched Snake play with almost no expectations. "I heard about Snake but the stories were so big, I wasn't sure if they were true," said Hennessey.

Then, like many who would watch Snake, the man named Dude exclaimed to the Foley coach: "We've got to have him."

Dude was an assistant coach at the University of Alabama. The attempt to catch a Snake had begun.

———

In 1963, Stabler was named homecoming king. On his arm was the homecoming queen, Judy Larson. The picture of them together is warm and quaint, and there is no hint of the Snake rebellion then, or the rebellion to come. Snake looked like any other young man at the pinnacle of his high school years. He wore a dark suit, buttoned to the top, and a thin tie clenched tightly around his neck. Judy stood to his right, a smile on her face, wearing a white dress and small crown.

She was the queen, but he had become one of the most popular students at Foley, thanks to his outgoing personality and athletic prowess. Judy would later pose with Snake in the minutes before the homecoming game. This picture was different. Judy still smiled widely as that crown was placed on her head, but Stabler's face, no longer content, was tense. He stared forward almost as if Judy weren't there or homecoming was just something to be dealt with, like grocery shopping. This would become a familiar expression for him. The fun. The games. The ladies. It was all something he loved, but none of it mattered once the games began.

Besides football, at Foley High School Snake was everywhere. As a member of the Key Club—a volunteer organization for students—he served lunch to his teachers at an appreciation banquet. Another day, he would hit a home run for the baseball team. Or paint pictures as a member of the art club. Or make all-county in basketball. Stabler was named "most athletic" by his class, along with Jearlean Petrey.

There was one thing missing from Snake's life, as was missing from the lives of many white school kids in Alabama at that time, and that was black faces, unless you counted the cast that put on the play *Showboat* in blackface—or the four-member janitorial staff. Snake grew up in the heart of the South, with Jim Crow laws still in effect.

In 1962, Snake's Foley team went 10-0 and was selected as the Class A champions by the *Birmingham Post-Herald* newspaper. As Snake was becoming a champion, parts of Alabama were imploding with racial strife and chaos. Just one year earlier, the Freedom Riders had blanketed the state. In 1963, in Birmingham, just a four-hour drive from Foley, there was a series of bombings, including the home of the brother of Martin Luther King, a civil rights office, and a Baptist church. Inside the church were four young girls who were killed.

Snake watched all of this unfold across his state and hated it. Later he would be angry at himself for not being more involved. Once Snake got to the NFL, he and Raiders teammate Gene Upshaw would sometimes talk about the civil rights movement. "I always felt like he almost wanted to apologize for what happened in Alabama," Upshaw said. "I told him once, 'You didn't become like those others. That's a victory in itself. Look at you now. It's great.'"

For all of Snake's eventual partying ways (which were indeed being formed in high school) there was always an introspective side. That is what kept Snake from becoming like the extremists that he saw while growing up. It armored him against racial prejudice.

⌐‒‒‒⌐

The clues to what Snake would become were scattered about his high school days. There was the May baseball game in 1963 against the UMS Cadets when Snake had three hits. The Foley newspaper, in October of that year, chronicled what was almost a regular occurrence. "Foley's first score came on their second play from scrimmage," the paper reported. "Quarterback Kenny Stabler went 41 yards for the touchdown. Stabler also added the point after. . . . In the second quarter, Kenny Stabler picked off an Alba pass and went 45 yards for a touchdown. The extra point by Stabler was perfect." In that game, Snake threw for a touchdown, intercepted a pass and returned it for a touchdown, and kicked two extra points.

Three months later, Snake scored a team-high 18 points playing basketball for Foley. In one game during a tournament, he scored 37, and was named to the all-tournament team. This is how it went for Snake in high school, maneuvering from excellence on the football field to the basketball court to the baseball diamond. "Stabler found halfback Jimmy Paul open in the end zone from 27 yards out for the first Foley TD," read one account. "The drive was started when Stabler recovered a fumble by John Johnson at the Crusader 45. Stabler's passing and Norman Moore's running carried the ball to the 27 in five plays, where Stabler hit Paul for the touchdown. Stabler kicked the extra point, his first of three in the game. . . . The second touchdown was made when Stabler circled end from a five yard touchdown loop following a 53 yard drive which took nine plays. Moore made a 31 yard run and Stabler a 10 yard pass to Paul to set up the Stabler touchdown."

By Snake's senior year, there were sometimes five thousand people at a game. It was also around this time that the nickname Snake began to appear in the Foley newspaper. There was almost a mythological feel to what Snake was doing. The Rotary club awarded the 1963 team golden footballs (not real gold, unfortunately). The mayor began appearing at all of Snake's football games. Snake didn't just kick extra points; he also punted. In one of his basketball games, a close 19–15 contest ended with the score 71–31, after Foley scored 23 consecutive points, with Snake scoring 12 of them on that run. In one baseball game, he struck out 12 batters and allowed only two hits. In another stretch, he pitched two shutouts in four days.

"Foley's win was largely due to the fine passing of Kenny Stabler," went one newspaper account of a Snake football game, "who completed 11 of 17 passes, made two touchdown passes and another that set up the final touchdown in the fourth quarter. His passing netted 162 yards."

It wasn't until August 1964 that the rest of the state saw the specialness of Snake. It happened at the North-South All-Star football game in Tuscaloosa. Leading up to that game, Snake was averaging 6.9 yards a rush. After that game, the Alabama media, which had heard of Snake but not seen him play, finally got a look, and the gushing commenced. After the game, a headline in the Foley newspaper proudly blared in large, bold typeface: "Sportswriters praise Stabler's performance."

"Comments of praise for Kenny and another Baldwin County headliner, David Chatwood of Fairhope, were carried by sports writers all over the state," said the newspaper. "Both players are signed to play freshman football at the University of Alabama and one game onlooker said, 'Bear Bryant was licking his lips.' Stabler was voted the game's outstanding back, and was described in one AP story as 'South genius . . .' It may be that Foley's Kenny Stabler Friday night played the best game of quarterback that's been played in this series which annually involves Alabama's top prep gridmen."

Wrote the *Anniston Star*: "The Snake is a young fellow out of Foley, Ala., who is headed for the University of Alabama on a football scholarship; much to the delight of Bear Bryant and Crimson Tide faithful. Listed on the roster as Kenny Stabler, a 175-pound, 6-2, left-handed quarterback, the boy from Foley dazzled 15,000 fans with the brilliance of his strike, his running, and his generalship afield. . . . Stabler opened up his own brand of lefthanded wizardry and turned what had been a dull show into a wild, 14-point performance."

Snake's final game at Foley was almost like a coronation and his play matched the moment. One story almost encapsulated the entirety of his impressive pre–Crimson Tide days. "Kenny 'Snake' Stabler closed out his high school career when he [led] his teammates to victory over the determined Fairhope Pirates. The slithering quarterback was responsible for 14 of the 20 points, passing 35 yards to Jimmy Paul for a third quarter score and slipping through the entire Fairhope defense on a 50 yard scoring run in the fourth quarter. He also made two out of three conversions. On defense, Stabler was a star too, when he cut two Fairhope drives short with pass interceptions and made a couple of key tackles."

It's important to note, however, that because of segregation, Stabler didn't compete against African-American athletes. It would have been interesting to see how he would have fared. My guess is he likely would have been just as dominant, because when he got to the NFL and went against the very best, he often beat the very best, no matter their color.

In one of my conversations with Snake, I asked him about his high school playing days, and how different it was not playing against black opponents. His response was thoughtful. "There were a lot of us that hated segregation," he said. "I despised it. Most of us wanted to play the black players. We wanted to test ourselves. But more than anything, most of us hated segregation."

The closest Snake came to playing with African-Americans was at the University of Alabama. An April 6, 1967, article in the *Tuscaloosa News* was highly discussed throughout the state. The headline: "Bryant checks Negro hopefuls." Bryant had invited five African-American players to try to make the team as walk-ons. This was an impossible mission for the players. Walk-ons rarely make any big-time college program, let alone at Alabama. They had little chance to make it but Snake remembers something Bryant told the white players before the five walk-ons arrived. "Coach Bryant told us that we were to treat them exactly as we wanted to be treated ourselves," Snake said.

Snake told his daughter Kendra that none of the white Alabama players would speak to one of the black players. What happened next was typical Snake.

"One day my dad saw him standing in the locker room alone and my dad went up to him and said, 'What do ya say man?' Basically, How's it going. They talked a bit and then went out to practice. After that the rest of the team welcomed and spoke to this particular gentleman. I love that my dad set the example that day to show [that] everyone is equal."

"My mom and dad met in college," Kendra added. "Both little rebels would sneak out of their sorority/frat houses and they would drive to the 'all black' clubs. That is where they liked to hang out. They both loved music, loved life, and loved people. Didn't matter the color. I love that they did that."

—————

By the time Snake finished his high school career in 1963, the results were impressive, particularly considering he never wanted to play football, and had to be bribed with a car to do so. He had rushed for 847 yards his senior year and passed for 862. He completed a record 64.7 percent of his passes. In 2016, fifty-three years later, that record still stood.

But it's important to remember the caliber of athlete Snake became in high school and how that athleticism manifested itself across many sports. In his senior year, he was just as dominant on the baseball field, where he won nine baseball games with a

blistering 125 strikeouts and five shutouts. At Foley, it was Stabler who handed the famous Don Sutton, from Clio, Alabama,
his only high school loss. In that game, Stabler had 16 strikeouts
and Sutton 14. Sutton would go on to win 324 games, including
58 shutouts and 5 one-hitters, in the pros. He's seventh on the
all-time strikeout list, and was beat by a future NFL quarterback. "When I was 17," Snake told *Sports Illustrated* in 1977, "the
Pittsburgh Pirates offered me $50,000 to sign. But by then I'd
gotten to like football. And I wanted to play for Coach Bryant. If
it hadn't been for sports, I wouldn't have gone to college. My dad
was a mechanic in a garage up to Foley, and I'd have followed
him, I'm sure. I went to college to play football, not for education.
That may have been wrong, but that's the way it was. I always
wanted to play pro ball, and I've done it."

"He was a wonderful pitcher," Brenda Hollis said. "We had
scouts calling day and night trying to get Kenny into baseball."
(The Yankees drafted Snake and he'd join an impressive group
the club would later select, including Bo Jackson, Deion Sanders,
and Daunte Culpepper. He eventually backed out.)

Then Snake met Bear Bryant. One of the things that first
struck Snake was how much his father and Bryant resembled one
another. They looked like relatives. They even dressed similarly,
with Slim often wearing tan slacks, a blue blazer, and the distinc-
tive hound's-tooth hat that Bryant would popularize.

Snake and Bryant would be one of the most successful duos
in the long, storied career of Alabama football. Their partnership
in some ways was the extension of the skill Bryant displayed as a
coach. He saw Snake's abilities and maximized them, and those
abilities were so considerable, Bryant had a great deal to work
with.

Snake would adapt as well, but only so much. On the field,
Snake embraced everything Bryant preached. Off of it, while he
had great respect for Bryant, he also still had an independent

streak. There was only so much conformity Snake could take. Even when it came to the mighty Bear Bryant.

"He was very imposing," Stabler told me, speaking of Bryant. "He kinda scared the shit out of me." Why? "He was a legend," Stabler said. "I don't know if there's an equivalent in college football today. He made you always want to do your best for him.

"I always did my best," Stabler added, "but I also had to be me."

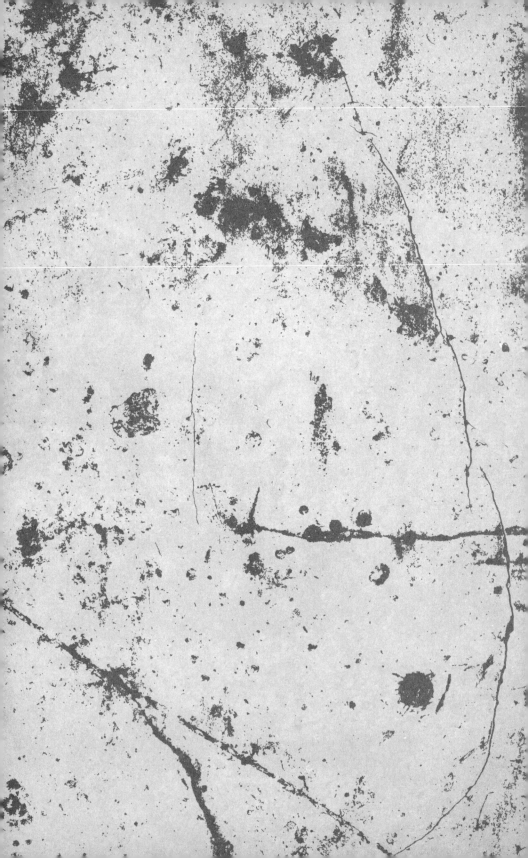

PART TWO

The Eternalness of Snake

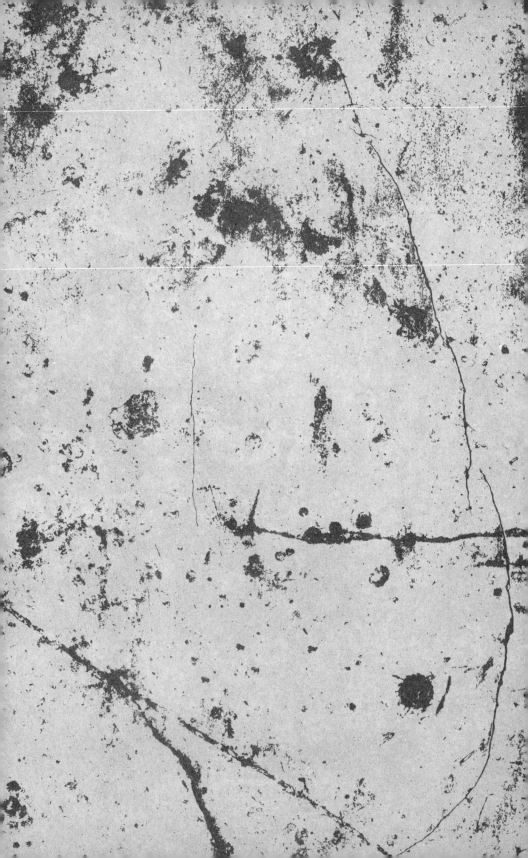

An act of bigotry, a stand against it, a moment of greatness in a life overflowing with them.

In all of the many things said about Ken Stabler, in all of the many things seen, in all of the things written and uttered, there have been a handful of Stabler moments that were never publicly chronicled. This is one of them. Over the years, Stabler forgot about it. Gene Upshaw never did.

Before Upshaw's death, he told me a story. He told me many stories about the Raiders days. Upshaw was the best guard in NFL history, and a member of the Hall of Fame. They were often conversation starters, or enders. Sometimes they broke the tension and in many cases the tension was thick. Sometimes Upshaw hated me. He believed I was a union-basher, but I never was. Eventually he would come to know this, and in several of our talks, once there was more trust, the stories would come. Many times, those stories were about race and the NFL. I kept notes (he was informed of this) with the hope of one day using his tales in a story or book. I collected stories from many 1960s, '70s, and '80s teams and players for decades, hoping to write a book on some of those personalities and franchises. I wrote one on the undefeated Dolphins. One on Jim Brown. Upshaw's only condition was that I not write stories he told me until after his death. Upshaw died of pancreatic cancer on August 20, 2008, at the age of sixty-three.

Upshaw was the African-American leader of a powerful union. I was an African-American journalist who appreciated his unique position, and Upshaw himself as an outstanding human being. I also suspected that not only did some NFL owners fail to respect him because he was a former player but also because he was black (he agreed with me). This was one of the reasons why we talked so bluntly about race.

Upshaw was, in fact, one of the smartest people I've ever known. He also knew the power of words. One of the things he would do with some owners (if not all of them) was decline to call them "mister" or "sir" the way many players, media, and others almost always did. Upshaw would call them by their first names. It was his way of beginning a conversation or negotiation with them, by letting the owners know they were all equals. No ground would be given. This is the mentality you would expect from the best guard in the history of football.

There was reason for Upshaw to be guarded about some of the owners. After one especially contentious meeting with a small group of owners, one of whom was Tampa Bay owner Hugh Culverhouse, the owners went to a different room. Culverhouse remarked to the other owners, "I will never be on another committee that has to deal with niggers."

Upshaw knew some of the owners felt this way about him. It's why he loved Al Davis and the Raiders. He knew Davis didn't feel that way. Upshaw also knew Stabler didn't. None of the Raiders did. This is one of the factors that made them such a close team.

One day, Upshaw told me a remarkable story about Stabler. Upshaw believed the incident happened in 1977, though he wasn't certain. He didn't remember the city exactly but believed it was San Diego. Upshaw and some of the Raiders players were meeting at a bar near the team hotel the night before the game. Upshaw remembers going to the bar with several teammates, getting there, and then soon after heading to the restroom. On his way out, he walked past a white man whom Upshaw remembers saying, "Get the fuck out of here, nigger."

Upshaw had seen the ugliness of racism before. He was born in 1945 in Robstown, Texas, and as a child, picked cotton. There was nothing Upshaw hadn't seen both as a child and a human being and it hardened his innards. It was that toughness that made him so prepared for football and a leader almost the minute he arrived at the Raiders.

But that moment . . . it unnerved him, Upshaw told me. The sudden and sheer nakedness of the racism—in a bar . . . Upshaw simply walking from using the restroom . . . doing nothing except breathing air and taking strides . . . it infuriated a man notorious for keeping his calm even in extreme circumstances.

When Upshaw played, he stood at six feet five inches and weighed over 250 pounds. Two of the most physically imposing men I've ever known were Upshaw and his fellow lineman Art Shell. There are few people who could have beaten Upshaw in a fight. The man, who had to be drunk in addition to being bigoted, was about to experience a world-class beat-down. Upshaw had started to move toward him when an arm came across Upshaw's chest, blocking Upshaw. It was Stabler.

"Hold on, Gene," Stabler said. "Let me get this."

Go back to Stabler and inside that Alabama locker room, when a small group of black players were invited to Crimson Tide practice, and the white players weren't speaking to one of the black players. Then Stabler intervened, and said hello to that player, walking with him to practice and defusing the situation. This was something similar. This was typical Stabler.

Stabler had entered the bar not long after Upshaw and, by chance, was standing near where the slur was uttered. Stabler knew what would happen if he didn't intervene.

"Gene would have beaten the hell out of that guy," said Stabler, "but somehow, Gene would have been blamed. The only thing I wanted to do was make sure Gene wasn't railroaded."

Stabler knew that if Upshaw defended himself, there was a possibility that Upshaw would be falsely accused. The instigator would walk away free and Upshaw would be imprisoned. That's how Stabler saw it and it's likely an accurate belief. The calculus of all this played inside Stabler's head. But he didn't need long to decipher the moment and all of its possible outcomes. After all, he'd heard of this kind of thing before. The idea of a black man getting treated poorly wasn't unfamiliar to him.

"Remember," Stabler said to me, "I grew up in Alabama."

Stabler told me his part of the story not long after Upshaw's death. Stabler had actually forgotten about the incident but it quickly came back to him once he was reminded of it. Upshaw remembered because it cemented something in his mind that he had always felt but was never able to fully digest until that moment.

"Snake is one of the most open-minded people I've ever known," said Upshaw. "He didn't care about race. He only cared about you as a person. All of the black players loved Snake. Loved him. One of the reasons why we were such a unified team in terms of race was because of him.

"I told him one time he had the racial halo."

What is that?

Upshaw initially laughed at the description, but then became serious. "When it came to race, he was an angel," Upshaw explained, "and like I said, he didn't care about race in any way."

This would become one of Stabler's quiet trademarks. It would be that way for the entirety of his life, from Foley, Alabama, to Oakland, California. The racial bigotry he witnessed as a child never took a foothold inside him. The opposite happened. The Snake persona was the one legends were built upon, but his ability to do something so many cannot—look only at the content of one's character—was in many ways his greatest accomplishment. This ability was also not restricted to race. Stabler was also able to look beyond gender.

Amy Trask was the first woman team executive in NFL history and worked for the Raiders for nearly four decades. She had many encounters with numerous Raiders greats, and her time with Stabler, she remembers, was always special. Not solely because of his football knowledge and connection to the past but because of how Stabler treated her.

"I had the tremendous good fortune of interacting with Ken a number of times over the course of my career," said Trask. "Each time I did, I asked him all sorts of questions. I wanted to learn and understand what he saw and what he thought when he played. Each and every conversation was utterly fascinating. And educational, wow.

"Also important to note this old-school Raider was utterly unconcerned by my gender. Never once—not one time—dating back decades did he ever interact with me in a manner that was any bit different than the manner in which he interacted with male Raiders staff. I loved asking him stories about 'old Raider ways.' When he spoke, it really was with a sparkle in his eye."

None of this is to portray Stabler as some kind of Martin Luther King. Other Raiders—in fact, all of them—would have also gotten Upshaw's back. Other white Raiders—in fact, all of them—also refused to see race. This was the Raider way. It still is. It will likely always be. It's the way Stabler did it that separated him. Stabler understood the harsh racial dynamics and acted accordingly.

After Stabler put his arm across Upshaw's chest, preventing Upshaw from pulverizing the man, Stabler moved close to the man's face. "Leave," Stabler said, "or I'll throw you out on your ass."

The man turned and left. The entire incident took just seconds.

CHAPTER THREE

5:30 A.M.

To understand just how far Snake came in his relationship with Bear Bryant—from adulation to defiance and back to worship—you have to first understand where he started.

The 1963 Sugar Bowl, between Alabama and Nebraska, was held in New Orleans. It had rained steadily all week, and right up until game time.

"We come out of the locker room and got right into the corner of the end zone," Snake said. "It had been drizzling and raining all weekend and I swear to God, he [Bear Bryant] stepped on the field, and it quit raining."

Snake obviously didn't believe that Bryant had stopped the rain. That moment did, however, add to the formidable and palpable legend of Bryant. This time Bear could stop the rain, but next time it might be a speeding train or the rotation of the earth. Snake would tell that story over the years and told it again, with great clarity, forty-six years after it happened.

Bryant is almost a mythical figure, like Paul Bunyan or Captain Kirk.

In 2001, Snake wrote the foreword for a book called *A War in Dixie*, about the Alabama-Auburn rivalry. Snake writes not just about his playing days at Alabama, but about what those days meant to him later in life. It's one of the few times Snake spoke this way publicly. "The Auburn people in Foley, Alabama, tried very hard to recruit me," he wrote. "Their style of playing in 1964 was very appealing. They had a quarterback named Jimmy Sidle who would sprint out and throw or run. That's how I played in high school. It was fun to watch Auburn play. Why, then, did I go to Alabama? Because Alabama won. When I was growing up in the early 1960s, in Foley—which is on the other side of the bay from Mobile—I followed Alabama football. I knew who Pat Trammel was, the great quarterback who died so young of cancer. I'd hear the stories of what it was like to play for Coach Paul 'Bear' Bryant. I knew who Harry Gilmer was and Bart Starr and Joe Namath, and I wanted to be part of that."

Snake also wrote: "When you have a special play, people are always coming up to you and talking about it. Even after all the plays I made as a pro quarterback, all those games against Pittsburgh when I was at Oakland, winning the Super Bowl, that run in the mud is one of the first things that people bring up. 'I was there when the umbrellas were turned inside out,' or 'Man, I was there at Legion Field.' Or, 'You know where I was on December 2, 1967?' I always say, 'I bet you were wet.' I get that a couple times a month."

A picture of Snake from one particular game while he was at Alabama shows almost a wide-eyed young man, in awe of it all. It was the Alabama-Clemson game in 1966 and Snake is on the bench, watching the defense; his left knee is secured in some type of wrap, and there appears to be blood around the knee, as the bandage is a moderate shade of red. The look on Snake's face is pure contentment. In that one picture, you can see Snake's feeling of joy, not just in playing the sport he loved, but in playing it for Bryant, and for Alabama.

One of the first things Snake noticed when he arrived at the University of Alabama was the women. This is common for many men upon setting foot on a college campus, yet to a man like Snake, whose pursuit of women was akin to another sport, it was a buffet. "Girls were everywhere," Stabler wrote in his autobiography: "blondes, brunettes, redheads. I had never seen so many great looking women in one place."

When Snake got to campus, one of the first players he saw was Namath. It was the summer of 1964 and both Namath and Snake remember the two played a two-on-two game of basketball in the Alabama gym. The two differ about how exactly that game went. "Snake was killing me, very physical game," Namath remembered. Said Snake, "He was the one who pushed me around."

It was at Alabama that Snake's penchant for independence was nurtured, which is fascinating because life under Bryant was strict, the opposite of Snake's personality. Yet, again, he would treat Bryant like he wasn't just a normal man, but something more godly. Part of the reason is how well Bryant treated his players. He was as loyal to them as they were to him.

Snake saw this early in his Alabama career. He played for the freshman team, and in one game against Tennessee, thinking it was third down when it was actually fourth, Snake was under pressure and threw the football out of bounds to stop the clock. The Volunteers got the ball back. It was one of the rare mental errors Snake ever made in college or the NFL.

After the play, Bryant approached Snake. "Have you lost your fucking mind?" Bryant yelled.

The team walked to the locker room. The door was locked shut. Initially, Bryant ordered the state trooper assigned as security to shoot the lock off. Bryant was told the bullet might ricochet off the lock and accidentally kill someone. Good point, Bryant thought, so he told everyone to get out of the way and used his shoulder to force his weight into the door, dislodging it off the hinges. He shoved the door aside, the team came in, and Bryant instructed everyone in the room that no player was to leave. That also went for the assistant coaches.

He turned to the team. Despite himself, he said, "I want to apologize for me and my staff for not preparing you people well enough to win the game today. It was us, not you, who lost that game. I'm sorry."

That was an example of one of the moments Snake would point to as why he felt so dedicated to Bryant.

That didn't mean Snake always listened to Bryant or respected authority. He constantly challenged Bryant when few players (not named Namath) would even dare think to challenge the coach or his staff. Bryant was an imposing and towering figure few people opposed. Hell, no one truly did. At that time, both on the college and pro levels, almost no player challenged a coach. The coach was judge and deity. He controlled everything and few disputed this power. Snake was different. He respected Bryant, greatly, and possibly even loved him as a second father, but this wasn't going to stop Snake from having fun. No one was going to get in the way of that.

Snake was in some ways ahead of his time. The country was changing as protests against the Vietnam War increased, and students, even in the South, began to insert themselves into the political discourse and civil rights movement. Snake's refusal to conform wasn't necessarily about those grandiose issues. It was, however, Snake expressing a form of independence.

Snake's harmless form of rebellion may have actually begun

with the manager of his dorm, named Gary White. The facility that housed the football and basketball players was originally not named after Bryant. There was a state law that prevented public buildings on college campuses from being named after living persons. The exception was made for Bryant and the dorm was renamed the Paul W. Bryant Hall after Bryant won his second national title. It was called the "Bear Bryant Hilton" because it was one of the more modern living spaces for college athletes. One publication described the building this way: "The facilities could house 136 athletes, two to a room, and contained all of the up-to-date conveniences of the day. It had central heating and air conditioning, two dining rooms, a color television room, four guest rooms, apartments for live-in coaches, a large recreation room, and several large meeting rooms that were also used as study halls. The rooms were equipped with 7-foot-long beds, dressers, lavatories, desks, bookshelves, and large closets. In 1970, telephones were installed in the rooms. Three meals were served daily, followed by a late snack usually served between 9:30 and 10:00 at night. In addition, a backyard patio with a number of grills was available for those who wished to cook out on special occasions. . . ."

Remember, this was the late 1960s. In some ways, even by today's standards, the facility was impressive. It demonstrated the level of commitment the university and Bryant had not just to winning but to the players as well. In return, players were to give their unwavering loyalty back to Bryant.

"Well, those were turbulent times," Snake once said. "The thing was the deal over the long hair and the hippies or beatniks . . . the Vietnam War was going on. There was a change of attitude all over the nation. I think that it got here down in the South a lot later. But we were faced with it and struggled with it. He [Bryant] made certain adjustments on things like hair length, but he did not change his fundamental philosophy. He told the players that,

'If you want to play, you're going to play the way I want you to. I know how to coach and how to win.' This would never change."

It wasn't just how they played that Bryant controlled—or wanted to control. It was how they practiced, how they lived, what they did in their spare time, and the rules he would create that needed to be followed. Snake didn't give a shit about haircuts or what he was supposed to wear on road trips. What he did care about was his ability to have fun and, yes, it started in the dorm.

White ran a tight ship. Publicly, he painted a mostly accurate picture of an Alabama team that followed the rules and obeyed the wishes of Bryant. "The boys are extremely proud of the dorm," White said in a 1965 newspaper interview. "You'd be surprised what good housekeepers they are and at the good care they take of the dorm."

Snake didn't always cooperate with the narrative. He and the other players called White Deputy Dawg behind his back, partly because of his slow southern drawl, but also because White was essentially the dorm cop. Players were required to be in their rooms by eleven at night and White would later come by each room, put his ear to the door, and listen for conversations among the players inside. If there were any, White would yell, "Cut the shit, get to sleep!"

One night, just before curfew, Snake and a teammate were heading up a flight of stairs to their dorm room, when one joke led to another, and Snake grabbed a fire extinguisher off a wall and aimed it at his friend. Instead, the hard stream of water hit White in the chest. "Stabler," White told him, "meet me at the practice field at five thirty in the morning."

The next morning, one of the great college throwers of all time, who would offer the best combination of charisma and talent the NFL would ever see in a quarterback, was on a grass field before sunrise, running two miles' worth of penalty laps around a track, and then doing drills on the grass field itself. It wouldn't be the first time White found Snake in violation of the dorm rules. There would be gassers for missing curfew or for refusing to wear slippers on the sensitive carpeting that would become scuffed when walked on.

As Snake developed into a star, his penchant for excitement grew, and not just on a football field or basketball court. He looked for it in other places and moments. Sometimes he found it in the simple act of looking for money. Stabler spent much of his early Alabama years totally broke but he found unusual ways to get cash. Because he was so intellectually stout—and as a physical education major wasn't required to do classroom heavy lifting—Snake sold most of his textbooks for money; the classes were so easy he didn't need them. He'd play roulette with cashing checks, doing so at one store, then going to another to get money to pay off the first place, and on it went until he made enough money, somehow and someway, to pay them all off, and he always did.

When Snake joined a fraternity, the weeklong initiation perfectly fit his adrenaline-seeking spirit. On the last day came the most interesting rite of them all. Snake was told to drop his pants and wrap one end of a long piece of string around his penis. Correct, his penis. After that, he maneuvered the other end of the string not attached to his penis up his shirt, and attached it to a pencil. Snake's mission, should he decide to accept it (and he did), was get twenty-five signatures of women around the Alabama campus. The problem was, each time one of them signed, the string, connected from pencil to penis, yanked on the latter, causing intense pain. Most of the women didn't know what was happening but one did. She misspelled her name—three times—so she had to write it over in each instance.

Snake would survive a tortured penis, and, later, an accident while drag racing at 110 mph, crashing after a part of the engine exploded, leaving him with three burned toes. The coaching staff made it clear, no more drag racing, and Snake complied.

Snake had fun but he worked extremely hard on the field. Before the 1966 season, Snake was named the starting quarterback. His search for fun and women was never outdone by one of the best work ethics on the team. Slowly Snake was learning what it was like to be a leader. "He [Bryant] was always tough but really fair," Stabler told me. "We did a lot of running and a lot of conditioning. I wanted to show him that I was a hard worker and that he could trust me. That more than anything. I wanted him to trust me."

———

There were many games in that 1966 season where Snake's impressive capabilities, and his dedication to the game, were evident. One of those contests was on the road at Tennessee. It rained for hours before the game, and then throughout it, but that didn't stop Snake. In what would be a foreshadowing, the worse the conditions, or the greater the opponent, the better Snake played. The Volunteers took a 10–0 lead in the first quarter and held it until the fourth. Then came Snake. On one play, he rolled right, and just as a Tennessee player tried to tackle him low, he swiveled his hips like a point guard, making the Tennessee player miss, then ran in the opposite direction to complete a deep pass. He later ran it in for the score from the one-yard line (and on the extra point attempt he saved the play by handling a poor snap).

As all of this happened, the rain started to fall even harder. The score was 10–8, and Snake would command another long drive, this one leading to a field goal. It was 11–10. Tennessee missed a field goal to win the game.

Alabama was 3-0, and had scored a total of 62 points. Snake accounted for 32 of them. He was rapidly impressing Bryant, but the Alabama coach wasn't going to let him know that. What made

Bryant perhaps the best college football coach of all time was his ability to get the most from players, and what made Snake so legendary was his constant desire to get better.

In the opener that season against Louisiana Tech, one play Snake called was a sweep to the left. Snake began rolling that way but noticed one of his wide receivers open down the field, so instead of running, he threw it deep. The play worked. Snake felt good about what he'd done. When he got to the sideline, Bryant was waiting to toss a slight jab right to Snake's chin. "One thing you should know, son," Bryant told him, "is you can't trust left-handed crapshooters and left-handed quarterbacks."

Bryant pushed Snake and chided him on occasion, but what he didn't do was shut him down. He allowed Snake the freedom to grow as a quarterback while also reminding him that he had to fit into his system and ways of playing the sport. One of the reasons for them butting heads, even though initially the conflicts were minor, was that Snake saw more than most first-year starters. Despite being so young, his knowledge of football was almost unmatched among his peers. He noticed how on the option plays and rollouts defenders would watch his eyes, and when he would turn them, or his head to make the pitch, they would move to attack where the ball was going. They could see where he was pitching the football.

So he made a change—he started utilizing no-look pitches. This was smart, though it added an element of risk that Bryant hated. Whenever Snake made the blind pitch, it worked, but Bryant would still apply that jab. "Stabler," Bryant would say, "you're luckier than a shithouse rat."

Snake wanted his life hacks and wanted to make the offense run more efficiently, but the truth is, the riskier play satisfied his sense of adventurism. The same adventurism that led to him joining a fraternity and having his dick attached to a string and puppeteered, and the same adventurism that would make him fearless and accurate in the NFL despite being concussed and straddled with bad knees. It would also manifest itself in something else Snake did: the jump pass.

Two decades before Snake, another Alabama quarterback, Harry Gilmer, had popularized the jump pass. When Gilmer was young he played with older boys, and because he was shorter, he needed to leap into the air as he threw the football. He continued to do this while with the Crimson Tide. Snake loved the move, and some twenty years after Gilmer, and about forty before Tim Tebow would repopularize it, he used it to great success. Except once. In one game, first five jump passes worked but the sixth was intercepted. Bryant didn't hesitate: "Keep your feet on the fucking ground."

Snake's Alabama team that year finished 11-0 and third in the polls. Alabama went to the Sugar Bowl and obliterated Nebraska by 27 points; Snake was named the game's Most Valuable Player. That season he completed 64.9 percent of his passes—at the time, a record. He threw for just under 1,000 yards and ran for almost 400. Snake did benefit from a rugged, stubborn defense but his year was nonetheless one of the most successful seasons a first-year quarterback ever had in the history of college football. Bryant didn't see it coming. Almost no one did . . . except Snake.

It was all going so perfectly. He was the quarterback for the Alabama Crimson Tide. He was playing for a coaching deity. He'd just gone unbeaten in a season. His face was prominent in every newspaper in the state. Pictures showed him smiling, wearing a dark jacket and tie, his hair slightly longer than it had ever been while at Alabama, holding the MVP trophy.

It could not be better for Snake. Then came that Corvette. That goddamn Corvette.

CHAPTER FOUR

Corvette Blues

There was a reason why Bryant came to tolerate some of Snake's antics. It's as old as organized football itself: Snake was too good for Bryant to totally dismiss.

Oh, Bryant would try, prompted by Snake's behavior. But in the end, he couldn't. The level of athleticism Snake possessed cannot be overstated. He physically didn't look the part but in the pantheon of college athletes—from Bo Jackson to Herschel Walker to Tim Tebow—Snake was as good as any of them. He was faster than people thought and stronger than people knew, and the core of his athleticism was a mind that could think quickly under duress.

As Bryant watched Snake practice and play at Alabama, this would become even clearer. Bryant knew what he had in Snake and Snake knew what he had in Bryant. Snake tried not to be Snake when playing for Bryant. He tried. He really tried.

———

The three highest-profile quarterbacks in Crimson Tide history are Snake, Bart Starr, and Joe Namath. Each quarterback, interestingly, had issues while at Alabama. In the case of Starr, the coaching staff at the time, and later even Starr himself, engaged in a cover-up over a series of brutal beatings Starr suffered being hazed while trying to get into Alabama's A-Club for varsity lettermen (Bryant wasn't the coach yet). Starr was beaten so badly it hampered his college career, led to his rejection for military service, and had an effect well into his NFL life. Starr kept his secret for more than sixty years and only recently did he disclose it. One of Starr's biggest crimes? He angered the A-Club hazers by eloping with a woman who attended rival Auburn.

He didn't disclose the severity of his injuries, which included weeks of traction, until 1968, when the school held Bart Starr Day, twelve years after he left the university. "What a difference twelve years makes," Starr said at a press conference then. "I had an escort into town today. When I was playing here we had an escort out of town." He added, "I left here with a bitter taste in my mouth. . . ."

Namath was suspended by Bryant because of one drink of beer. The team had a bye week prior to its last regular-season contest. During that week, Namath went to a local diner, and had just several sips of beer. Not an entire beer. Just a few sips. This still violated Bryant's policy that players were not allowed to consume any alcohol during the season. Since Bryant had sources in every diner, outhouse, farmhouse, and henhouse in Alabama, it was only a matter of time before he heard about Namath's beer-sipping exploits.

What happened next is the kind of thing that led so many players to cherish Bryant. After the suspension was announced, and as every newspaper across the state began looking for Namath, the coach who had suspended him hid him in his house. Namath ate home-cooked meals and enjoyed the hospitality of the man who suspended him. On the surface, such an arrangement seems, well, awkward. Not at Alabama. To Namath and Bryant, the punishment was transactional, not personal, and Namath was mature enough to understand that.

"Everything he did was to make you a better player and a better person," Namath explained. "This is why so many players truly loved him. You understood this just from spending a little bit of time around him." Namath laughed and added, "This is something I later explained to Kenny."

Okay, but back to the Corvette . . .

Snake decided that after beating Nebraska in the Sugar Bowl, he was going to treat himself. Most players under Bryant went out to get a burger to treat themselves. Snake was different. A burger wouldn't do. A car would.

And not just any car. Snake wanted a new 1967 Corvette. The gall needed to think that he deserved a Corvette when he didn't have credit . . . or money. Not even a damn dime. But this was Snake. The fact he wanted a Corvette wasn't arrogance. It was exuberance together with an understanding of the system. He understood the college game, and how much money (even then) it generated for the school. To Snake, he figured he'd get a piece of the action. He caught a ride to Birmingham and went to a car dealer, one that he knew had strong ties to Alabama. When Snake walked in and introduced himself, the salesman's eyes lit up. "Snake Stabler!" he exclaimed. "I saw you win Most Valuable Player in the Sugar Bowl. You guys just stomped the shit out of them Cornhuskers."

So, yes, the salesman was an Alabama fan. This was going to be easy, Snake thought. "You know the contract Joe Namath got when he went pro?" Stabler wrote in his biography. "I'm going to be a top pick, too. When I sign, I'll have a bunch of money. You just carry me till then and I'll pay off the whole note when I get my bonus." Snake wasn't lying. He did indeed pay off the car note once he was drafted by Oakland. The car cost about $5,700, or $40,000 in today's dollars.

Then while driving to Mobile to show off the car to a woman he liked, and hoping to utilize it like an aphrodisiac, he drove into a car stopped at a red light. There was extensive damage to the front of the car. Nothing was going to stop his date in Mobile, so he borrowed another car and made the trip. He arrived and told the woman it had been quite a morning already. "I started out today in a new Corvette that I bought without a cent down and no known credit," he told her. "You don't happen to know anyone who's good with fiberglass, do you?"

"No," she said, "but I'm good with some other things."

It was good to be Snake. Most of the time, anyway, the only thing that could slow him—truly the singular thing—was Slim.

"I really believe my father was a good man at heart," Snake told me. "I think if he lived today, he'd have gotten help. But men then didn't do that. They didn't get help. He lashed out in part because he was unhappy with his life. He also got jealous."

Jealous? "It bothered him that I was beginning to become famous," Snake explained.

As Snake's final season at Alabama approached, the talk was that Snake would go high not just in the NFL draft, but in the baseball one as well. From the *Anniston Star*, January 28, 1968: "Alabama quarterback Kenny Stabler has a problem. He doesn't know whether he wants to get rich playing professional baseball or football. Stabler, who guided the Crimson Tide to an 8-1-1 record this season, was drafted by the Houston Astros in the second round of the baseball draft Saturday as a left-handed pitcher. To complicate his life, he likely will also be a high draft choice in the pro football draft next Tuesday. Stabler obviously is aware that the football teams want his services and probably will be willing to bid for him with the baseball establishment. 'I will just wait and see how things go in the football draft before deciding what to do,' Stabler said from his home Saturday."

Instead of being proud of his son—and there was certainly an element of Slim that was—he began hating the fact that Snake was going to make millions and was already driving a Corvette, while he was still struggling with money. Some of this would again manifest itself in Slim's drinking and subsequent attacks against his wife and his daughter, Carolyn.

In Stabler's biography, he recounts a story Carolyn told him. Slim had come home late one night, drunk off whiskey, and began beating Sally. He had asked Carolyn, who was sixteen at the time, to make him dinner at that late hour. She refused. Slim assaulted her, too.

There would come a time, later in Snake's life, when the cruel abuse would stop. As he had done for decades, one warm afternoon in August 1970 Slim was mowing the lawn. This day, however, was different. He suffered coronary failure. Slim's immense physical strength and toughness—the opposite of his cowardly treatment of his wife—still allowed him to pick up the lawn mower and drive some fifteen miles to the doctor's office where Sally worked. Slim had suffered from severe indigestion for almost a month but ignored the symptoms. Snake has said that when his father arrived at his wife's office, Slim gave Sally his wallet and keys to the truck, and then was rushed to a hospital several blocks away. He was dead on arrival.

There were more than two hundred people at his funeral. "Funeral services for Leroy Stabler, 47, of Foley were held August 24 at 3 p.m. from the First Baptist Church of Foley," reported the *Foley Onlooker* of August 27, 1970, "with Rev. Bryant Scott officiating. Internment followed at Pine Rest Cemetery. He is survived by his widow, Mrs. Sally Stabler, Foley; one daughter, Carolyn Stabler, Foley; one son, Kenny Stabler, Foley; Mrs. Betty Sue Roland, Nashville, Tenn.; two brothers, Harold Stabler, Foley; and James Stabler, Lubbock, Texas; and one grandchild."

Twenty-eight years later, at seventy-four, Sally would die. "Mrs. Stabler . . . had worked for many years as a nurse's aide for several local doctors," wrote the *Mobile Register* in October 1998. "'She was just a wonderful, very simple lady,' recalled Dr. Marvin H. Taylor of Foley of the woman he said everyone called 'Miss Sally.' Mrs. Stabler had worked for Taylor for about 20 years, he said. In addition to her son, survivors include her daughter, Carolyn Bishop of Foley; two sisters, Annie Langley and Effie Lee White, both of Foley; four grandchildren; and four great grandchildren."

Slim and Sally were buried next to each other.

⌈————⌉

The telegram from Bryant to Snake was almost bone chilling in its succinctness:

YOU HAVE BEEN INDEFINITELY SUSPENDED
COACH PAUL W. BRYANT

Again, it all started with that Corvette, which gave Snake mobility. It allowed him to reach women in all corners of the state. This is not said in judgment. It is a simple fact. Snake did what college men have been doing since college began. He just did it better, with more ease.

The woman's name? It's unclear. What is clear is that Snake was infatuated with her. Initially he took the Corvette to see her in Mobile just once a week, but then it became three or four nights a week. Initially, Snake followed the rules at Alabama. Hell, he earned the award for the neatest dorm room, but there was always a part of Snake that was a self-saboteur. Off the field, there would be no conforming.

Snake's trips to Mobile to see the young lady became expensive in both dollars and capital with Bryant. He started skipping more and more classes. The reason was the commute. As fast as the Corvette could travel, it still wasn't a rocket ship. His first class was at eight in the morning, and he'd leave for Mobile at nine the night before. Snake would spend two hours with her and then head back. He'd miss that first class. In the beginning, just a few. Then more. Then all of them. The same with some of his other classes. Soon he was flunking them all.

"It was not easy for football players at Alabama to fail courses, particularly education majors," wrote Stabler in his biography. "All you had to do was show up. I took such classes as audio-visual aids, where I learned how to plug in and turn on a movie projector, and industrial arts, where we were supposed to learn how to make various doodads. I took that class because the teacher was a friend of the coaching staff who got to go on trips with the team. You could go into his classroom, jack around, and still pass. I never did make a doodad. But as I said, you did have to show up."

(Namath had one of the best jokes about Alabama and academics when he spoke to reporters on a plane ride to New York for his first press conference. "What was your major at Alabama, Joe, basket weaving?" Namath didn't miss a beat. "No, basket weaving was too tough. So they put me in journalism instead.")

There were, also, six speeding tickets in two months during Snake's trips between the dorm and Mobile. Eventually he did something almost fatal: he stopped going to football practice.

This was Bear Bryant. You thumbed your nose at his rules at your own peril. As much as Snake deified Bryant and respected him, Snake didn't fear him. After all, Snake had had a violent, alcoholic father. After that, there's little that scares a young man.

"My dad saved me," Snake would say, years later.

Slim had demons that even his close friends didn't know

about. This allowed Slim to function normally in society and have friends he might not otherwise have, had they known about his violence. One of Slim's friends was an attorney who composed a fake letter that read like a letter from the army. The letter stated that if Snake didn't return to football, he'd be drafted and sent to war. It was an immaculate lie, and it worked. Snake panicked and began to try to work his way back into Bryant's graces.

The first thing Snake did was reregister for classes to gain back his eligibility. Bryant wasn't impressed. They saw each other one day on campus, and when Snake told Bryant he'd make up for his transgressions, Bryant didn't believe him. "Maybe you should play baseball," he said, and the conversation was over. Stabler had a long way to go before Bryant would forgive him.

Snake was trying hard to return. It was genuine. The women were still there—there was a new one, in addition to the woman in Mobile—but nothing was going to stop Snake from working his way back on to the team. The switch that caused Snake not to give a shit, the rebellious Snake, was flipped back to the off position. Snake regained his eligibility and in the summer, two weeks before the start of camp, he went into Bryant's office. He'd rarely been so nervous.

Bryant was sitting and smoking a cigarette. Snake remained standing. "I'm ready to return, Coach," he said. "I worked hard all summer."

Snake recalled Bryant just glaring at him, silently, smoking and spitting tobacco into a cup. "Stabler," Bryant told him, "you don't deserve to be on this team."

Bryant was angry with Snake, but he knew Snake was one of the most talented players he'd ever seen. Bryant just needed to reestablish who was the boss and he needed it to be extra clear for Snake—that no matter how much he despised the rules, on a Bryant team there was no exception to them. It didn't matter how special a player was. Once Bryant saw that Snake understood this, he sent word to allow Snake back on the team.

Snake celebrated by buying a six-pack, hopping into the Corvette, and driving to Foley. He took the empty beer cans and tossed them out of the sunroof, aiming for stop signs. He hit most of them.

CHAPTER FIVE

Mudder

I was really fortunate to play for great, not good, but great coaches.
I have to admit that I gave them more aggravation off the field than
they deserved. But they all had a way of getting the best out of me on the
field. And every time I went out there, I gave them everything I had.

—KEN STABLER

n January 1968, Snake was named a co-captain. In the state at that time, this was like winning a Senate seat, perhaps even bigger. The decision was met with great pomp and circumstance. "Alabama's Kenny Stabler and Bobby Johns joined an exclusive club recently when they were chosen by their teammates as co-captains of the Crimson Tide," wrote the *Anniston Star*. "Membership in the club includes some of the brightest football names in Alabama's recent past. Such Tide All-Americans as Dr. Pat Trammell, Billy Neighbors, Lee Roy Jordan, Joe Namath, Stave Sloan, Paul Crane and Ray Perkins have been chosen as captains since Paul Bryant took over the football (reins) 10 years ago.

"For Stabler, the selection means final vindication for his abrupt suspension from the squad last spring. The young man from Foley, Alabama, has come a long way since he was put off the team for what his coach labeled 'non-conformity.' After going to summer school and earning a second chance to play football, the Snake performed brilliantly throughout the season. His fine play earned him a berth on the All–Southeastern Conference first team and the award for SEC Back of the Year by both the Birmingham Monday Morning Quarterback Club and the Atlanta Touchdown Club."

That's not how it all started, however. Snake initially wasn't a star or a part of history. He was, as Bryant constantly called him before he was named a captain, a turd.

His brown jersey matched the nickname. Bryant had a certain way of building hierarchy on his teams. Players wearing a red jersey in practice were starters, players who sported white were second team, third team was blue, green was fourth, orange was fifth, and the last team, sixth, was brown. Stabler was given a brown jersey and had to crawl his way back from the sixth team. It was a remarkable state of affairs, especially since Snake was coming off a brilliant Sugar Bowl performance for which he was named the MVP.

Snake's mental toughness was never more on display than those four weeks that hot Alabama summer, working his way back from the penal colony that was the sixth team, all the while Bryant exacting punishment for Snake's behavior. Bryant called players that made mistakes "turd," and that summer Snake didn't hear "Snake" from Bryant as much as he used to. Each time Snake made an errant throw or wrong read, Bryant would scream the word *turd*, along with a few other choice words. No matter how hard Bryant made it, Snake continued to fight. By the time the regular season arrived, he had worked his way back to the first team. This wasn't a shock. His talent would have vaulted him past almost anyone in college at the position.

But before Snake earned his way back into the good graces of Bryant, there was a penance. That season, the first game was against Florida State in Birmingham, and it was on national television. Snake was the backup in what was Bryant's last moment of humiliating him. The game started, the offense sputtered, and one series later, Bryant turned to Snake. "Let's see what you can do," Bryant said.

With those words, the punishment was over. Snake's season—his last one at Alabama—had begun.

Years later, Snake would write about his suspension at Alabama, and his rebirth, in the book *Always a Crimson Tide*: "I don't think I realized what he was doing for me until I was old enough to look back on it. In my case, I was young and dumb and wild, and when I became a disciplinary problem, Coach Bryant disciplined me. At the time, I couldn't see it, but he was teaching me a life lesson. I was close to throwing everything away, and he saw something worth saving. He suspended me then gave me the opportunity to get back. Don't think I got off light. I got the hell beat out of me at practice, but he didn't let me throw it away."

Then Snake once again showed how much he cherished Bryant despite the suspension: "Coach Bryant had a knack for treating everyone fairly, and in a way that everyone thought was the same. You believed that he was polite to the janitors cleaning up the stadium as he was to the president of the university, that he treated the fourth-team guard the same way he treated the All-American. He was taking care of me. He saw I needed a kick in the pants. I was just about to throw away my college career, which led to a 15-year career in the NFL and to a lot of other good things in my life. Without Coach Bryant saving me, I guess I'd be a bartender somewhere."

Snake wasn't going to be anyone's bartender without football. He was too smart. The low grades, the suspension, the poor decisions weren't due to a lack of intelligence.

Snake's self-depravation was an attempt, even years after Bryant's death, to continue to pay homage to him. Loyalty was a Snake element, a fundamental one, like oxygen. He always felt the need to pay back Bryant for having faith in him—and practically saving him—with kind words. "He gave me two opportunities," Snake said. "The first was when he offered me a scholarship to the university. The second was when he saved me from myself with his discipline. He prepped me for the next level, the next level of football with his teaching of fundamentals and understanding, and the next level of life with lessons that seem to come back at me all the time."

Bryant also had a lot to be grateful for. Snake's teams would go 28-3-2 at Alabama. The ultimate moment in Snake's Alabama career came in 1967 against Auburn. "What I remember most about that game was the mud *and* the wind," Snake told the author. "Most people just think about the mud. I get that. But the wind was just as big a problem."

Gusts approached 40 miles per hour. Many of the umbrellas became useless since the wind twisted them into upside-down messes. "When the rain hit you, it stung a bit," Snake remembered. "The mud on the field was up to your ankles. You could barely move."

Snake remembered Bryant telling the team before the game that since the weather was so bad, Alabama was going to have difficulty moving the football on offense, so they would play conservatively, and wait for Auburn to make a mistake on special teams. That's exactly what happened. Auburn had a series of special team miscues, including one that gave Alabama the football on the Tiger's 47. Alabama trailed 3–0 at that point.

What happened next would become one of many electric moments in the life of Snake. Just as some people remember the first time they saw the Beatles or Beyoncé, or remember watching the first moon landing, many football fans remember Snake's run in the mud. It would immortalize him.

In typical Snake form, he deflected a lot of the credit for the run to his teammates. "The thing that really made the run work was all of the great blocking that sprung me loose," Snake said. Some of that is true but there's little question when you watch the run and hear the reaction to it from Snake's teammates, that it was Snake who truly made the run work.

Initially, Snake and the Alabama offense weren't doing much of anything. "Kenny Stabler stood in the middle of the muck in the middle of Legion Field," wrote Benny Marshall in the *Birmingham News*, "and at this moment, this was Auburn's football game because John Riley had kicked a 38-yard field goal in the third quarter and because Auburn had been master of the day, which grew darker and wetter and windier."

The two best parts of the run are the very beginning and very end. He starts off rolling to his right for what is called an option play. For a left-handed quarterback, a pitch play to the right is far from easy, yet Snake's fluidity and ease of movement (as well as speed) make it look ridiculously so. Particularly when he transitions from potential pitch man to definite runner.

At the end of the play, Snake bolted for the corner and initially outran three Auburn defenders, and then a fourth who had the perfect angle of pursuit. What isn't generally known is that that year, Snake had begun to experience almost constant swelling in his knees, which required getting them drained frequently. While Snake always believed the knee issues slowed him, the run in the mud demonstrated it hadn't slowed him all that much, since he outran the Auburn defense in mud six inches deep.

After the game, Bryant approached Snake: "Son, I am as proud of you as I am of anybody who's ever been here. You've done a great job for me on and off the field."

Author Allen Barra was at the game, and wrote about the reaction of the play in his biography about Bryant: "It was the most spectacular play I have ever seen live in a football game. My mother had driven me to Legion Field to buy some souvenirs for cousins visiting from out of town, and as I jogged through the rain up to the souvenir stand at the gate, I realized the gate was wide open. I decided to go in just as the security people, hot dog vendors, and everyone else yelled and ran towards the end zone. I had a bird's eye view of Stabler streaking down the sideline, and thousands of fans leaving their seats as he ran past them—perhaps the first version of 'the wave' ever seen at Legion Field."

In his autobiography, *Bear*, the Alabama coach mentioned his complicated relationship with Snake. It was clear Bryant cherished Snake and appreciated what he did at Alabama. It's also clear Bryant felt he wasn't tough enough on Snake after he allowed Snake to return to the team. Bryant refers to the time he suspended his quarterback. "Snake Stabler had been great, and he was great for us for three years, but I've always felt I made a mistake with Kenny that hurt us later on.

"In the spring of 1967 I had to discipline him, much as I had to discipline Namath. It was over a combination of things. They just kept piling up and I couldn't overlook them. I finally suspended him from the team. But that fall—1967, his senior year—I took him back. We made an agreement. If he lived up to it, he could play. And he did. And he was a fine player, no doubt of that. But I've always felt my not being firm with Kenny—and I think he's a warm friend of mine now—had a bad effect on our morale."

It was a curious choice of words by Bryant. For his part, Snake never came close to saying anything negative about Bryant. It was always the opposite. "When I first got to Alabama, I hung on every word Coach Bryant said, but I got away from that and made some bad decisions," Snake said in the book *Bear Bryant on Leadership*. "Looking back, Coach saved me. He suspended me and stressed to me that no one is expendable. He taught me to be part of the group; it's the only way you'll succeed. I can still hear his voice today: 'You must sacrifice and persevere and if you do, you can do anything you want to do.' Coach saw something good in me and saved me from myself. He allowed me to be part of his football family, but only if I would conform to his rules and always put the team first."

Snake was magnificently talented, but not everyone in the NFL was convinced. Left-handed quarterbacks were viewed with great suspicion (some teams still view them this way now) because the ball leaves the pocket at a different angle when thrown, though the differences are minor. The lack of interest in Snake as a first-round selection was likely because of a more tangible reason. There were concerns about Snake's attitude and his devotion to football. This was an odd concern for a player who was draining his knees of fluid so he could play. Teams worried that his partying ways would hamper his NFL career. NFL teams knew he'd been suspended, and why, and this made some of them nervous. The Raiders, however, weren't one of those teams.

It was actually a close call as to whether Snake was going to play football or baseball. Closer actually than many knew. The reason was the money. Snake's first thought was that if he played baseball, it would be more immediate cash, but his love of football won over the money. The Raiders made him the last pick of the second round, fifty-second overall, in 1968. Davis signed him to a four-year contract that called for base salaries of $16,000, $18,000, $20,000, and $22,000. There was also a signing bonus of $50,000.

Did Snake's partying ways bother Al Davis at all? In his interview with me, Davis laughed. "He was smart and dedicated," Davis explained, "and that was easy to see. All you had to do was know just a little bit about him. I knew what we were getting even when things got tough initially after we drafted him. I knew there would be some early ups and downs with him, but I also knew what we had. We had a guy who had the potential to be a great star. We would just have to figure out how to manage him and the way to manage Kenny was to not manage him. Let him be himself."

Davis added: "We loved that Kenny was Kenny. With us, he could be Snake all he wanted."

PART THREE

Game Changer

CHAPTER SIX

The Perfect Raider

"We were the only team in football whose picture showed both a front and side view."

—STABLER ON THE RAIDERS' BAD-BOY IMAGE

DECEMBER 21, 1973
Mr. Al LoCasale
Executive Assistant
Oakland Raiders
7811 Oakport Oakland, Calif. 94621

Dear Mr. LoCasale: I have tried to reach both you and Al Davis for three days now, but my calls have not been put through. I understand that this may not be the best time in the football season to try to reach you by phone. Playoffs, travel arrangements and ticket purchasing procedure do not make it easy for you to answer a phone call from a magazine, so I decided to send you this letter.

We at Rolling Stone *were taken a bit by surprise when you decided to bar Hunter Thompson from covering Raider games and practice sessions. We decided to allow Hunter to deal with the matter himself, but when he informed us that he did not receive any substantial explanation for the move the matter became most disturbing. As I understand it from our brief conversation and from Hunter, the reason that you have barred him from covering pro football is "because of his personal involvement in the drug scene." I am sure that you understand that such an unspecified charge, with not even a hint of evidence to back up the charge, raises some serious questions about journalistic freedom and the First Amendment. If we were to allow such a vague charge to stand up, we would be certainly remiss in our pursuit of journalistic integrity and freedom. The same kind of generality could prevent Norman Mailer, Gore Vidal and even William F. Buckley, Jr., from covering major sporting events. We at the magazine feel it is our duty to defend our and their right to cover such events. As a matter of fact, I personally have been involved in sports for four-and-a-half years on a day-to-day basis. During that time, publications I worked for had a circulation of less than 7,000 and were still credentialed to cover pro football games and World Series games. As a matter of fact, I don't recall being turned down for credentials. Now a reporter for a national magazine with a circulation of around 350,000 has been told that not only can he not cover practice sessions, but that he cannot have even a pass for the press box.*

This letter is not meant to be a threat; Rolling Stone *has not decided to take any kind of action at this time against the Oakland Raiders or pro football. Journalistically, Hunter Thompson was going into the assignment with an open mind about the sport but, unfortunately, the events of the past two weeks, I suspect, may be changing his attitude. I have no reason not to believe him when he tells me that he has no intention of writing a negative article about the Raiders or pro football. As a matter of fact, as I explained to you a couple of times on the phone, the experiences of the Raider games and practice sessions were going to be used merely to background Hunter so he could cover the Super Bowl. I get the impression from talking with Hunter that he feels he is being forced to write a negative article. I hope it doesn't turn out that way.*

We still hope that Hunter can cover the Super Bowl and I hope that our requests for credentials for any future games are fulfilled.

I look forward to hearing from you as soon as possible about this matter. I think you can understand our viewpoint: We just can't let an unspecified attack like this prevent us from doing what we consider our journalistic duty.

Sincerely,

John A. Walsh

Managing Editor

Yes, the Raiders even managed to infuriate one of the greatest writers and magazines of all time. Like Snake, they didn't have many fucks to give, either, which made him and the Raiders a perfect match. Initially, however, it didn't seem that way.

———

In July 1969, just one year after he was drafted by the Raiders, Snake's phone rang. It was a reporter from the Associated Press. He wanted to ask Snake why he had quit the Raiders.

Now, decades later, the idea that Snake would quit at anything related to football seems absurd. He was, without question, one of the most supremely confident players in history. There was no cockiness or arrogance. He was well endowed with the belief that he would always win—either a single play, or a single game, or a Super Bowl. Thus the reason he considered quitting is more complicated. Snake loved the game but the politics around it was poison to him. The business aspect of football was to be despised, Snake believed, like shingles, and, more important, it drained him. It took his energy, which had the kilowatts of a burning sun. But even a sun can lose its brightness.

"Why'd you quit the Raiders?" Snake was asked by the reporter.

"There's not much sense in staying in it if I can't enjoy it," came the response.

"I know that it's hard to tell a football fan you're tired of the game," Snake continued. "I'm not tired of playing football. I just hope that people will understand."

Few did. The Raiders had used a second-round pick on Snake, and to make matters worse, no one on the Raiders knew Snake was quitting. It was a total shock to coach John Madden and the entire team. After Davis found out Snake had quit, he referred to Snake for several weeks after that as "that fucking guy." What made matters worse was that Snake was scheduled to play Kansas City in an exhibition game in Birmingham. On the plane ride to the game, unbeknownst to anyone on the Raiders, that fucking guy had been contemplating quitting the entire time.

Snake next indeed left the team. After a Monday practice in California, he caught a flight to Birmingham, and then drove to Tuscaloosa. No one knew he was gone until it hit the media.

What the media didn't know was exactly how Snake left. After that practice, he asked Raider defensive tackle Dan Birdwell if he could borrow his car. Snake drove the vehicle to San Francisco International Airport, parked it in a long-term lot, turned off the ignition, and put the key under a mat in the front seat. He then phoned the Raiders and informed them he was going home.

"I really enjoyed playing for coach Paul Bryant at Alabama, but I'm not happy now," he explained to the reporter. "At Alabama, I looked forward to the game and doing well. I could really get fired up. It's not there now."

And that was it. He was gone.

———————

Of course, we know that's not how the story ended. A Super Bowl win would come. The Hall of Fame would come. Yet that moment, like at Alabama, was instructive. It had mostly been easy for Snake to be great. He was immensely capable at Foley and Alabama. The NFL was different. Everyone was skilled. Everyone was fast, and the violence was far nastier. A part of Snake had believed that his skills would transfer to the NFL the same way they did at Alabama. They didn't initially, and at certain points it seemed to him they never would.

But that lack of confidence was momentary. Snake also didn't want to do the alternative—be a normal guy. In his year away from the NFL, Snake sold insurance in Tuscaloosa. He went from 190 pounds to 218. He was incredibly bored. It is not hyperbole to say that a man like Snake would have gladly lost a limb rather than work a nine-to-five job. Insurance sales was light-years from who he was and what he loved to do.

Thus, the inevitable happened. In late November 1969, the media buzzed of a Snake return. Snake made the announcement and was his usual loquacious self. "I'll be back in pro football come June with the Raiders, in Canada, or perhaps somewhere else," he told the media. "But I'll be back. . . . I've really missed it that much. Watching Alabama practice and watching the pros on TV, well, it's really bothered me. . . . I want to let the people in Alabama and the South who watched me play know I can do just as well for Alabama and the South in pro football as I did at Alabama."

Snake would talk publicly about going to Atlanta to play, but the seeds were already planted for an Oakland return. The Raiders knew his abilities were vast; they never gave up on Snake. John Madden and Al Davis saw his potential. All Madden had to do was convince Snake to return, which actually didn't take much effort.

"In my coaching career, I never met someone who loved football as much as he did," Madden told me.

When Snake and Madden met, Snake had the same demeanor

he had after meeting with Bear Bryant when trying to come back from the suspension. There was almost a desperation, a hunger, to play football. Like Bryant, the Raiders coach could see it as well.

In one of their first practices together, Madden stood over Snake's shoulder and watched him throw routes. Even in those ordinary moments, Madden saw Snake's smarts and accuracy in throwing the football.

Snake's NFL career began remarkably low-key. In many cases, a future star at quarterback has a moment, or series of moments, that show the greatness to come. That didn't happen early in Snake's Raiders career. He had surgery to repair torn cartilage in his knee, after which he needed crutches. He saw friends. He worked out with the Raiders in the weight room. There was a great deal of nothing, of averageness, at least in football terms.

He began dating a woman named Isabel Clarke. She wasn't one of the women who would temporarily enter Snake's orbit only to be flung into deep space later. She was different. Isabel drove Snake around in the Corvette, sometimes as Snake's legs and crutches hung out the side window. Isabel was smart, and loved fun the way Snake did, but she was terrible at driving a car with a clutch. When they pulled into one of the Alabama campus bars (Snake often traveled back to campus in those early days), Isabel accidentally left the clutch engaged, and the Corvette—parked in front of the bar, directly in front of a large glass window—went careening through the window and into the bar. It was like something from a comedy movie. No one in the bar or car was hurt, but shattered glass covered the hood of the car. They sat in the car for a moment, speechless; it was one of the few times Snake was utterly shocked. He panicked. "Let's get outta here," he said.

They left the scene and decided to wait things out at a local motel. The problem was, Snake was one of the most well-known faces on campus. He couldn't drive through a fast-food lane without being recognized, let alone through a window in his Corvette. It wasn't long before the police found him. There were no arrests, Snake paid the damages, and not long after that, Isabel and Snake were married. Snake sold the Corvette.

"I thought I was in love and didn't want to leave her," Snake would write in his autobiography. "But I'm sure I didn't know what love was about then. I think I felt I'd be lonesome, going off alone to a whole new environment. I hadn't been out of Alabama for any extended period of time, and now I was going to California."

That type of openness is what makes Snake so easy to like. He was *always* open. Snake is one of the few sporting greats who were resolute and fierce but also in touch with their feelings, before it became popular for men to be that way. It's also true that at times he had no regard for the institution in which he constantly engaged: marriage. When Snake was away from football, he took those frustrations out on Isabel, getting drunk and starting verbal altercations that would last hours.

———————

What's often lost about the Raiders in that era is that the team was a group of intellectuals. Davis and Madden were the top big brains, but the players weren't far behind when it came to high IQs. Snake and a host of other Raiders fit neatly into this construct.

In the biography *Madden*, author Bryan Burwell describes the coach's relationship with Davis, which was based on testing and pushing intellect.

"The one thing that Madden understood and appreciated about Davis . . . was that Davis was a firm believer in the Socratic method," Burwell writes. "He wanted to turn every conversation into a heated debate. Davis' management style was to provoke someone into defending himself and scrutinizing his position by offering an often-harsh opposing viewpoint. It was always business, not personal, unless you wilted under the intensity of the argument. Then it became very personal, because Davis saw that as a personal failing, and he hated weakness in the men he chose to be leaders.

"Al liked a good argument," Madden told Burwell. "He would say things just to see how you really felt about it, and I enjoyed arguing with him, too. It always seemed to me like they were academic arguments."

Once, Davis asked Madden this hypothetical: "Would you trade Ken Stabler for Jack Youngblood?" referring to the defensive star and future Hall of Famer.

"No fuckin' way," Madden responded.

That type of more intellectual approach—you will rarely hear the words "Socratic method" in association with a football team—is what Madden would use with his players. Madden would challenge their minds, and while it was understood by the players that he was the boss, he allowed them to be them, in whatever form that took. This is a coaching philosophy that is almost nonexistent in football today. Coaches and the league want to exert as much control over players as possible. In contrast, the Raiders in Stabler's era didn't just loosen the leash on the players. There was no leash.

As a result of Madden allowing them that freedom, the Raiders players responded with smart and hard play. Madden coached the Raiders for ten years, and in five of them the Raiders were among the least penalized team in football.

Snake was one of the best examples of the freedom Madden provided. No one drank harder, or caroused more, than Snake, but Madden didn't care, because no one on the team played harder, or better, or cared more, than Snake did.

One of the men who quickly recognized Snake's talents was

quarterback George Blanda. He emphasized to Snake that since Snake didn't possess the strongest of arms, he should work on his accuracy, and since Snake was very smart, he should focus on knowing everything about his offense, and every possible wrinkle a defense could toss at him. Blanda was an excellent teacher and it's easy to see why. Blanda played 26 seasons, the most ever in the NFL, and finished his career having thrown for over 26,000 yards and 236 touchdowns.

Blanda was also a drinker, which was another factor in them becoming close. He would put mixed drinks in Pepto-Bismol bottles and strategically store them in the training room for easy access.

Madden knew a tutor for Snake when he saw one and encouraged Blanda to teach young Stabler the ways of the NFL. Blanda was happy to oblige and soon the two became road buddies, hanging in various bars, clubs, and any other place that stayed open late and served lots of alcohol.

"I remember one of our road games [in 1975], I think it was Denver, and I had bed check duty," remembered John Robinson, an assistant coach on the staff. "Well, Kenny and Blanda and Pete Banaszak were all late. I had to go tell John, who was always nervous anyway. They're all out forty-five minutes after curfew, and when I tell John, he starts cursing up a storm. So now we're both out in the courtyard of this hotel just waiting for them. And here they come strolling in like they didn't have a care in the world. Well, John starts screaming at them."

Madden was less upset about them being so tardy for curfew as he was fearful that something had happened to three of his star players. "What the fuck were you thinking?" Madden yelled.

Snake didn't wait for the other players to speak. He took the lead. "Don't worry about it, John. We'll kick these guys' asses easy."

That's exactly what would happen. The Raiders beat Denver,

42–17, and Snake, who was possibly drunk just hours before the game, was 11 of 15 with two touchdowns and a passer rating of 121.1. He was practically flawless.

Madden would come to a specific place when it came to the Raiders and football players in general. Wrote Burwell: "This was the sort of compromise Madden seemed to be willing to make with his players. If you could stay out half the night and play like hell on Sunday, that was an allowance he could afford. The art to coaching the Raiders was to deal with the craziness of it directly or indirectly led to winning football games. Madden believed there was something in the culture of pro football that bred men who loved living on the edge. If you took that renegade edge away from them, restricted them with too many rules and regulations, it might take away some essential trait in their competitive personalities. So even if it drove him to nightly anxiety fits, he'd just grab a bottle of Pepto-Bismol and deal with the angst." Madden's approach was much different from every other NFL coach's at the time, and from almost every coach's now.

It didn't take long for the organization to see Snake's mental prowess as well as his superhuman drinking abilities. As Snake's knees healed (mostly) and his confidence regained its original form (totally), Madden grew to trust Snake more. One of the things that amazed Madden the most was Snake's recall. In planning for specific games, both on the practice field and in the classroom, Madden's offensive concepts and plays would stick inside Stabler's cranium and stand ready for instant recall. Snake often joked that he studied the playbook by the light of a jukebox.

The truth, like many things with Snake, was far more complicated. Snake was a voracious and quick study who not only almost never forgot a play but also had a talent for keeping the play and all of its intricacies clean when under the duress of a pass rush. "So Kenny . . . may have been calling the plays, but it wasn't 'their plays,'" says Madden. "It's *your* plays and it is a whole-week process where you are basically feeding the information into their heads every day in meetings and practice. Short-yardage situations, this will work. Two-minute offense. Red zone. This is where working with Stabler was great. You could give him something, and it was in his head. 'This is the first goal-line play we want to use. This is the first play-action you want.' I was able to prioritize all of these for him so that whenever he got into a particular situation . . . BOOM . . . it's in his head."

And it stayed in his head. No amount of bourbon or carousing erased it.

Madden and Snake's relationship was initially problematic, but the cause was an external one. Stabler initially toiled on the bench, for almost five years (in 1970 Snake threw a total of seven passes), playing mostly behind the aging Daryle Lamonica. In the history of the NFL, few players threw a more gorgeous—if not always accurate—deep pass. His nickname was "the Mad Bomber," after all. Davis had traded for Lamonica and wanted him at quarterback over Stabler, because Davis wanted the Raiders' main tactical approach on offense to be deep passes, something Lamonica did well but Stabler didn't. Stabler's greatest strength was his accuracy in the short and medium passing game. He picked defenses apart instead of carpet bombing from the pocket.

Madden saw the emerging Snake and wanted to start him but knew he'd get a fight from Davis. Raiders players told Snake he was only on the bench because of Davis, not Madden, so Snake stayed mostly quiet, waiting for his chance. When the end of the 1972 season came, the buzz inside the locker room was loud, as veterans wanted Snake to start. They had watched as Madden would sometimes bench Lamonica for George Blanda or Snake. They players wanted Snake and knew the only reason he wasn't starting was Davis.

Snake eventually lost his patience. In the preseason of 1973,

Snake believed he'd be the starter. It didn't happen then or when the regular season started. Again Lamonica would eventually be benched in a game by Madden for playing poorly. The Raiders opened 1-2 and were getting ready to play in St. Louis. There was a cloud hanging over the franchise, since the week before, Madden sat Lamonica in the second half against Kansas City. That Tuesday, before the Cardinals game, Snake went into Madden's office to confront the coach about how he was being utilized. In many ways, the meeting was typical Snake and Madden. Snake was passionate but respectful; Madden was understanding but stern.

Snake spoke first. "John, that situation you sent me into on Sunday, down by thirteen with just a few minutes to play, I don't want to go into one of those again. Start me, and I'll go all the way. But you can't count on me to go into situations like that again. I think I'm playing well enough to start, and I want to."

Madden was calm. "I hate to hear you say I can't count on you in those situations."

There was momentary silence. It's likely Snake was rethinking his choice of words. No coach wants to hear the words *you can't count on me*. And no player actually ever wants to utter them. Ultimatums also usually went over poorly with Madden.

Snake slightly rephrased his words. "You can count on me, John, but you can count on me to play regular and do the job. I just don't want to go in and mop up somebody else's mess."

"Well, I'm sorry you feel that way, Ken," Madden responded. "But we haven't decided to change our starter. That's the way it is right now. What you have to do is go out there in practice and just keep working hard."

Snake left the meeting frustrated, but he followed Madden's advice. As the primary backup, Snake played the quarterback on the scout team, which consisted of him imitating that week's opposing thrower against Oakland's defense. Some Raiders players remember a handful of practices where Snake never threw an incomplete pass, something that is almost unheard-of. The practice after the meeting with Madden was one of those moments. Snake wore a red jersey, signaling the scout team quarterback, and imitated the Cardinals' Jim Hart, a four-time Pro Bowler (who also holds the record for interceptions in a Pro Bowl game, with five).

Snake was so startlingly efficient, Madden had no choice. He had to start Snake.

The next day, after that initial terse meeting, came a second one. Snake, as was often the case, was the first player in the locker room. Madden and Snake walked into Madden's office and the coach's message was clear and succinct. "You're gonna start this week in St. Louis," Madden explained, "and win or lose, you're gonna play. It's your ball, Kenny."

It is difficult to explain how crucial that moment was, not just for the Raiders, but for the entirety of the NFL, and its history of elite pass throwers. Football teams are synergistic forces, to be sure, and the Raiders epitomized this. Yet, while Oakland's defense was the engine, Snake was the ignition. His ability to lead, and throw with accuracy, is possibly the biggest reason the Raiders would undergo a fairly rapid transition from mediocrity to championship.

For the next seven years, all in Oakland, Snake would cajole, dominate, amaze, fascinate, feud (with Davis and one journalist), and party (with many) as the quarterback for the Raiders. He was a comet, flashing across the night sky, but the result was eternal: a legend.

Outside of the Raiders, there was an almost mythical quality to his life. Snake's reach would go beyond football—from the sublime to the absurd. He'd pose for a magazine shoot with a bare-chested woman model. He'd hang with musicians. He'd hang in a hot tub nude with teammate John Matuszak and several flight attendants. He'd be on the sets of television studios as an analyst. Or, when he was eventually traded to Houston, he'd talk to reporters while sitting at his locker naked, one leg crossed over the knee, smoking a cigarette. As a radio analyst for Alabama, he'd go out to the bars the night before a game, drink and chat, and then go to the field the next day wearing the same clothes he had on at the bar.

He always said hello. He was always kind. He was always smart. He'd show up in some of the most pivotal moments in NFL history. Not because he was fortunate but because he made his own luck.

"I have such deep respect for him," says Baltimore Colts defensive lineman Joe Ehrmann, who played against Snake. "He was kind of the personification of cool. Whether they were in the first quarter or the two-minute drill, his heartbeat and blood pressure stayed the same. You could just look over [on the field] and see how he was so cool and calm. We had such great respect for him. No matter what was happening, he never changed. His voice never changed. You were always listening to that Alabama twang of his."

All of it began that day in Madden's office. Madden was always honest with his players. He'd keep his word. Snake was his starter. Then again, Snake made the initial decision easy, and the subsequent promise to keep him as the starter an even easier one. The team with Snake at the helm went 3-0-1. In his fourth game as a starter—*his fourth game*—he completed fourteen consecutive passes. That notorious accuracy was there from the beginning.

In the locker room after that game, the Raiders' fullback Marv Hubbard made sure to pull Snake aside. "There's nothing that makes a club go to hell faster than a quarterback who loses his cool," Hubbard said, "and you are one cool country boy."

There are only a handful of quarterbacks in the history of the NFL who displayed the kind of chill that Snake did when quarterbacking. Players like Joe Montana and Aaron Rodgers are among them but Snake was even better at keeping his calm than they were. The violence of the game didn't scare Snake, and that coolness was genetic, not a learned trait. Maybe some of the bravery came from a father who fought in a great war. Maybe some of it came from a distant grandfather who took part in the American Revolution or a mother as tough as any of them. Whatever it was, there was a reckless but admirable fearlessness to how he played football.

"Getting close to all my teammates helped my quarterbacking," Snake would write. "The best part of the game was the brotherhood, laughing and working together. It was my personality to be part of all that, to go out for drinks with the guys, jack around, chase and carouse with those who wanted to. I asked everyone about their injuries, their families, whatever they wanted to talk about. I made sure that everyone knew that I was interested in them not just as players but as people. Again, it was important for me to be liked and it was important that my teammates knew I liked them."

Snake was far from the only one who would enjoy life on the Raiders. In 1975, during training camp, the Raiders signed linebacker Ted Hendricks. He was known as the Mad Stork, and took part in one of the more amusing moments in Raiderdom. As players were readying for practice with their stretching routines, Madden noticed that Hendricks wasn't there. He basically had just one rule: don't be tardy. Just as Madden was asking about Hendricks's location, Hendricks, in full practice gear, and wearing a German helmet with No. 83 painted on both sides, entered the field on horseback. He approached the center of the field and dismounted. It remains the greatest entrance in NFL history.

"It's things like that where it's just easier to go along with it," Madden said of this incident, in Burwell's biography of him. "You have to remember back then, we were in training camp for over two months. We had six preseason games. Every practice was in pads, and there were two-a-days every day. So sometimes you needed things to break the monotony of training camp, and that sure as hell did."

What did Snake think? "We all just looked at each other and said, 'Yep, fits right in.'"

CHAPTER SEVEN

Throw Deep

O n October 7, 1973, in Snake's fourth year in the NFL, Madden met with the media after the Raiders beat the Cardinals, 17–10, on a brutally hot day in St. Louis. Snake's insertion into the starting lineup was working. Madden began talking about the offensive troubles early in the game and how Snake was able to solve them. "It would have been easy to figure we were snakebit," said Madden. Then, realizing his interesting choice of words, he caught himself.

"Maybe that's not the best way to put it, but it would have been easy to get down because we made those early mistakes and didn't score. But we just kept going and Snake didn't let those things bother him. He mixed up his plays well and did things exactly the way they should have been done. Everything he did worked right."

Snake was humble. "I'm just happy we won," he told the media. "But I don't think one game means that much. I'd like to wait four or five games to evaluate my performance. The Cardinals are a good team, but we gave them a lot of life with our mistakes. We made it tough on ourselves. But our line deserves credit. They whipped them up front."

Snake truly understood the media. He used them as much as they did him when writing about his exploits on and off the field. What Snake most understood about it was how to appear like a leader. In many of his quotes—except a few notable ones—Snake praises teammates and coaches. He used the newspapers to communicate to teammates, knowing many of them read everything. Snake knew a well-placed compliment in the papers could go a long way in the locker room.

It was also becoming clear that Snake was like nothing they'd ever seen in Oakland. One of the reasons was his toughness. During a game against Denver on Monday night, October 22, 1973, Snake was sacked six times as the Broncos blitzed him on almost every play. Despite the pressure, Snake was still able to find the open receivers, torching the Broncos with both short and long throws. He finished with 322 passing yards.

The *Oakland Tribune* headline about the game read: "Snake Betrayed by Mates' Errors." Another story in the *Tribune* highlighted Snake's ability to take a beating. "If there is justice, it should have been Kenny Stabler's finest hour as an Oakland Raider," the story read. "The Alabama Snake had his finest game as a pro, guided his team through adversity to the brink of sole possession of the division lead and should have solidified his spot as starting quarterback. Instead, Stabler isn't even sure if he'll play this week in Baltimore after Denver's Paul Smith jarred him out of the game as Kenny drove the Raiders toward momentarily tie-breaking points late. . . ." On the flight home, Snake spoke to reporters. "I was scared at first," Snake admitted. "I thought something might be broken. They already X-rayed it, and they say it's a dislocated second toe and turned ankle. They gave me a shot so it really doesn't hurt now."

Smith hit Snake so hard on that play that after the game he approached Snake and apologized.

There was never a chance Snake would sit the next week. If he could walk, he was playing. The Raiders played six of their first seven games of the 1972–73 season on the road. It was almost unprecedented for a team to open its season with that many road games; still, they had managed a 4-2-1 record at about the midway point. "Stabler Engineers a Victory," read the *Oakland Tribune* headline. Against the Colts, his ribs sore, and his ankle still smarting from the game six days earlier, Snake completed 25 of 29 passes for an 86.2 completion percentage. That broke a twenty-eight-year-old record set by Sammy Baugh. The 25 completions tied a team record.

The following week, the only thing that proved negative about the Raiders' 42–0 thumping of the New York Giants was the fan reaction to the CBS simulcast of both the Raiders and 49ers game broadcast in the Bay Area. The network flipped back and forth between Raiders and 49ers coverage. There were 353 complaints about the coverage, the majority of them Raider fans who felt not enough airtime was given to Oakland.

————

Joe Greene is one of the most talented and vicious defensive linemen in NFL history. He appeared on the cover of *Time* and was a ten-time Pro Bowler, a two-time defensive player of the year, and a four-time Super Bowl champion, and is a Hall of Famer. Greene was the destroyer of bodies and dreams, and on November 11, 1973, all 275 pounds of Greene crashed into the leg of Kenny Stabler.

The Raiders were at home, playing against the Steelers, and Oakland would lose the game, the third time in one year the Steelers would get better of them. The reason this time was Greene's hit. It sent Snake crashing to the ground and out of the game in the first quarter. Once Snake was gone, the Raiders didn't stand a chance. "Stabler is the hottest quarterback in the league," said the Steelers' quarterback coach, Babe Parilli, who was a former Raiders quarterback. "Getting him out of there was a very, very, big break for us. . . ."

Among all the things written about Snake, this moment is one of the more underrated. "Everything would change for us the few times Snake got hurt and he couldn't play," remembered Gene Upshaw, the Hall of Fame guard. "The offense would be completely different. Defenses were always afraid of how he'd pick them apart. When he wasn't in the game, they weren't as fearful. His absence always cemented in our minds how valuable he was and how he was our quarterback."

(Upshaw played brilliantly in that game, as he did almost every game, despite getting punched in the back of the head. Upshaw was going against a former Raider defensive lineman, Tom Keating, and the two were friends. Just not during the game. "Gene grabbed my jersey," Keating explained. "He was holding and I said a few obscenities. He jawed back, I lost my composure, and hit him on the back of the head. He punched me in the mouth the next play, then Jim Otto jumped in between us. I just lost my temper.

Said Upshaw: "We're still friends. Keats went all out and I respect him for that. Yeah, he hit me on the head and I punched him back but it was an emotional thing that happens in the heat of battle." A smack to the back of the head. A punch in the mouth. Followed by an apology. No refs throwing players out of the game. No shaming of the players on social media. No being called into the commissioner's office. This was football in the 1970s.

Lamonica replaced Snake. He was sacked four times and booed relentlessly by Raiders fans.

In December 1973, one of the best coaches of his generation made a significant mistake: he insulted the Oakland offense.

The Chiefs won the pregame coin toss and coach Hank Stram decided to kick off. He clearly wanted to avoid what was a burgeoning and powerful Raiders defense. The offense took Stram's decision to kick off as an insult. "He was telling us he had a lot of respect for our defense," Snake would say later, "but very little for our offense. It jacked the guys up."

The result was an angry Raiders team that obliterated the Chiefs, 37–7. The game was effectively over at halftime. Stram said he'd never been beaten so badly. "They just kicked the hell out of us," he said.

The season was almost over and the Raiders were 8-4-1 and in control of the division. The next week, against Denver, the Raiders would capture the division after beating the Broncos. Oakland players were again miffed at a perceived slight. That week, the Broncos players were talking about purchasing their playoff tickets, as in, they'd get them after they beat the Raiders. That didn't happen. "They were talking about their playoff tickets. . . ." Upshaw told the media. "It looks like they'll have to use those tickets for a tax deduction."

The Raiders had made the playoffs for the sixth time in seven years. They were happy to make the postseason but doing so wasn't the primary thing on the Raiders' minds. That was the Steelers. Pittsburgh, then and now, is one of the great dynasties in the history of sports. The Steelers from the 1970s had ten Hall of Famers, including the coach, Chuck Noll. Some of the names are eternal: Terry Bradshaw, Franco Harris, Lynn Swann, Jack Lambert, Mel Blount, Jack Ham, and others.

Pittsburgh had beaten Oakland three times in two years. The Raiders were obsessed with trying to reverse that. "I felt," Snake would tell me, "we were going to dominate them. That was the only time before we played them when I felt that way."

Before that huge game came a small moment of appreciation for Snake. The Oakland Raiders Booster Club named Snake "the player who best exemplifies the pride and spirit of the Oakland Raiders." Fullback Marv Hubbard was asked his thoughts on Snake winning the award. "Kenny's not a rah-rah type," Hubbard said then. "He's just a good old country boy who knows what to do. I can't say enough about him."

CHAPTER EIGHT

Lifting the Steel Curtain

When Snake was asked about the Steelers and those battles—those bloody, historic, and brutal battles—he told the stories of those fights like he was still in them, all those years later.

"We really respected them but I don't know how much they respected us. They'd look past us to another team. They dismissed us. We knew that and it really angered us."

Angered you? "They thought they were superior to us," Snake continued. "We took that personally."

The Raiders didn't need to manufacture anger when playing Pittsburgh the way they did against lesser opponents. The dislike of the Steelers was genuine. No, the Steelers didn't respect the Raiders. At least not initially. Then the Steelers would learn what everyone else did, and what history would show: the Raiders weren't a franchise to dismiss. You underestimated them, and Snake, at your own peril. It would take some time for this to prove true against the Steelers, but it did.

One of the criticisms of the Raiders from this era is that they won just a single Super Bowl, while the other dominant teams from that conference in that time period, the Steelers and Dolphins, won multiple ones, with Pittsburgh winning in 1975 and 1976, and two more in 1979 and 1980. That stretch of football in the AFC, the 1970s, was one of the most competitive periods in football history. The only one perhaps fiercer was the NFC in the late 1980s and early 1990s, when you had Bill Walsh's 49ers (with Joe Montana and Jerry Rice), Bill Parcells's New York Giants (with Lawrence Taylor), and Joe Gibbs's Washington Redskin teams (with Darrell Greene and Dexter Manley), and later the Dallas Cowboys (Troy Aikman, Michael Irvin, and Emmitt Smith).

As great as that 1980s football was, the Raiders were in perhaps an even more competitive era. Miami produced seven Hall of Famers from that time (including coach Don Shula) and two championships, including the only completely (that is, including the playoffs) undefeated season in the modern era. The Steelers generated ten Hall of Famers (including coach Chuck Noll). It's no wonder it took so long for the Raiders to break through. They were fighting some of the best teams in the history of professional football. The rivalries, particularly between the Raiders and Steelers, would generate hatred, legendary plays, and respect. Their brawls created dynasties and an eternal play. They also produced a near riot.

The riot story was first described in *Badasses* by Peter Richmond and it is worth retelling. The Raiders' tight end Bob Moore and another teammate, linebacker Greg Slough, went to a movie the night before their December 23, 1972, playoff game at Pittsburgh's Three Rivers Stadium. The game, and this moment, would set the tone for what at times was intense hatred between the two franchises. When Moore and Slough returned to the team hotel, they found a throng of Steelers fans gathered outside, as well as a significant number of police officers, some in riot gear, assigned to protect the Raiders inside and the hotel itself. Moore approached one of the officers, thinking there'd be no problem. After all, *they were simply trying to get to their hotel room.*

"We say we're with the Raiders and we want to go up to our rooms," Moore explained. "This policeman kind of hits me and says, 'I don't care who the fuck you are. You're not getting to the front of this line.' I didn't think a cop with a nightstick was going to beat up an Oakland Raider in town for a playoff game. So I make a comment I regretted pretty quickly."

The comment? "Look, motherfucker, I'm going to my room."

Even for a Raider, that was insane. "So then, boom. This guy comes down on top of my head with a nightstick, which is like a baseball bat. Solid wood. The next thing, I'm on the ground. And I got a guy on my chest trying to beat the shit out of me, and another guy holding my legs. I'm trying to cover up, and I get my hands pulled away, and bang, I get it again. You get hit by one of these things while you're conscious, you think you're going to die."

Things for Moore were just getting started. "They drag me away to a paddy wagon. I get in the back. The first guy comes in. I went after him. Just attacked him. Hit him with everything I had. He goes out and they slam the door. A couple of minutes later the driver comes back and says, 'We're going to take you down and book you.' I said, 'Book me for what?' Then he sees I'm drenched in blood. He says, 'No, we're going to rush you to the hospital.' Turns out it wasn't bad. Seven stitches, cuts on both sides of my head. I was swollen like a son of a gun. I'm on the operating table and the young surgeon says, 'You're real lucky.' I said, 'You have to explain this to me. I don't feel lucky.'"

Blood and stitches even before the contest was played.

Then came the game itself.

The Immaculate Reception has been called the greatest play in NFL history. It remains, to Pittsburgh and its fans, the best symbol of the destruction the Steelers created during their lengthy reign. To the Raiders the play was a cheat: it never happened. More than a few of them call the play the Immaculate Deception. What's inarguable is that the play also represents how long it would take Snake and the Raiders to finally surpass the Steelers. "I don't think any of us had an idea of the battles that would come," says Snake.

The Raiders had lost in the season opener to the Steelers, 34–28, and all week the media both in Oakland and Pittsburgh billed the contest as a revenge game for the Raiders. Oakland's speedy and powerful defense had held Franco Harris and Bradshaw to just two field goals. Madden decided to bench Lamonica and go with Snake. There were six minutes left in the game.

"Was I nervous?" Snake said. "No, not really."

Snake started his possession at the Oakland 20 and would maneuver the offense all the way to the Pittsburgh 30-yard-line. What happened next is a chapter in Snake lore. "One of the things I remember the most was how much my knee hurt," he said. Years of running, at Foley and then at Alabama, had eroded his knee strength, and when he ran—hell, sometimes when he walked—the knee felt like someone was smacking him with the same club that officer used on Moore.

Snake ignored the pain and as the Steelers blitzed, with the pocket collapsing, he took off running. There are so many Snake runs where it looks like the entirety of the defense will catch him. Then, they never do. He was always faster than he looked on film, and defenders didn't realize it until it was too late.

Snake ran and ran. The Steelers were caught by surprise, and once they realized what he was doing, it was too late. He went 30 yards for the go-ahead score. It was 7–6 with one minute and thirteen seconds left. No, he wasn't nervous.

Two head-shaking things about that play. First, when Snake talked about it, he downplayed it, and spoke more about how it was the Raiders as a team that made the moment possible. Many times, whether it was high school, or the pros, Snake often deflected praise. He saw that as a valuable form of leadership, and it was always sincere.

Second, Snake didn't think the game was over at that point, despite the fact there was so little time left on the clock. "I was on the sideline and bracing for something crazy to happen," he said, "but I didn't think it would be *that*."

The play is the most famous in NFL history, one of the most famous in sports history, and needs no retelling. Franco Harris has a statue in the Pittsburgh airport. I've seen Steelers fans hug it. I've seen non-Steelers fans give it the middle finger. For the Raiders, there would be no statues. There was, however, a picture in the *Tribune*. It showed Snake standing in disbelief, his head in his hand, his helmet in the right. In another picture, George Blanda has his arm around Snake, consoling him, and yet, in another picture, Madden has his hand up to his head, his mouth agape, an expression on his face of total disbelief.

"Black Day for Bay Area," read the *Tribune*, referring to the fact that the 49ers also lost, though in less dramatic form, to the Dallas Cowboys.

The Raiders lost to the Steelers, and it seemed like they would never beat them.

———

The season after that devastating loss, the Steelers beat Oakland again, 17–9, in November. The media would again talk about how it seemed the Raiders would never beat the Steelers. That conversation changed in the playoffs, on December 22, 1973, in Oakland, thanks in large part to Snake.

"If I remember correctly," Snake explained, "that was one of the few times I didn't go out much the week of a game."

Snake didn't throw an interception and the rest of the Raiders' offense was also essentially perfect. The Raiders' defense, led by Willie Brown's pick-six off quarterback Terry Bradshaw, was even better. It was a complete demolition.

Snake completed 14 of 17 passes and two of the incompletions were drops. The fact Snake was able to throw so accurately and effectively opened up the running game and kept the vaunted Steelers defensive line from running downhill on its pass rush.

Before the game, Snake had told some of his offensive teammates that the key would be not turning the ball over. "Hold on to the fucking ball," he told some of them, calmly. After the game, Snake expressed his pride to reporters in how mentally sturdy the Raiders were. He focused on the team's lack of turnovers. "We felt if we could eliminate the turnovers, we would beat them. They didn't beat us those other times, we beat ourselves. When two good teams play, it's decided by big plays. We made them. We played with a lot of determination and confidence. We weren't going to be kept out. We'll be in any game we line up for if we don't make mistakes. We knew what we could do, and we beat them badly."

Something else Snake said after the game spoke to the relationship he had with Madden. At times, the Oakland offense would get a little too conservative, and it's understandable why. Madden knew he had a formidable defense and solid running game. He could turn both loose and the Raiders would win most of their games. Snake generally agreed and never let his ego get in the way. This remains one of the Snake traits that isn't discussed enough. He was remarkably unselfish. He ran the offense Madden wanted even when it could have been more effective with Snake throwing the football more. But on occasion, Snake would energize the offense with his arm, and revolt against the conservatism, and Madden had no problem with it. After all, Snake called his own plays. Madden also had no problem with Snake discussing it publicly, as Snake did after the Steelers win.

"It has seemed to be the character of the Raiders to become a little too conservative sometimes, and it's up to me to not let it get that way," Snake said. "Last week against Denver we stayed too conservative in the second half and they caught up with us, and that happened a couple of times earlier in the season, where we got a little lead and got conservative and it hurt us. This time we came out in the second half and loosened it up a little. First down is the most important down in football. What you do then dictates what you're going to do on second or third down. We had to get big plays on first down and we did it. So I'd have to say that's part of the Raider character, too."

Tom Keating, the former Raider who gave his old team fits, spoke for many of the Steelers defenders when he talked about Snake. "Stabler had a great day, he was super," said Keating. "Everything he did was right. He had us off-balance. . . ."

After the game the Raiders couldn't wait to return verbal fire against a Steelers team they felt had disrespected them for the past several years. "I don't know [who it was], Joe Greene or Dwight White, telling some writer last week that they had thought we were pretty good last year but 'Something's missing. The Raiders don't impress me as a No. 1 team this year,'" the Raiders' Upshaw told the *Oakland Tribune*. "Man, we're No. 1 in defense, No. 1 in offense, setting all kinds of club records, and this cat's having a rip. I wanted to beat these guys by 50 points. I know how bad they feel to come all this way through a tough season and go home with nothing, but in the game I just wanted big pieces of them. We didn't beat them by 50, but they know we beat on them pretty good. I hope they had a nice vacation at Palm Springs. I think they came in here a little bit overconfident."

They were going to enjoy this one a little bit. It was a long time coming. Snake would say years later that moment was one of the proudest of his football career. He remembers going back to his locker and sitting there quietly for a few minutes as other teammates celebrated. He took it all in, but Snake was also contemplating the next playoff game. For one of the few times as a Raider, he was slightly worried. Why? The Miami Dolphins were next and their defense was a matchup nightmare for Oakland.

⸺

On December 31, the day of the conference championship game against the Dolphins, and eight days after the huge win against Pittsburgh, the Raiders woke to a newspaper story that said Madden was contemplating leaving the organization.

Madden immediately refuted the story. "Madden Denies He's Leaving," read a small headline in the *Oakland Tribune*. "John Madden emphatically denied early today that he is considering leaving the head coaching post with the Oakland Raiders. 'There's nothing to it,' Madden said of the report in a San Francisco paper. 'The Raiders are my life. I've been very happy here and I'm looking forward very much to next year, coaching this team which I feel was just starting to come together.' He said that, despite views expressed in a San Francisco column, his relationship with Raider managing partner Al Davis is wholly amicable."

Madden was telling the truth . . . mostly. He wasn't ready to leave, because he felt strongly the Raiders would one day break through and get to a Super Bowl. Yet there's also no question that Davis could wear on his coaches.

Madden had more immediate problems. They went into the AFC title game on Sunday, December 30, 1973, as one of the hottest teams in football, and left defeated yet again. They lost to the Dolphins 27–10. "For yet another time," wrote Raiders beat writer Tom LaMarre, "the Oakland Raiders will be just spectators on Super Sunday."

There was, in fact, nothing shocking about that day, except, perhaps, the bullets that were fired into the hotel rooms of two San Francisco journalists who were in Miami to cover the game.

One of the bullets bounced under a bed, barely missing them. No one was hurt.

In the Raiders' locker room, pride was a casualty. The Raiders had believed they'd be able to handle the Dolphins but underestimated what was one of the most talented teams of all time. That Super Bowl was Miami's third straight. They lost their first to Dallas and in the hours, days, and months afterward, Don Shula swore they'd not only never lose another Super Bowl, but they'd go undefeated. He was right on both counts. Not only did the Dolphins win a second Super Bowl in three years, but they went undefeated in the regular and postseason.

The Raiders had, in part, eradicated the Steelers' curse, lifting that curtain, but there was now another realization. Maybe, just maybe, they weren't good enough yet to win a Super Bowl of their own.

CHAPTER NINE

Sea Change

In an interview once, Snake was asked an odd question: What are your dreams like? "I had one the other night," he said. "I dreamed that I was on this river with my friend Randall Watson. He and I are pretty close. And we're up there in this place where we can get away from people. And we're sittin' and fishin' and all of a sudden Dan Rather comes out of the woods. Honest to God! And he's wearing a coat and tie and tennis shoes. He came up there and shot the bull with us. And I kept waitin' for a camera crew to pop out of the woods and ask about my tax returns."

S nake often stayed late after practice. His love of football was one reason why. His love of camaraderie was a second. His deteriorating marriage was a third. He was in no hurry to get home to more fighting and arguments.

Snake had come off the previous season leading the AFC in passing and was the established starter for a franchise on the rise. His salary? Just $37,500. Then came a dramatic offer.

After the Dolphins won their second Super Bowl, the World Football League, one of many leagues to try to compete with the NFL, only to fail, offered three of the Dolphins' star players massive contracts to join—Larry Csonka, Jim Kiick, and Paul Warfield. All three went to the WFL. It was seen as a potentially historic move and the WFL wasn't done. They made a run at Snake, too.

The Birmingham Americans offered Snake almost $900,000

in salaries and bonuses over seven years. Snake was astounded. He signed the deal but wouldn't leave the Raiders until his contract was up in two years. It turns out, however, there wouldn't be a two years, because the WFL didn't even last that long. The Birmingham team folded after just one season and the league went down the tubes partway into its second. Coaches were evicted from their motel offices for lack of payment and in one stretch, players weren't paid for five weeks.

Snake would have to settle for being the quarterback of the Raiders, where he continued to demonstrate the ability to both play football and party on almost unmatchable levels.

The Raiders lost their season opener but on September 22, 1974, they atomized the Chiefs, 27–7, which began one of the best stretches of football Snake ever played. The Chiefs opened the game using a five-man front, anticipating a heavy dose of Raider runs, since Oakland the year before had rushed for over 300 yards against them. When Snake saw the five-man front defense, he slyly motioned his runner from the backfield to edge on the weak side. This forced the weak-side safety to move from the middle of the field to cover the back, and left the middle wide open for Snake's passing attack. For a passer as accurate as Snake, this was easy pickings.

That was the beginning of a seven-game winning streak, including a once-unthinkable 17–0 shutout of the Steelers on September 29, 1974. This time there was no Oakland player getting a club to the head. Instead it was the entire Steelers franchise. The game was in Pittsburgh and the Steelers hadn't been shut out at Three Rivers since 1951. When the Raiders beat Cincinnati on October 20, winning in the final eight seconds, the legendary coach Paul Brown, who hated Al Davis, held a press conference after the game. "The Raiders have it all," said Brown. "[T]hey're excellent. That's all I'm going to say."

Then Brown slammed an object onto the ground and walked off.

Those Raiders teams were remarkable in their ability to transform from a finesse team that could outrun an opponent into one that could play physical and bash the hell out of their adversary. Their game against the 49ers on October 27 involved the latter approach and was one of the bloodier games of the season. "There's only one way you can tell if a game is extra rough," Upshaw said afterward: "by the number of guys they carry off the field."

There was plenty of that. In the 49ers locker room after the game, players were bloodied and limping. Seven San Francisco players left the game because of injury, many of them carted off. One player had his left arm broken. Another had such a severe concussion that when he spoke to reporters he couldn't remember anything about the game. This was the carnage of 1970s football. The only protocol was survival.

On November 3, 1974, against the Broncos, it was Snake who had one of the best regular season games of his career. But the story of that game actually begins the night before.

Snake, who roomed with wide receiver and Hall of Famer Fred Biletnikoff, described the evening in his autobiography: "We beat the 49ers, 35–24, then flew to Denver, looking for our seventh win in a row. In Denver we stayed at an old, cold ratty hotel called the Continental. Everyone hated it, except Al Davis, who apparently kept the team at the Continental because the Raiders had always been successful while staying there. Al, of course, denied that he was superstitious. Freddy and I checked into our room and saw a roach had a mouse backed up into a corner. Neither of the lamps on the night tables had shades on them. The bare bulbs poked out of them like lights in a flophouse.

"Some of us never worried about our accommodations on

the road. We came to town to have a little fun and win a football game. The fun was aided by the endless number of women we got to know in every town we played in. They all enjoyed coming out and playing with us. You had to watch the partying the night before a game a little bit, not wanting it to run too late. But as I didn't need a lot of sleep, I didn't worry about the good times too much. And sometimes the pregame partying would make you feel loose the next day and you'd come up with a real good game. I know a lot of players who would agree with that. . . .

"Anyway, in Denver Freddy and I called a couple of girls we knew after dinner and asked them to come over and bring four bottles of wine."

Yes, that was *four* bottles of wine.

"Freddy was between marriages at the time, so what the hell?" Snake wrote. "We already had a nice glow from our dinner wine and wanted to keep it alive. No problem. We got so ripped that by 4 a.m. we were all sitting around nude, making shadow puppets on the walls using the harsh light cast by the bare bulbs. And laughing like there was no tomorrow. There was, and we finally went to bed about five."

They woke three hours later. Snake and Biletnikoff went to breakfast and grabbed some coffee, and in the game Snake threw four touchdowns against the Broncos. He was almost flawless.

Snake left one critical part of the tale out of his book. That night, before Snake's display of superhuman concentration against the Broncos and equally impressive simultaneous consumption of wine and women, teammate Monte Johnson couldn't sleep, so he left his room and decided to get a soda at the nearby vending machine. It was three in the morning and just returning to the hotel were Snake and Biletnikoff. "I can't remember what Fred had in his hand," said Johnson in *Badasses*, "but Kenny had the small portion of a bottle of Wild Turkey, I think. I thought, 'Oh, my God, we're not going to have a very good game tomorrow.'"

The next day, just hours later, Snake would throw those four touchdowns. There's a high degree of probability that Snake was still, at the very least, slightly inebriated. It's not unheard-of for players to play games under the influence of alcohol or some other substance. It is, however, unheard-of for a player to play under the influence and do well. It is virtually impossible for a quarterback to do it. The precision required to throw the football, particularly in that era when defensive backs committed felonies against wide receivers, making throwing windows extremely tight, *without* being somewhat drunk, is remarkable. Yet Snake either had a liver from Krypton that could drain alcohol from his system at warp speed, or he was simply good at managing the requirements of drinking and throwing a football. Or both.

"After the game," Johnson remembered, "we're cleaning out our lockers. Kenny walks by me and goes, 'That's not too bad, right?' He knew I'd seen him. It was like, 'I can do what I can do: I can drink, and I can throw touchdown passes, and I can win.'"

If that kind of story ever became public in today's NFL, there would be calls for the player to be suspended. Or be put into the NFL's substance abuse program. And maybe that's the right approach. What we do know, what will always be true, was that Snake's time was a simpler time.

Snake would endure his share of violence on the football field. But for now, in the 1974 season, he was playing some of the best football of his career. The Raiders were 8-1, and players and media used to watching Snake's excellence were seeing an entirely new level of it. "You know what's great about the Raiders?" wrote columnist Ed Levitt in the *Oakland Tribune*. "They've got a Sandy Koufax pitching for them every time they play. This one isn't Jewish. He doesn't have black hair and dark eyes. And his left arm never pulls up and needs to be dropped in an ice bucket after every game. But like Sandy Koufax, Ken Stabler throws strikes. He may become the most accurate passer in the history of the game. Ken keeps throwing, his receivers keep catching and the Raiders keep winning."

Then came December 22, 1974. At first, it didn't seem like the notorious play was actually going to happen. The Dolphins led fifteen seconds into the game after Nat Moore ran a kickoff back 89 yards. That excitement would be unmatched by what happened at the end of the game. With thirty-five seconds left, and no timeouts remaining, the Raiders lined up at the Miami eight-yard line trailing by five points.

When that final drive began, Upshaw had a moment of pre-science. "We can do it," he said in the huddle. As the Raiders drove down the field, that mantra would be repeated before almost every play.

On the game-winning play, Snake dropped back, and one of the best offensive lines in history gave him almost five seconds to attempt a pass. All of Snake's primary receivers were covered to the right. So Snake did what'd he done since his Foley days: he used his feet to buy time to throw.

He rolled left and the receiver with the worst hands on the team, Clarence Davis, flashed in front of Snake. Dolphins defender Vern Den Herder stuck his hand out to grab Snake but was only able to swipe at his ankles. It was good enough and Snake started to fall. Then he flipped the football forward and even with that awkwardness, the football still moved forward with great accuracy. Not only that, the football went between three Miami players. "And then came a sight that turned the stadium into the wildest scene since the Oakland A's clinched their third straight World Series last October," reported the *Tribune*. "Stabler, nose-diving to the turf, looped a pass to Davis amid defenders Mike Kolen, Larry Ball and Charlie Babb. Clarence outclutched the trio, putting a half-Nelson on the ball to keep it from being ripped away. Then came Davis' most perilous moment. He was buried by an avalanche of delirious teammates and fans, most of whom spent the afternoon waving black hankies at the Dolphins. The 5-9 scatback from USC pulled the ball away from the frenzied mob, waved it to the crowd and danced joyously back to the Raiders' bench under what amounted to an escort of stadium police who were trying desperately to keep the fans away from him."

After the game, Shula met with reporters. "I hope Oakland goes all the way," he said. Shula added: "It's the toughest defeat I've ever suffered as a coach. A lot of dreams went down the drain but I'm proud of my football team." For Shula to say he wanted the Raiders to win was highly unusual for him. It's not the kind of thing Shula normally stated. Why did he say it? "I was impressed with them," Shula explains now. "It took a really good team to beat us. I was also so impressed with Snake. The poise he demonstrated is the kind of thing that every coach appreciates. It's really the kind of thing anyone who loves football can appreciate."

"I'm asked about that play all the time," said Snake. "The big thing is, it showed just how tough our team was." Again, he redirected attention to his teammates.

Then he laughed: "That was the worst throw of my life."

"That throw was a sign of how great he was," says Shula. "He never gave up. I don't think he ever gave up."

The Sea of Hands game did so many things to so many people. It did, in fact, end the Miami dynasty. More than anything, the game would launch Snake as a miracle generator, even more than the Run in the Mud or his Prelude to Immaculate.

What's often lost in the Sea of Hands play is that on the final drive, Snake was a perfect six-for-six, for 61 yards. Yet this, too, was what Snake almost always did. The bigger the moment, the more he rose to meet it, and then surpass it.

Then came another loss to the Steelers, this time in the AFC Championship game. "Defeat," Madden said afterward, "is a bitch."

"Two things you can bank on every December," wrote columnist Levitt, "Christmas will be on the 25th, and the Raiders will lose in the playoffs."

Raiders defensive end Horace Jones, his right hand still taped, slammed it against his locker. "When we were beat last year by Miami," Jones said at the time, "we broke down and cried. But look around this dressing room now. Nobody's crying. There are no tears because we didn't deserve to win. We have people here who make the same mistakes. Then we get socked with those ridiculous penalties. We're not supposed to make such silly mistakes. In a championship game you've got to use your head. Why cause a penalty? Yet we keep causing them. It's happened in so many games. And damn if it didn't happen again when we're shooting for the title. It came in key situations. It destroyed us. It's totally uncalled for. But it may be for the best. If we had won over Pittsburgh with these silly mistakes, we'd go on to make them against Minnesota and get humiliated in the Super Bowl."

There would be yet another loss to the Steelers the following season. It's not that Snake had a transformational moment after yet another postseason defeat. It was nothing so complex. Snake simply decided he'd had enough of the losing. "I wanted to be remembered," Snake wrote, "and I knew the only way that was going to happen was to win the Super Bowl."

Breakthrough

There's no single starting point for deterioration of the relationship between Snake and Al Davis; it was a gradual process. In fact, after the 1975 season, Davis did something with one of the Raiders beat writers that he'd rarely done: he gave Snake a public compliment.

"I never said this before, but I think Ken Stabler might be the most accurate passer in football today," Davis said. "Other than that, the only thing I can say about him is that he is a winner."

Davis rarely spoke to the players, and he normally said little about them to the press. When Davis did speak to the players, it was usually in an attempt to motivate them using verbal gamesmanship. This was no different with Snake. In fact, Snake may have gotten it the worst. Snake writes how once, after throwing a touchdown to Biletnikoff, he saw Davis after the game, and Davis remarked about another receiver, Cliff Branch. "You know, Clifford was wide open on that play," Davis told him, "nobody near him."

Stabler later said, "I couldn't see what difference it made if I'd had three other receivers wide open. You can score one touch-down per pass. But Al liked to nudge you."

That nudging began when Snake first became the permanent starter with the Raiders. "Young man," Davis asked at practice one day, "do you know what you're doing this week?"

Snake was momentarily taken aback. He had an unmatched wit and his synapses fired as quickly as any human's. "Well, if I don't, we're in a helluva shape," replied Snake, "because I understand I am playing quarterback."

In another instance, the two men were on the practice field engaged in a rare conversation. Snake started discussing the high productivity level of the offense. It was encouraging. Snake simply said that the Raiders were scoring a lot of points. "Well, you should," Davis said; "you're driving a Cadillac."

"Even a Cadillac needs somebody to steer it in the right direction," Snake shot back.

These moments were the beginning of a cold war that would last decades, and would only be settled in a room, the two men burying their dislike and showing great appreciation and—yes—love for one another. But this would happen later. Much later.

In his 1986 book, Snake wrote of his relationship with Davis: "Al Davis had been a successful coach, the commissioner of the AFL who had forced the merger with the NFL, and the shrewd-est owner in the game, a man who put together teams that had won more games in the last nine years than any other club. In my mind Al was the biggest man in football. And as a guy who worked for him, I kept wishing he would loosen up a bit and be more like John Madden."

It was difficult to be Madden. No one was Madden but Mad-den. Snake, like all the players, cherished him. Even then. It was easy to understand why. In NFL history, the three coaches who were able to get the most out of their players were Madden, Shula, and Bill Parcells. They each reached locker rooms in different and effective ways. Madden's was treating each Raider like a human being, and not just a chess piece to be maneuvered. That's the main reason why, so many years later, every Raider who played for Madden still feels a great closeness toward him. "He was a good guy," Snake says in his book, "the ideal coach for the renegade Raiders. Everybody liked John and got along well with him. I never heard one player ever cuss him seriously. Guys would bitch and moan when he kept us out for an extra hour of practice, but it was soon forgotten.

"In training camp, John would come into your room, sit down, and chat. He liked to talk, he liked to get to know all his players and to let them get to know him off the field. I was always among the first guys to come into the dressing room before home games (on the road we all bused in together). John would come by and drop down on the stool next to me, and we'd sit and talk about anything but football. John showed everyone that he cared, and I think that set a tone among the Raider players that brought everyone closer. Pro football teams are made up of competitors, guys who have already been starring in the game for ten years— in junior high school, high school, and college. In the pros, not everyone is a star; almost half the players are not even starters. For the first time in their lives, they back up someone else and work like hell hoping to get some playing time, to prove that they are good enough to be regulars. The reserves are often unhappy. I know how they feel because I was one of them for over three years. But there were always guys on the Raiders who encouraged me. . . . Many of the veterans on the Raiders did that with other younger players. And John Madden was the man who fostered that attitude."

The pairing of Madden and Snake was as good a coach and quarterback match as any that ever existed. They were driven, methodical, and brilliant but what made them work, and why the Raiders were so successful, was their combined humanity.

The breakthrough began with a mesmerizing win against the Raiders' nemesis, the Steelers, on September 12, 1976. Snake was the key, as always.

The Raiders trailed 28–14 with about three minutes to play. Then Snake threw one score to Dave Casper and ran in another. Suddenly the score was tied, and after Oakland forced a turnover, a Raiders field goal won the game. Afterward, Snake and his wife went to dinner at a San Francisco restaurant. They celebrated the win by eating shrimp and drinking bottles of Johnnie Walker Red.

"Kenny Stabler's right knee seems to be OK," wrote LaMarre. "There can be no question about his left arm."

Snake was hurt while throwing a touchdown pass that game, and never seeing his tackler until he was on the ground. He completed his first nine passes but his knee was worse than he thought and he sat out the next game. He'd watch the Raiders barely beat Houston, 14–13. The Raiders were pummeled by New England the following week. Then, before the San Diego Chargers game the week after that, Snake had another long night out, drinking and carousing. No matter whether Snake won or lost, played well or didn't, he viewed going out as a necessity.

"Several of us partied pretty good before the next game in San Diego," Snake said. "We had some girls who just wouldn't quit, and nobody likes a quitter. We all realized that football was a serious business and that our performance affected a lot of other people. If I went out on Sunday half-assed and didn't do my job I was capable of doing it, I would be letting down forty or more teammates. But I knew what I could do in the pre-game hours and still perform at a peak on the field.

"I also knew that if I let football totally dominate my existence it would overwhelm me. If I didn't stretch the rules and dodge a few curfews, I would have been bored stiff and distracted from the real task at hand. I felt the need for diversions because, having so much energy and needing so little sleep, what else could I do with the empty hours. The partying relieved the pressure and kept the tension at bay. I was always 'Cool Hand Ken' during games. It was the night before them when time moved so slowly that I felt the tension building. But I never had trouble pitching it away."

The day after that night of partying, Snake threw touchdowns of 41 and 74 yards.

"There were times," Upshaw told me, "I thought Snake was superhuman."

Snake was getting so good, he was second-guessing himself, even after playing well. After the Raiders went 7-1 by beating Denver, a reporter asked Snake about the game. Snake was shaving, a towel around his waist, as he appraised his performance. "I was mediocre," he said. "I'm healthy but I wasn't sharp. They grabbed two of my passes. I didn't even like the passes I completed. That 52-yarder to Cliff Branch wasn't a good throw. He had to run back to catch it. I threw the ball late. You can't do that with Cliff. He's so fast, once you hesitate he gets out of range. Then you need a cannon to reach him."

That win against Denver on October 31, 1976, made the Raiders 7-1. Snake led the NFL with fifteen touchdown passes, and while the rest of the football world knew how good he was, it was beginning to sink in that he was beyond good. That he was quickly working his way into the conversation with the greatest quarterbacks of all time. "Oakland used to have a quarterback I never thought was a winner," said Denver kicker Jim Turner, who would later be elected to the Broncos' Ring of Fame. "Now they have Ken Stabler—the best quarterback working on any field."

One of the things constantly mentioned with Snake, then and now, was his toughness. Players would get knocked out cold, and then return to the contest as soon as the haze cleared. That's what happened to Snake in Chicago in early November 1976, on a chilly Soldier Field. He was picked up and tossed on his head. When he awoke, he was helped off the field, only to return in time to help the Raiders win.

After the game, the Bears' Walter Payton approached Snake as he was walking off the field, and then came one of those small but powerful moments that often go unnoticed. "You're such a great fighter," Payton told Snake, "it was an honor to be on the same field as you."

The following week, Snake threw four interceptions. It's quite possible, even likely, that he was still being affected by that hit to the head. There would be more such hits and every time, all the time, Snake would pick himself up and look for the next play.

Four weeks before the postseason began, on November 21, 1976, the Raiders trampled the Philadelphia Eagles, 26–7, to win the AFC West. In the locker room afterward, there was happiness, but not the giddiness of other division wins. That's because the Raiders had been there many times before. In the previous decade, they'd won nine AFC West titles, including five straight. Winning the division was nothing new. The team wanted bigger and better things. "We've been here so many times," Snake told the media after the Philadelphia game, "I'm happy for the guys who have never been on a winner before, but we all realize that our season is in front of us."

The only notable moment of the game came from Philadelphia linebacker Bill Bergey. The Raiders' offensive line was so dominant, Bergey got frustrated and began hollering at his own defensive front. "Why don't you just lay down!" he screamed. Later, still frustrated, Bergey threw a punch at Raiders running back Mark van Eeghen. Upshaw approached Bergey. "I'm just tired of being blocked," he told Upshaw, before laughing. Bergey wasn't the only player frustrated by the best guard-tackle tandem in history. Upshaw at guard and Shell at tackle drove many of the best defenders to mumble to themselves.

In the Philadelphia locker room, defensive end Blenda Gay said something many around the NFL were thinking. The Raiders were good but there was still a good chance the team would again choke in the postseason. "It remains to be seen how far they'll go in the playoffs," he told reporters. "Who knows? They might fold again."

There was indeed a strange mind-set when it came to people outside the Raiders. Following that Eagles game, while waiting at the Philadelphia airport to catch their plane, a journalist asked Madden what was wrong with Snake. "Are you kidding?" Madden shot back. "Stabler completed 14 of 18 passes. What do you want from the guy?"

Columnist Levitt summed up the attitude of many Raiders fans and even some in the media. "Perfection," he wrote. "People think Ken Stabler shouldn't miss a pass, the Raiders shouldn't lose a game, the coach shouldn't make a mistake. Oakland fans are so used to the Raiders winning that when the club arrived at the Oakland Airport last night—after clinching their fifth straight division title—I counted fewer than 25 people there to greet them. Rooters and rivals have a tough time knowing how to handle this Oakland team."

Eagles runner Dave Hampton would say "the Raiders are arrogant. But they have a right to be arrogant. They're that good."

Inside Oakland's locker room, players were ignoring the outside noise, instead choosing to focus on their mentality approaching the playoffs. None of the Raiders' key starters, including Stabler, wanted to rest and sit out some of the final games. "Until we end up with the best record," Snake told the media, "to give us home field advantage in the playoffs, we'll still go all out in every game."

The next week, on the same day Reggie Jackson left the

Oakland A's for the New York Yankees, the Raiders went 13-1 after dismantling the hapless Buccaneers, 49–16. It was their eighth consecutive win. "I want to be the quarterback of the team with the best record," Snake told the media after the blowout, "and we have it now."

Some of the Raiders players, always looking for a mental edge, manufactured outrage at the talk in the press that the Raiders would lose their final regular season game to the Bengals. Snake, who threw four touchdown passes, was one of those players. He played the disrespect card with great efficiency. "Even though we had the best record in football before tonight," Snake said, sitting at his locker, "a lot of people doubted us. This ought to shut up that kind of talk. We handled a fine team which had a lot more to play for than we did. People have been saying some absurd, crazy things. You know, that we've had an easy schedule and that we're going to lay down. This team doesn't know how to do that. But talk doesn't fire us up. We come to play no matter what."

What likely bothered Snake was the speculation by some media that Bengals quarterback Ken Anderson was better than him. "I never thought there was any question," Madden said. "But to anyone who thought otherwise, I think Kenny showed tonight that he's the best quarterback around."

Davis, as was his penchant, felt differently from his players and coaches. He understood the skepticism about the team, particularly when it came to the playoffs. In fact, Davis embraced that skepticism. "Don't get too excited," Davis explained after the Bengals win. "Sure, we played well. We did what we had to do. But don't you remember? We've been here before. Three times in our history we've had this good feeling about our team. And each time it didn't pan out. So you know what I'm thinking now? I'm thinking of our first playoff opponent. I'm thinking how New England beat Pittsburgh and Oakland back-to-back. I'm thinking of that 48–17 score against us. I'm thinking how New England beat Baltimore. I'm thinking New England is playing the best football of anybody."

Beating the Bengals meant the Steelers were also in the play-offs. The irony wasn't lost on the Raiders. "Merry Christmas, Pittsburgh," said Upshaw. "Now we can go home and lay down."

Then offensive lineman George Buehler quickly added: "After the postgame party."

Playoff tickets went on sale. The prices: $8, $11, and $12.

———

To understand how far the Raiders had come, you must go back to 1966, when John Rauch was the head coach and a race riot nearly broke out in the locker room.

In training camp that year, as the Raiders players were in the locker room getting ready for practice, Rauch was in his office. The phone rang. It was the equipment manager, Dick Romanski, who was frantic. "Somebody get over here!" he yelled. "There's a guy with a gun and he's threatening to shoot!"

Rauch ran to the locker room as fast as he could. What he saw was frightening. On one side of the locker room were the white Raiders players and on the other were the black ones. In the middle was a player brandishing a gun. "I had never experienced anything like that before, so I just walked into the middle of that thing and said, 'What are you guys doing? Are you all crazy?'" Rauch told writer Mark Ribowsky. "Like a fool, I reached out and said, 'Give me that gun,' and the guy handed it to me."

It was over. What started it? "This had stemmed from what happened in the dining hall involving a black guy and a waitress," he said, "and one thing led to another, and we had a couple of white guys on the team that were notable rednecks. But here's the thing: it happened, and 24 hours after that there was a little talk about it here and there, but we never saw anything more of it, and I think Al had a lot to do with that."

Davis called a team meeting soon after the incident and made it clear there would be no tolerance of bigotry. It would be one of many high standards Davis set for the franchise. That racial lesson would remain for Snake's Raiders. That group also had southerners, like Snake, but no player or coach tolerated racism.

This isn't to say the Raiders were perfect in every way. In the Madden biography, author Burwell writes of the difficulty faced by the first woman beat writer for the Raiders, Betty Cuniberti, one of the great pioneers in sports journalism history. She worked for the *San Francisco Chronicle*.

"There was a phone call made to the *Chronicle* not to send me," Cuniberti told Burwell. "This was more Al Davis than John, although John never defended me. Al Davis didn't want me on the team plane, never mind that the other male writers were on the plane. You know that old navy superstition about how a woman is bad luck on a ship? Well, Al thought I would be back luck on the plane. Never mind that there were female flight attendants and never mind that Al brought his wife."

Madden told Burwell a different story. He says the Raiders didn't call the paper, the paper called him.

"Our beat writer is going to be a woman."

"Okay," Madden said.

"She's going to be at practice every day."

"Okay," Madden said.

"She's going to travel with the team."

"Okay," Madden said.

"She's going to be going into the locker room at training camp."

"No, she won't," said Madden. "The locker room at camp is too damned small. Barely enough room for the players. No writers come into the locker room at camp."

Madden says he had no problem with Cuniberti covering the team. She said something different. "Like most men in sports at that time," she said, "particularly in football, he was very upset that I was with the team at all. . . ."

Madden and Cuniberti had one major issue. It was when she wrote about the Raiders' annual air hockey tournament at the end of camp. The tournament actually had little to do with air hockey. It was more about bonding, and had some specific rules:

1. Cheating is encouraged.
2. It's only cheating if you get caught.
3. Drunkenness is mandatory. Urine must be clear.
4. Verbal abuse of opponents is encouraged.

No journalist had ever bothered to write about the tournament before. Madden was furious. He called Cuniberti to his office. He screamed at her. "I can't believe you wrote this story!" he said. "It has nothing to do with football! This is why women shouldn't cover football. This has nothing to do with football!"

Cuniberti stood her ground. "I said it has everything to do with football," she explained. "It has a lot to do with football. It has a lot to do with these guys working hard all through training camp, sticking together, and looking forward to this tournament every year. This is part of team cohesion."

Cuniberti was right and a part of Madden knew it. He called Cuniberti into his office again a few days later. "You know what I really hated about the story?" Madden said to her.

"No, John, what did you really hate about that story?"

"My wife really loved it," Madden said.

I've been told that when Cuniberti came on the beat, Snake did something that only a few people know. He went to a handful of players on the team he felt might be against Cuniberti covering the Raiders. Snake asked them, I'm told, to treat her with respect. There were no grand statements or players-only meeting called. Just a few words to several players. Low-key.

Things would change for the Raiders. Davis, decades later, hired Amy Trask to help run his team. He'd hire the first African-American and Latino head coaches in the modern era. Overall, bigotry wasn't tolerated, but on Snake's Raiders, shenanigans were. To a point. But Madden's credo remained a core point. "I'm interested in what you do Monday through Saturday," he'd say. "But I care greatly about what you do on Sunday."

That philosophy wasn't always easy to follow. "It was a pretty tight ship in one way but a fairly untight ship in so many other ways," Cuniberti remembered to Burwell. "Let's face it, they were the coddlers of guys who were not totally unfamiliar with the criminal justice system. In that way, it was a very loose ship. But because John always made it all about football, he didn't care about anything else. Nothing. If you could perform on Sundays, allowances were made for the rest of the week. You were fine if you did that, but you had to do it. I believe he looked the other way on a lot of things like [drugs and alcohol]. I don't think he gave a shit about stuff like that."

The Raiders had mostly good citizens and intellectuals but they also had reclamation projects like John Matuszak. Prior to joining the Raiders, the Tooz already had a reputation in the sport as a wild man. George Allen, after cutting Matuszak from the Redskins, when asked why he released him, said, Vodka and Valium, the breakfast of champions. Matuszak was funny and, when it came to football, like all of the Raiders, he played with relentless fervor. He could, however, go too far. His background before the Raiders included an arrest for punching, and seriously injuring, a man he thought was sleeping with his girlfriend.

Matuszak teetered between the extreme of being a warrior in a violent sport and a drug-addicted sociopath. One incident in particular involving teammate Pat Toomay, while the Raiders were on the road, was especially troubling. Toomay described what happened in a 2007 ESPN.com story he wrote for the site.

"I grabbed a bite from the team buffet before heading up to the room to relax," explained Toomay, who roomed with Matuszak. "My roommate, I noticed, had met some friends in the lobby. After making only a token appearance at the buffet, Tooz headed out with them."

Midnight arrived and Toomay was in his room, reading and, later, watching television. "Then a key sounded in the lock, the door flew open, and in staggered Tooz," remembered Toomay. "He was ripped. Hardly able to stand, he was slurring his words. Quaaludes was the word that popped into my mind. Weaving as he stood there, Tooz looked around, as if to get his bearings. He had the appearance of a man who'd been hit in the head with a hammer. To his right was our open closet, in which hung a single shirt. The shirt belonged to me. A Pendleton flannel, it was one of the few nice shirts I owned and the only one I'd packed for the trip.

"'Ohhhh! What a puuuurrrty shirt!' Tooz exclaimed. At which point he took off all his clothes, yanked my shirt off its hanger, and tried to pull it over his head. Of course Tooz was 6′8″ and weighed more than 300 pounds, while I was 6′5″ and weighed a little under 250, so my shirt wasn't going to fit him—and it didn't. As Tooz struggled to squeeze his massive biceps through the shirt's skinny sleeves, both armpits ripped out, leaving the shirt in tatters. I groaned as Tooz, still naked except for my shirt, wandered out into the hallway and began banging on doors."

At this point, if all of this had happened in twenty-first-century football, the CIA and FEMA would have been called. But this was the 1970s.

"In the room, I lay there, wondering what I should do," Toomay continued. "Before I could make a decision, however, Tooz was back, only now he seemed more disoriented than ever. Staggering over to the window, he tripped, losing his balance. For an instant, it appeared he might slam his head against the wall, but he recovered, grabbing the curtains for support. But then the curtains ripped away, and down went Tooz, crashing through the table to land with a thud on the floor. I helped him up, pushed him toward his bed. Collapsing on the mattress, Tooz reached for the telephone. 'Gotta . . . call . . . Tammmmpaa . . .' he mumbled. Then he murmured the name of his ex-wife."

Later the team doctor would show up and Toomay would get an apology from Madden, who felt terribly about putting Toomay in the room with Tooz in the first place. Another notorious Raider story was in the books.

The Raiders championed difference but also pushed togetherness. That closeness drove them. It was one reason why they beat the Patriots on December 18, 1976, in the opening round of the playoffs.

This close game would again come down to Snake. More specifically, a Snake run.

Under a headline that read "Even Stabler Calls Finish 'Unbelievable'" was the opening sentence of LaMarre's game story: "Perhaps the Oakland Raiders do believe in miracles and Santa Claus, but most of all they believe in themselves and Kenny Stabler."

The Patriots had been the only team to beat Oakland during the regular season and they showed no inkling of succumbing to the Raiders in the playoffs, either. They fought Oakland hard and were leading the Raiders with about two minutes left. That's when Snake took over.

On that final drive, Snake's coolness was perhaps never more evident. During one timeout earlier in the game, when the Raiders were trailing, Madden approached Snake. "Let's get them back one at a time," he told the quarterback. Upshaw would repeat that mantra in the huddle. But it wasn't necessary. That was Snake's plan all along.

To end that final drive, Snake bootlegged around the left side, following behind Upshaw, and scored with less than ten seconds remaining. Oakland won, 24–21. Snake had done it again.

There are several notable things about that game and that play. First, Snake had been sick all week with a bad cold and was still feeling the effects of it during the contest itself. Second, in the game, Snake was hit with an elbow to the face, which knocked him hard to the ground. Again, Snake would get up and keep playing. Third, the coaching staff wanted Snake to run that play on first down. He didn't. Instead, he ran a different play, which failed.

One of many things that endeared Snake to his teammates was how he publicly took blame for plays that failed. After the game, Snake admitted it was him, not the coaches or players, who was responsible for the play not working.

In the moments after the game, Upshaw expressed a similar notion. "Snake came in there and he had ice water in his veins," Upshaw told the media. I thought to myself, 'This is why we do it all the time, because he's like this. . . .'"

The Patriots were furious after the game, believing a series of controversial calls gave Oakland the win. They would also say, rather bluntly, that the Raiders were dirty. Patriots tight end Russ Francis spoke to reporters despite a broken nose that was snapped toward the left part of his face, courtesy of safety George Atkinson's forearm. Patriots wide receiver Darryl Stingley said he was "ducking forearms all day. The Raiders better clean up their act. There's nothing wrong with jamming or bumping a guy, but they'll stick a finger in your eye or collar you with a forearm. I was coming over the middle once and Willie Hall tried to throw a forearm at my throat." Stingley's words about the Raiders were nearly prescient. Two years later, Stingley was paralyzed after a hit from Raiders defensive back Jack Tatum.

After the game, Snake sat at his locker. All of the media had left the room except one reporter. Snake looked at him, still contemplating the great win. "Wasn't that unbelievable?" he said.

In the AFC Championship game, a game against the nemesis

Steelers that would actually turn into a route, Snake threw a pass in the second half that went for a touchdown. Just as he released the football, linebacker Jack Ham, one of the hardest hitters in history, put his helmet right into Snake's ribs. The hit was so jarring, it didn't just bruise Snake's ribs, it knocked a cap off his tooth. And what happened after that hit? Snake got back up.

After the game, Snake eased the pain of the ribs with a heavy dose of partying and scotch. But the 24–7 win . . . the win to finally get to the Super Bowl . . . was the best elixir of all.

Snake deflected praise to his defense, but there's also no question that Snake's efficiency and smarts were another reason why the Raiders succeeded. Snake had audibled out of several plays once he noticed a Pittsburgh blitz was coming and made the right throw each time. He was again cool and poised, so much that the Steelers were impressed. Greene even asked reporters if Snake was okay from the hit. Greene was relieved after being told he was. "I want Oakland to win it all," Greene told the media. "The Raiders deserve it. They finally found out what it takes to win the big one. They met the challenge. . . ."

Finally, they had done it. "Going to the Super Bowl is an incredible feeling," said Snake after the Steelers game, "but I want to savor this one because we shut up all that stuff we've had to live with about not winning the big one. It's something you can't understand unless you're involved with it. I can't express it in words. This team deserves everything it gets."

The front page of the *Oakland Tribune* carried a large picture of Madden celebrating the win, and below it a story on the victory, with both placed above stories on the Saudis boosting oil output and Gerald Ford reminiscing about his presidency, and warning President-elect Jimmy Carter that promises made during a campaign were hard to keep once in the White House.

The night before the game, Upshaw had a dream. He dreamed the Raiders would win big. Upshaw was so confident, he wrote on the blackboard in the locker room the word *BIG*. His dream, mostly, came true.

———————

Jim Murray, the late columnist for the *Los Angeles Times*, composed one of the best lines ever written about Super Bowl participants, the Minnesota Vikings and the Oakland Raiders in Super Bowl XI in Pasadena. "The Vikings play football like a guy laying carpet," he wrote. "The Raiders play like a guy jumping through a skylight with a machine gun."

Decades later, Snake said the media got many things wrong about that Raiders Super Bowl team. "We were always portrayed as renegades, as the bad guys," Snake told the author. "What we didn't get enough credit for was how hard we worked and how we were actually a pretty smart group of players."

In fact, the Raiders had some of the highest-IQ players in the history of the sport, players like Shell, Upshaw, and Snake, among others. The media, however (and not the Oakland media, the national one), focused mostly on the partying that went down.

When Snake looked at film of the Vikings, he saw a defense and secondary that was vulnerable to the run. So the Raiders were going to run the football, that was for certain. Yet Snake noticed something else when studying film: the Vikings' league-best pass defense played a great amount of zone defense. This played into Snake's strength. Both then, and in history, few were better at slicing up a zone. Because Snake's mind worked so quickly, and Oakland's offensive line was so formidable, Snake could sit in the pocket and dissect a zone—any zone—with ease.

The irony of that week is that Snake—by Snake standards—decided to stand down from his Snake ways. Mostly, that is. One night, in the week before the Super Bowl in Pasadena, Snake and Biletnikoff went to the Playboy Mansion. "It was full of beautiful women who gave us a tour of the place," Snake wrote in his biography. "We had so much fun that we didn't leave until about 4 A.M. The next night, after a short, crisp meeting, I went to the condo of a girl I'd met at the Playboy Mansion. I stayed with her till morning. On Wednesday, Freddy, Pete, and I just barhopped in Newport Beach. That ended the partying, except for a little scotch sipping in my room to relax. I never got to sleep before two."

Sleep was irrelevant. Snake and the Raiders were going to win whether he slept twelve hours or none.

Before Madden would give a simple, brilliant, and inspiring pregame speech, and before Snake would slice one of the most formidable defenses ever assembled into tiny little pieces, it is important to understand how far Snake and the Raiders had come before that dominating Super Bowl game against the Vikings.

"49ers Upstage the Raiders, 38–7," read the December 21, 1970, headline in the *Oakland Tribune*. "It was the worse licking the Raiders have taken at home in their five-year history in the Oakland Coliseum," wrote the newspaper, "surpassing a 32–10 loss to Kansas City on the Coliseum's opening day in 1966."

Seven years later, the Raiders were seen as good, but not great. In November 1973, they lost to Cleveland, 7–3. After the game, runner Marv Hubbard sat at his locker, naked and stunned, a small splattering of blood on his forehead. He sipped a soda. "Cleveland 7, Oakland 3," he muttered to reporters. "It never should have happened. The Cleveland Browns are good. But they're not the best. We're the best. It said so in all those preseason stories. It read so nice. We've got consensus All-Pros at just about every position. On paper we're outstanding. On the field, we're something else."

He continued in what was a blunt but accurate assessment of the Raiders at that time, just four years before their Super Bowl appearance. "Every time the Miami Dolphins play somebody

they always hear the same old line: they're really not that great,"
he added. "But then they go out and prove they belong on top.
With us it's just the opposite. We know we're the best. But then
we go out and prove we're not. Two straight losses now and we're
still making alibis. Every week we keep blaming our troubles on
penalties. But if you're the best you shouldn't have to hold. You
shouldn't have to clip. You shouldn't have to push. Now somebody says the Oakland crowd wasn't noisy enough. Since when
do pros need fans to do part of their job? I remember enjoying
one of my greatest days with only 6,000 people watching. I didn't
hear a thing. I just did what I had to do. That's what we need to
do here . . . before it's too late."

Hubbard then said something no one would ever say about
those Raider teams—they were soft. One of the nastiest, boldest,
and toughest teams of all time was *soft*. "During the game," he
said, "we heard Denver and Kansas City both won. We knew if
we lost we'd fall to third place. But even that couldn't arouse us.
Only once could we move beyond the 50-yard line in the first
half. We couldn't even score a touchdown all day. Just think of it:
the mighty Oakland Raiders held to 12 points in two games! It's
embarrassing to the offense. Heck, you can't blame the defense.
It only gave up seven points to Cleveland. How many teams
beat the Raiders by scoring just seven points? What's wrong?
I'll tell you what's wrong. We're not battling hard enough for
everything. You must have 11 fighters out there. We don't have
11 fighters. You have to play this game mad at the world. We're
not mad at anybody. We're not even mad at ourselves. We're just
searching for excuses."

It was a startling statement but it was true. But then came the
slow, steady climb. The Raiders would merge their talent, and
the mental toughness would follow. There was a 28-point rout
in 1972 of the Los Angeles Rams. "All right, dammit," Madden
said afterward, "you wanted us to start out fast, so we did."

Things began to turn around on October 26, 1975, when they routed the Chargers, 25–0. This was two years before the Super Bowl against Minnesota. It's an odd game to point to as one of the keys for the Oakland success. There would certainly be bigger victories. Much bigger ones. Yet that game was one where you started to see the Raider offense, especially Snake, begin to believe they could play with any team, anywhere, anytime. That game sparked a belief in Snake that would last for years. The game also showed just how much Snake understood that the mental game of football was as important as the physical part.

"We needed to win big for the morale of our team," he told reporters. "Our offense has been erratic, sputtering. I don't know what people expect. But I know we can do better. With our talent we should be more consistent. But we mess up. We fumble. We lose the ball on interceptions. The opposition doesn't stop us. We stop ourselves. We're a high-powered offense. But sometimes it's not easy to blow the other team out of the stadium—especially if you keep giving away scoring chances. . . . Against the Chargers we wanted to prove something. We wanted to prove it not to the people who have been criticizing our offense. We wanted to prove it to ourselves. We wanted to go out and get a lot of points so each guy on the club could feel we still could do it."

Snake's confidence would grow so exponentially that on November 7, 1976, with the season not even halfway over, and the team holding an 8-1 record, Snake predicted the Raiders wouldn't lose another contest. "That's the only way I can approach it," he said after the Raiders beat Chicago. "A quarterback must believe in himself and his team. We'll finish the season with a 13-1 record."

So much would happen to the Raiders, and they'd overcome it all. They'd overcome reports of a divide between Madden and Davis. They'd survive accusations from Lynn Swann and the Steelers that Raiders defenders were cheap-shot-taking renegades. They'd survive Immaculation. They'd end the Miami dynasty. They'd disprove the notion that they were just thugs and criminals, instead showing, mostly, that they were honorable warriors. A legion of historic names would emerge: Tatum, Casper, Shell, Upshaw, Biletnikoff, Branch, Brown, Guy, Atkinson, Madden, Davis, and Stabler.

So, Madden's speech in the locker room before the Super Bowl was in many ways a reflection of their long climb. The quote would resonate with every single Raider there. "I was never big on speeches but John's was great," Snake told me. "It touched all of us and it was so simple."

This will be the single biggest event in your whole life. As long as you win.

Those were Madden's words, and with them, the Raiders would go on to obliterate the Vikings.

Oakland would gain 429 yards of offense behind one of the greatest offensive line performances in Super Bowl history. Shell and Upshaw physically humiliated an NFL defensive line. That was the biggest factor for the 32–14 Raiders win.

Snake's Raiders finished the season 16-1. Few teams in history would surpass it—only the undefeated 17-0 Dolphins, in 1972; the 49ers, who went 18-1 in 1984; and the 2007 Patriots, who went 18-1.

Snake showed with one play the precision and smarts that had made him so formidable. His 48-yard pass to Biletnikoff, one of the key plays of the game, occurred after he recognized the speedy receiver was isolated one-on-one. The Vikings blitzed a linebacker, leaving the middle of the field open. One safety went with an Oakland back, and the other moved to cover Casper. Snake recognized the single coverage immediately and threw a strike.

Snake also made one of the slickest moves of the game. "After the Alabama Snake connected with Biletnikoff for five yards and a first down at the one on a comeback pattern," wrote LaMarre, "Stabler fooled the Vikings and half the country. Stabler play-faked, then found Casper by his lonesome in the left corner of the end zone, where he made a leaping catch."

When Snake was asked why that play was called, he turned the question back on the journalist. "Why not?" he said.

In typical Snake fashion, he gave credit to teammates. "It's difficult to express," he said after the game, when asked how he felt. "It's more of a feeling inside me. I'm happy for the other guys on this team. Guys like Fred Biletnikoff, Willie Brown, Pete Banaszak and Upshaw who didn't win the Super Bowl nine years ago. And for guys like Willie Hall, John Matuszak, Dave Rowe, Floyd Rice and Carl Garrett, who were castoffs when they came to this club and now are champions."

There was also the typical Al Davis. He was joyous, but also used the occasion to wag a finger at the NFL and Commissioner Pete Rozelle. "I still have that AFL-NFL feeling," he said. "I grew up with it. I remember the obstacles put in our way." Also in typical Davis form, he refused to explain what those obstacles were.

The great sports journalist Dan Jenkins bluntly and correctly portrayed the game as inevitably lopsided, partly because the Raiders were so good and partly because the Vikings were so bad. "The only fascinating part was how ingeniously easy Minnesota made it for the Oakland Raiders this time," Jenkins wrote. "It was perfectly evident that the Raiders came to play a superb game.

"When Stabler took over and drove the Raiders 97 yards for their first flicker on the scoreboard—a 24-yard [Errol] Mann field goal—a pattern began to emerge. Casper was going to be open, so was Biletnikoff, and [Clarence] Davis was going to burst through openings—most often to his left against the overaged and undernourished right side of Minnesota's defense—and compile statistics similar to those that Miami's Larry Csonka (145 yards) and Pittsburgh's Franco Harris (158 yards) had amassed against the Vikings in previous Super Bowls."

The Raiders' offense was a splendid symphony not only in the Super Bowl but for the entirety of that season. The offensive line created running lanes. When defenders started creeping up to stop the run, Snake's accurate passing beat them deep.

The day after the Super Bowl, the entire city of Oakland erupted in joy. The front page of the *Tribune* ran the news of the win above stories about Governor Edmund Brown Jr.'s tax relief plan, an oil tanker that split apart off the eastern seaboard, and a plane crash. The newspaper ran an editorial on the front page. "Any doubters left?" asked the paper. "The 1977 Super Bowl reflects the spirit of this City of Oakland where things happen that don't seem possible."

Fans flooded into Jack London Square, located on the Oakland waterfront. "Strangers were kissing in the streets," wrote Peter Clark of the *Tribune*; "conga players beat out rhythms in symphony with the horn-honking, pickup trucks packed like telephone booths with young people cruised around; and hands stretched out from passing vehicles were greeted with slaps of joy."

Back in Pasadena, an Associated Press photographer took one of the more iconic photos of Snake as the game concluded. It was of him standing next to Biletnikoff, both of them holding their right index fingers up, signaling the Raiders were number one. Snake's helmet is off, his hair wet and disheveled.

He had never looked so good.

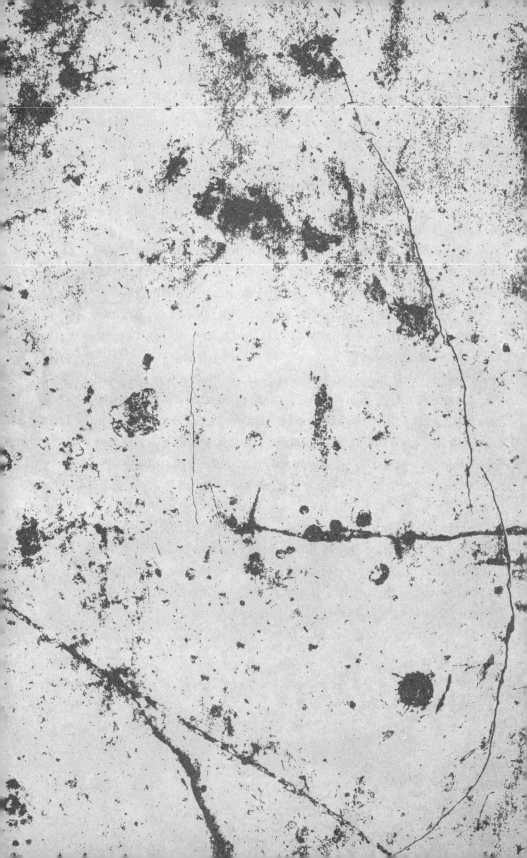

PART FOUR

Dadskers

CHAPTER ELEVEN

Lot Four

T he letter begins simply, succinctly and, in the end, partly symbolizes that at times messy life of a brilliant legend.

I, Edward J. Thomas, hereby declare:

1. I am an attorney duly admitted to practice law in the State of California and am associated with the law firm of Sheppard, Mullin, Richter &Hampton, attorneys for Petitioner herein.

2. Petitioner is a young woman 22 years of age who has no business sophistication, no formal education beyond high school and no records in her possession regarding the financial matters of the parties. Respondent is a professional football player for the Oakland Raiders, age 31, who handled all financial matters during the marriage and whose actual residence is unknown by Petitioner or her counsel.

3. The law firm of Sheppard, Mullin, Richter &Hampton was retained as counsel by Petitioner, Deborah Ann Stabler, in April of this year. We immediately established contact with Henry Pitts of Selma, Alabama, who purported to be the attorney of Respon-

dent, Kenneth Michael Stabler.We immediately filed an action in Los Angeles County and sent Mr. Pitts copies of the appropriate pleadings. A copy of our letter to Mr. Pitts, dated April 22, 1977, forwarding the pleadings and requesting documentary information is attached.

4. Mr. Pitts contended that California did not have jurisdiction to entertain this matter and proposed we try to settle the matter by negotiation without effecting service on Respondent, thereby necessitating what could be a counterproductive court battle. He assured us he would provide us with any information we requested, including the information we requested in our letter of April 22, 1977. Although he has repeatedly made this representation, we have yet to obtain the required documents. The few documents we have received have been incomplete and, in some instances, inconsistent with other documents and what was orally represented to us to be true. Pursuant to Mr. Pitts' request, no attempt has yet been made to serve Mr. Stabler. Petitioner's attorneys have, however, made unsuccessful attempts to find out where Mr. Stabler is living in the event service became necessary.

In the summer of 1977, Snake's first wife, Deborah Ann Stabler, and her lawyers, searched for Snake. They couldn't find him. He'd disappeared.

Deborah and Snake had married on June 20, 1973, in Bay Minette, Alabama. They had separated on March 26, 1977.

Deborah and Snake both filed for divorce—Deborah in California and Snake in Alabama. Negotiations to settle the divorce began but, as in many divorces, things proceeded slowly. Eventually Deborah's lawyers wanted to serve Snake notice but he was as slippery off the field as he was on it. It was the off-season and he didn't have any obligations with the Raiders in Oakland. Even Deborah was unsure where he was.

Snake being out of touch was not totally unusual. "The Snake was never given to wild mood swings," wrote author Mickey Herskowitz in *The Quarterbacks*. "Casual observers were seldom aware when he was feeling low, or even when he was wildly happy, partly because it was hard to read the mood of a fellow who, for weeks at a time (during the off-season), could only be reached by telephone, except on those days when he wasn't answering the phone."

Her lawyers made a bold move. On August 27, 1977, the Raiders were playing the Chargers at Oakland–Alameda County Coliseum in an exhibition game. The Raiders won, 35–7.

Snake emerged from the stadium some hours after the game. As he walked to his car, a man approached.

"Mr. Stabler?" the man asked.

"Yes?" Snake said.

Stabler was handed a hefty batch of documents: copies of a summons; an amended petition; a confidential counseling statement; an ex parte application; a declaration from the judge; a first request for production of documents; a first set of interrogatories; and a notice that a deposition would be taken.

Ken Stabler had been served . . . in a stadium parking lot . . . after a game.

———•

The common ground in some of Stabler's marriages and relationships—until his last relationship with Kim Ross-Bush, which was loving and substantive—was the Snake-ification of them. His courting of the women moved fast and unapologetically. Marriage was simply another extension of having fun. Stabler enjoyed the chase and the idea of romance, but the work required to keep a marriage intact simply didn't matter to him. This is harsh, perhaps, but it's also accurate.

Debbie met Stabler in 1973 in Foley. "Foley, Alabama, is a very small town," she said, "like Mayberry. There is one main traffic light and if a new car arrives in town you know it."

When Stabler returned home that off-season, he drove to Foley in a white Corvette. She just happened to be at a corner where Stabler was driving. They waved to each other. In Foley, everyone waved to each other. They'd later meet at a club. Stabler asked her to dance. She said yes. Six months later, with about ten days until Raiders training camp began, they were married. "When I met Kenny, I didn't know who he was," she said in a 1975 interview. "I didn't know who the Oakland Raiders were. You could have told me they were a soccer team and I'd have believed it. But Kenny was a Southern gentleman and that was what attracted me to him. He treated me like a lady and still does."

Stabler's marriage to Isabel ended bumpily. In January 1981, a bench warrant was issued for Stabler's arrest. Stabler had been ordered to increase child support payments from $500 to $1,400 a month but Stabler kept paying the former amount and now owed $9,750. Since judges tend not to look favorably on people who ignore their orders, Stabler was to be arrested. The arrest order was only valid in California but Stabler, now with the Houston Oilers, was heading to the Golden State for the season opener against the Rams. He could have been arrested before or after the game. Stabler reached an agreement with Isabel and the court, and the warrant was rescinded.

⸺

It's the early 1990s, and O. J. Simpson is a broadcaster for NBC, not yet accused of murder. He is standing at an elevator at Giants Stadium, in East Rutherford, New Jersey. He introduces himself to me and proceeds to tell lots of stories. One of them is about Snake.

They were at the Pro Bowl. Simpson asked Snake if he wanted

to hang out after the game. Snake said no. He just wanted to relax. Simpson says he was shocked.

"Ken had this reputation as a party guy," Simpson recalled. "But every time we spoke, I always got the feeling that Ken was conflicted. I think he wanted to be a family guy but a part of him just couldn't help himself."

Snake definitely wanted to change, and he would. Just not yet. After the Super Bowl, a story appeared in *People* magazine under the headline: "The Super Bowl Was 'a Meat Market'—No, Not the Game, the Women After Ken Stabler."

The story was, well, very *People*-y.

"I've got bad ways. Part of me wants the dog, TV, kids and fireplace, the other part wants to chase," admits Oakland Raider quarterback Ken Stabler while sipping whiskey at Clancy's, a team hangout. After home games the Raiders often take over the mike and entertain the crowd. Alabama-born Stabler's contribution is to yodel Dixie. "Drunk, you can do anything," he reckons, then adds thoughtfully, "Even when I've been bombed the night before a game I've played good."

At 31 Stabler has led the Super Bowl champion Raiders into a tie with the Denver Broncos for first place in the Western Division of the AFC. One of the highest-paid quarterbacks in the league (a reported $1.2 million over the next four years), Stabler is known for his accurate, bullet-fast passes. In high school he was also a scrambler whose zigzagging runs downfield earned him the nickname "Snake."

"I've got choicer names for him," says Wanda Blalock, 26, an ex-model from Jackson, Ala. and his current honey. Maybe another animal? Like "Stallion"? A friend talks about the Super Bowl last January in Pasadena: "It was a meat market. Women came up wanting Snake to sign their breasts. They would do anything to be with him for a night." Stabler protests: "I'd rather have a challenge than someone just coming on."

Twice divorced, Stabler feels burned by marriage. His first, at 22, was to Isabel Clarke, a fellow student at the University of Alabama. It ended after two and a half years, and his daughter, Kendra, now 7, lives with her mother in Phoenix. At 29, Stabler tried again with Debbie Fitzsimmons, the daughter of a policeman and 10 years his junior. This time it lasted two years; the divorce will soon be final. Stabler concedes that his marital disasters can be blamed partly on his preoccupation with football and his strong feelings for the South. "Both wives loved California," he says, "while I'm hellbent to get back home. They were jealous of the time I spent with buddies talking boats, trucks and women."

Born and reared in Foley, Ala. (pop. 4,000), Stabler was the son of a garage mechanic and a nurse. Nine years ago his father, Leroy (6′5″, 220 lbs.), died of a heart attack at 46. "I've thought about it," says Ken of his boozing and womanizing, "but I'm not going to change my ways." A natural athlete, he was offered a baseball contract as a pitcher with the Pittsburgh Pirates at 17, but headed instead for Tuscaloosa and the university. "I studied just enough to play football," he admits. "I am not proud of it."

By the end of his junior year he was cutting classes, ignoring football curfew ("I made the acquaintance of some ladies in Mobile") and smashing up cars with such zeal that coach Bear Bryant suspended him. Wisely, Stabler settled down, and at graduation Bryant praised him as "the best passer I ever had." Stabler claims, "He'll say the same thing about his quarterback this year . . ."

In the September 1980 issue of *Inside Sport* magazine, Snake elaborated on Wanda. "Stabler once ruled the stove off limits to Wickedly Wonderful Wanda after she tried to heat up some TV dinners without removing them from their boxes," the story said. "Wanda, 'nice with a little spice,' was always a good foil for Stabler's sense of humor."

He would write more about his relationship with Wanda in his own book:

> Wanda was coming out of a marriage just as I was when we met, and I thought she was looking for some unrestricted fun like I was. Now, I liked Wanda, I really did, and we lived together almost two years, as she went back to Oakland with me. But soon after she moved into [Snake's house] she seemed to think she had full dibs on my person. "Hell, my wives never achieved that kind of arrangement," I explained. Wanda was not interested in the past.
>
> As it turned out, "Wickedly Wonderful Wanda" could also be "Terribly Tempered Wanda." The situation was that while she always slept at my house, I did not. Sometimes I wouldn't come home for two or three nights. When I did mosey in, Wanda would start throwing things at me. Bottles, ashtrays, whatever was at hand. As a quarterback, I had learned to duck pretty good. But Wanda's missiles were not limited to small items and once I had to play receiver. Wanda heaved a large expensive glass table lamp and, rather than see it smashed, I had to stand fast and catch it.

Stabler described another scene involving her. He was at a friend's house with a woman who wasn't Wanda. In bed with her, actually. "The stereo was on and I didn't hear anyone enter the house," wrote Snake. "Wanda had not only slipped in, she had come into the bedroom behind me. She didn't say a word. She just picked up a metal trash can and cracked me in the back of the head. *Quarterbackus interruptuous!* For a full minute my head was filled with those black stars you see when a flashbulb goes off in your eyes. I jumped up naked, grabbed my clothes, and locked myself in the bathroom while I got dressed. It was 4 A.M. and Wanda was beating on the door and screaming as loud as she could."

Snake says he ran for his car, and as he bolted, Wanda tried to push him down a flight of stairs.

On the practice field, where Wanda couldn't hit him with a metal trash can, Snake picked up his game where it had left off after the Super Bowl. But before the season began, he gave his offensive linemen custom-made cowboy boots, their numbers embroidered on the sides. Typical Snake.

The afterglow of the Super Bowl didn't last long. The genius of the Raiders was still there, but for Snake, the game was beginning to take a dramatic toll on his body, particularly his knees. They'd long been bad but now the only thing lubricating the joints in his knees was guile. Playing through that knee pain was actually one of the more courageous chapters in a life full of them.

Outwardly, it was the same old Snake. He elegantly summed up his feelings about playing football. "I think I'm one of the luckiest guys in the world," he said. "I'm doing what I love and getting paid for it. How many guys go to work every morning and feel like they are bleeding inside? Playing football is more than being a celebrity. It's creating something. You blend people of different size, shape, talent, and personality. You all work together for a common goal. And when you achieve it, that's it. Perfection. You own the world."

Privately, however, Snake's world was far more different than most knew; he was in constant pain because of his knees. Following the Super Bowl season, he had them drained after every game. The team physician would stick a six-inch needle into each one.

———————

On September 18, 1977, the Raiders clubbed the Chargers, 24–0. It was the first of four straight wins, putting the Raiders' streak at 17. After the game, San Diego's head coach, Tommy Prothro, lodged a complaint with the officials saying he wasn't informed that the thirty-second clocks were inoperative.

"Probably nothing will happen," the coach told the media following the game, "but I told the officials I was playing under protest. I guess the world champions can't afford to rig up 30-second clocks."

The accusation played into the belief that the Raiders didn't always play by the rules, even though most of the time they did. They were renegades, but *renegade* doesn't necessarily mean "cheater." The Raiders had permission from the NFL not to have the play clocks because the field was still configured for the baseball season. Controversy over.

Snake and the Raiders would embark on one of the most physical, and physically devastating, seasons any team has ever played in the history of the NFL. The at-times-horrible brutality of the sport was on full display that year. You were starting to see the effects of performance-enhancing drugs concurrent with the absence of NFL player safety measures. Concussions were seen as small dings and players routinely played with broken bones.

On September 25, 1977, the Raiders played their nemesis,

the Steelers, on the rock-hard turf of Three Rivers Stadium. The Raiders won, 16–7, but the team lost five key contributors, including Jack Tatum. On the flight home to Oakland, which arrived at midnight, the Raiders used a team record twenty bags of ice to calm the various contusions and other injuries. When the team plane came to a stop, four attendants pulled alongside it with wheelchairs at the ready.

"The Oakland Raiders came home last night from Pittsburgh," wrote Bill Soliday from the *Daily Review*, "alive if not particularly well."

After the game, Joe Greene gave the Raiders one of the best compliments they'd receive all year. "When you talk about the Raiders, don't you talk about the cheap shots or about [George] Atkinson . . . talk about the way they run to their left, about how Shell and Upshaw block. Talk about the way they throw the ball. That's what makes this a great rivalry . . . not all that other BS. What caused us to lose the game was that they outplayed us."

"The biggest thing about Stabler," Greene would tell me years later, "is that he never gave up."

Meaning? "You'd hit him as hard as you could and he'd pop right back up," Greene explained.

Greene remembered once when he hit Snake "and I thought for sure I broke him in half. He was on the ground for a minute and then looked at me and said, 'Nice hit, Joe.' That's the kind of competitor he was."

Another example of that toughness came two games later in Cleveland. The Browns, far outmatched in terms of talent against the Raiders, pursued an unusual strategy. They decided to antagonize the Raiders with verbal assaults and late hits, hoping to drag them down to their level. The problem was, the Browns weren't good at that, either.

Early in the fourth quarter, Browns defensive end Turkey Joe Jones, the brother of Ed "Too Tall" Jones in Dallas, clubbed Snake in the back of the head after Snake had completed a pass down-field to Cliff Branch. The hit was particularly stinging because Snake didn't see it coming. "Usually, when you're around people and think you might get hit," Snake said, "you stay tensed up. But in this case, I'd already relaxed and was watching the flight of the ball when I got hit from behind."

He was temporarily enveloped by blackness. He'd explain after the game the hit took him down for the "mandatory eight count." But, as he always did, he stood back up.

When Snake got to his feet, the Browns players were laughing at the sight of the dazed quarterback. "Told you we were going to get him," one of the Browns said; "told you."

In one of many signs of the closeness of the Raiders, the affection players had for Snake, and a reflection of the times, Upshaw decided he was going to get revenge. Jones already had a reputation for questionable play. His unnecessarily brutal hit on Terry Bradshaw the previous season had led to the Steelers quarter-back missing seven weeks.

Jones escaped on-field justice for that hit but not the one on Snake. The next play, after the hit on Snake, Upshaw tracked Jones. "I was downfield and I heard Uppy and then this 'oomph,'" remembered Shell. "I looked up and there was Turkey lying on the ground. I think Up got him pretty good."

"Yeah, I got him," Upshaw remembered. "I wasn't gonna miss."

He didn't. Upshaw had driven his helmet into Turkey's back. Redemption had been achieved.

In the locker room afterward, Snake thanked Upshaw. "No one does that to you and gets away with it," Upshaw said.

Snake and the Raiders were 4-0. The Broncos were next and Snake would have one of his roughest games yet. Broncos coach Red Miller was able to do something few coaches were ever able to do: decode the Snake.

Miller spent months deciphering where Snake threw the ball when he was under duress. That game, Snake ended up throwing seven interceptions—mission accomplished. It was officially the worst game of Snake's career. One of his interceptions went to a damn defensive end. On the fifth pick, he turned to referee Jim Tunney to say that the Broncos had fourteen players on defense. They didn't. It just seemed that way.

After the game, Snake stood at his locker and answered every question from reporters without snark or attitude. He vowed to win the next game. They did, beating the Jets in New York. The most interesting part of that game was how Raiders defensive back Jack Tatum totally lost his mind, both in the game and afterward. After Jets receiver Richard Caster caught a pass, Tatum tackled him, and then threw a punch. "A few plays later," Caster recalled, "I had finished running a route and Tatum appeared out of nowhere and said, 'Hey, man, I'm going to kill you, you blinkety blinking blinker. I just said, 'I got no time for this,' and went back to the huddle."

Then, after the game, Caster was shaking hands with Snake when Tatum again approached him. "Snake's a good friend of mine," Caster said. "I reached out and shook his hand and told him he had a good game. Tatum all of a sudden throws himself between us and starts screaming, 'You blankety blanker, you don't talk that way. You blankety blank.' Otis Sistrunk is a good friend of mine and jumped in and grabbed Tatum and restrained him. I said I wasn't ready for any of that and I told Kenny, 'See you later.'"

There were likely many times the Raiders of the 1970s were called blinkety blinking blinkers or even blankety blankers. Just that week, in fact, Tatum had an altercation with journalist Larry Merchant, known now for his role as a boxing announcer for HBO Sports. Merchant did a story on Tatum and the hard-hitting Atkinson. After Tatum thanked Merchant for allowing them to tell their side of the story, Merchant showed them a tape of Tatum's hits. Tatum became enraged, got in Merchant's face, and ordered him out of the Raiders' training facility. Merchant told the *Daily Review* that as he left, Tatum spit in the spot where Merchant had been standing. Merchant was apparently also a blinkety blinking blinker.

Snake, as expected, rebounded from his seven-interception game by slicing apart a good Jets defense to the tune of completing 19 of 26 passes for 230 yards and three touchdowns. After the game Snake couldn't help but think back to his Alabama days, and the effect Bear Bryant was still having on him, years after he departed the program. Richard Todd, the Jets' quarterback, like Namath, was a fellow Crimson Tide quarterback.

"Todd put a lot of pressure on our offense to play catch-up," Snake told the media. "He had an outstanding game. It's hard to explain [the success of Alabama quarterbacks]. It must just be something Bear Bryant instills in his players . . . and I'm not just talking about quarterbacks. I'm talking about anybody who's ever played for him. He gives you something, a never-say-die thing. You've got to be competitive or you're not going to ever play for him."

The following week, amid reports that O. J. Simpson was contemplating retirement, Snake would get revenge against the Denver defense that intercepted him seven times just two weeks earlier, by beating them, 24–14. Snake and the Raiders saved some of their best shots, however, for after the game. "I've never seen such fan enthusiasm since I've been in the pros like Denver's," Snake said then. "But there's one difference between their fans and Raider fans. When they got behind, I heard the boos come out. Our fans would never do that." Said Upshaw, displaying his excellent sense of humor: "When Denver wins a game, they get 10,000 people at the airport. You know why? Because it's a miracle. When we win a game, 100 people show up. That's because we're expected to win."

On November 6, 1977, news of the Raiders' next win appeared on the front page of the *Daily Review*, alongside stories about the end of a teachers' strike, a flood in Georgia, and a material called collagen, which could lead to the building of a bionic man.

The Raiders were at times so dominant, opponents were left to use reverse psychology on them. In some cases, that was their only hope. As Snake started to riddle the Seattle Seahawks with his accurate passing, the Seahawks made the curious decision to talk a huge amount of trash during the game, and so the Raiders decided to pour it on even worse for them. Snake threw three touchdown passes in the 44–7 shellacking despite playing only three quarters. Seahawks defenders told Raiders receivers they would get hurt if they kept catching passes. The Raiders kept catching passes, and the only thing injured was Seattle's pride.

They were rolling, until near disaster struck.

It was November 20, 1977, and they were playing at San Diego. A defensive end for the Chargers, Louie Kelcher, who weighed 282 pounds, rolled onto Snake's bothersome left knee.

Snake was helped off the field. The Chargers used the moment to take advantage of the Raiders, and the Raiders themselves seemed completely thrown. Snake took massive beatings. They were beatings that would have lasting effects, for the remainder of his life and even beyond. Each pounding he took, we know now, caused small protein deposits to form inside his brain, and he would join a legion of other players who would advance science in their deaths. But for now, Snake's toughness was almost unmatched, and the players were so used to him always being there that when he wasn't, it felt as if the Earth had shifted orbit.

When Snake left that game, it didn't just impact the offense; it also made the defense uncomfortable. "I'd be lying if I said we weren't aware that Stabler wasn't in there," linebacker Monte Johnson said after the game. Madden agreed: "Stabler means an awful lot to us. I think some of it was pretty evident. Yeah, from that time on [following Stabler leaving the game], we did kind of look dead in the water."

The team's physician, Dr. Robert Rosenfeld, didn't think the knee was too problematic. Snake actually tried to see if he could play at halftime, but the knee stiffened. That night it ached, he said, "like a headache. It just throbbed."

At the beginning of the season, ABC Sports thought the Monday night matchup between the Raiders and Buffalo Bills would be one of the most anticipated of the year because of Snake and Simpson. But when the game arrived, Simpson was a guest announcer in the booth, thanks to being out for the season with a leg injury, and before the game, Snake was trying the knee, seeing if he was ready. He was.

Snaked limped onto the field and the entire Oakland Coliseum erupted into applause. The ovation was more than appreciation for Snake. It reflected the love affair between him and the fans.

"There was only one reason Ken Stabler was on the football field last night: his teammates needed him," wrote Dave Newhouse in the *Oakland Tribune*. "Stabler has pain in his left knee, which he admits to, only he doesn't say how much. Yet in a magnificently courageous performance, he came, he limped, he conquered—left-handing Buffalo to defeat, 34–13."

In the locker room afterward, Raiders players were effusive. "Stabler is the guts of this team," defensive lineman Pat Toomay said. "He's one in a million. You can't say anything else about the man."

"What does he mean to us?" said offensive lineman Henry Lawrence. "When he plays, we have the best quarterback in the league out on the field. Stabler's one of those guys who can go out and play with pain."

The players knew Snake's value. They had awarded him the

Gorman Award three times. It was given to the player who "best exemplifies the pride and spirit of the Oakland Raiders." But the outpouring surprised even Snake after that game.

Snake threw just twelve passes, but three of them were for touchdowns: 28, 12, and 44 yards. Each was perfectly thrown. "Durability is something that separates people in this business," he said after the game. "You have to play when you're in pain. . . ." Snake wasn't the only player who did that. Many did. But if you were to pick a player who defined the toughness of that decade, Snake would be near the top of the list.

Often, when he was aching, he would wait until the locker room was empty of players. Usually, it was late at night. He'd then meet with the team trainer, and together they'd go over the various ailments. He'd do it that way so none of his teammates ever saw him in the training room. That was part of being Snake, too; he didn't want anyone to see him weak.

That season, the Raiders made the playoffs as a wildcard with an 11-3 record. They led the NFL in scoring (351 points), first downs (305), and offensive plays (1,030).

Oakland entered the playoffs the most injured of any Raiders postseason team. "Their secret is out," wrote the *Oakland Tribune*. "The Oakland Raiders made the playoffs this year on hospital cooking. Never before have the Raiders had so many injuries and still reached the postseason tournament—yesterday's 35–13 crushing of Minnesota marks the 10th time in 11 years. This proves beyond a doubt that John Madden doesn't just push a button in September and out pops a playoff team in December. . . ."

On a cool Saturday in Baltimore, the night before Christmas, in 1977, Snake would get into a shoot-out with Bert Jones, who some people at the time thought was actually better than Snake. The game would be not just one of Snake's best—if not the best;

the contest would be one of the greatest in NFL history. The game lasted an epic four hours, over six quarters, including the two overtimes.

It started out as a defensive fight and then, suddenly, the points started coming. Oakland's opening drive began with Snake throwing 15 yards to Biletnikoff. A short time later, however, Snake threw an interception that was returned 61 yards by the Colts for a touchdown. The game was tied at 7 early in the second quarter, and at halftime the Colts led 10–7.

"What I remember about that halftime," Snake said years later, "is that everyone was calm. We felt pretty strongly we were better than them and we were going to win."

Snake was like other great quarterbacks in that when he made a mistake, even one as significant as throwing a pick-six in a playoff game, he shrugged off the error and moved on. This is what happened early in the second half. He hit Branch for 41 yards in one of the prototypical Snake-like throws—the precise deep pass. Then he connected with tight end Dave Casper—the Ghost—for an eight-yard touchdown.

This is how the game went. The Raiders went ahead. The Colts went ahead. Baltimore led, 24–21, with about ten minutes left in the game. Snake was getting hot now. The more intense the game became, the more relaxed he got. That was particularly accurate in this playoff game. The Raiders were trailing 31–28 with 2:55 left in regulation. Snake's first pass went for 14 yards to the Oakland 44-yard line. Next came an incomplete pass. Then came history.

Madden described what happened next in a 2015 interview for the Raiders' website. "We have a pass called '91 In,' the two outside receivers ran 'in' patterns, and on that the tight end would run a post, which was kind of a clean out," Madden said. "He would go deep and clean out the middle and the two outside receivers would come to the inside. So [assistant] Tom Flores noticed when we would throw the 'in' that the safety was sneaking up. He said, 'on 91 In, take a peek at Ghost to the Post.'"

There are three key components to the play. First, the catch by Casper—outstretched, looking over his shoulder, drifting right and craning his head—was, frankly, impossible. Just flat-out impossible. Yet Casper did it.

Next, the throw itself could not have been better. Snake was able to place the football in a position where only Casper could make that impossible catch. Lastly, and often forgotten when this piece of history is discussed, is that a Colts defender, defensive end John Dutton, was directly in Snake's face as he released the football. Snake had spent much of his career being fearless in the face of attack, and making pinpoint throws despite knowing a player was about to club him in the head, which happened often.

"I don't think I caught a pass on that play all year," Casper told the site. "I did some maneuvers to set him up [the defensive back], and I faked an out and went underneath him to the post and I had him going the wrong way and I was open. Because I was late, Snake had already thrown the ball, guessing where I was going to go. When I looked up over my shoulder, I took one look and said 'the ball isn't going where I'm going.'"

A field goal tied the game and the next score would win. There have been a few different descriptions of what Snake told Madden near the end of the fifth quarter. The most reliable is likely what Snake wrote in his autobiography. As Madden was chaotic and flailing during that timeout, and the more than sixty thousand Baltimore fans were screaming, Snake approached Madden. Snake looked up at the fans and told the Raiders coach: "You know, John, these sonsabitches are getting their money's worth today." It was as if he were playing flag football on a high school field.

"Where in the hell are you?" Madden responded. "We got a game out there."

"We've got that under control," Snake responded. "No problem."

He did. And it wasn't.

After a flurry of punts and defensive stops, Snake took over. He threw passes of 9, 11, and 8 yards to Biletnikoff, then hit Branch again, this time for 19. The first overtime was done. Soon after the second began, Snake's fast-working brain came into play. Remember, Snake called his own plays, and he did so without the help that so many quarterbacks today possess—analytics that accurately predict trends, a litter of coaches giving advice, speakers in helmets, tablets on the sideline that break down defenses frame by frame. Snake's mind had the analytical power of a dozen tablets.

"Calling plays is probably the most fun a quarterback has," Snake wrote in his biography. "It was a chess game between me and the middle linebacker, who usually called the defensive alignments. I called the plays by feel. Remembering what had worked and what hadn't, I'd put myself in the linebacker's spot and try to guess what he might be expecting in the situation we were in.

"I figured now the Colts had to play us for the run because all we had to do was run three plays and kick a field goal. We used a three tight end formation on first down and picked up two yards on the ground. The Colts had everyone bunched in the middle. A lot of things can go wrong on a field goal when the wind is swirling. So on second down we play-faked, Casper drove inside, then went outside, and I flipped the ball to him in the corner."

The game was over. Oakland won, 37–31. Snake finished the game 21 for 40, with 345 yards and 3 touchdowns. Casper caught all three of them. Jones, who some before the game thought might be the equal of Snake, had just 164 yards passing and was sacked six times.

Madden and Snake walked off the field together. Madden resembled a man who had just fought off a wild animal and lived to tell about it. Snake was smiling.

"That was kind of fun, wasn't it?" he asked the coach.

———

The Raiders lost in the AFC title game to Denver. The following season came the Holy Roller, another legendary Snake play. But that would be one of the few highlights. The media began saying Snake was to blame for the Raiders' struggles. Mostly, though, that year saw the offense face more injuries than possibly ever before in Snake's Raiders career. Also, Snake's interception totals were up—he would end up throwing thirty interceptions—and those troublesome knees were worse than ever.

Then something truly shocking happened. Al Davis met with reporters that season and blasted Snake. "You've got to point to someone, so blame Stabler," Davis told the media. "He makes the most money. He gets paid to take the pressure. I'm certainly not going to make excuses for him, but he doesn't do any work in the off-season. I'm dissatisfied with the condition of the team and with the coaching staff for allowing the players to get out of shape. It has been our offense that has controlled the game. The defense played the same this season as it always had. But this year Cliff Branch caught only one touchdown pass. If you can't get the long ball to your wide receivers, you can't win. It all starts with the left-hander."

Davis's words were harsh. He would later get into a notorious, long, and bitter feud with another Oakland great, Marcus Allen, but his public and harsh words about Snake marked the first time he criticized a player. Davis would next criticize Madden, and not long after that, Madden retired. The Hall of Fame, a legendary broadcasting career, and video game history awaited.

Snake, however, was still there, and he wasn't happy. He did an interview with the *Birmingham News* and didn't hold back: "I have lost all respect for the organization. I don't want to stay where I'm not appreciated. I have contractual obligations to the Oakland Raiders and I will fulfill them. I'd be letting down my teammates if I took a powder. I will play as hard as I can because I have loyalties to my teammates and myself. I have two years left on my contract and option year. I'll honor that and go from there."

Snake was definitely right in one sense. His off-field shenanigans were now being used against him. When Snake was winning Super Bowls, those same shenanigans drew a chuckle and pat on the back from the media and others.

Snake didn't take the criticism from Davis or the press well. No one would. The extraordinarily friendly Snake stopped talking to the media. This was only the beginning of his troubles with some in the press. There was one story in particular that was especially crazy. Even for Snake.

"Every time I think of Kenny Stabler," wrote journalist Bob Padecky in a recent story, "I think of handcuffs, submachine guns, a jail cell that stunk because of that clogged toilet, standing half-naked in front of laughing cops and, of course, about seven-eighths of a gram of cocaine."

Padecky covered Snake during both men's Raider days, doing so for the *Sacramento Bee*. After the 1978 season, Snake, who had been feuding with Padecky, invited him to Foley for an exclusive interview. The story is long but it comes down to this: Padecky had cocaine planted under the fender of his car and police were called. Padecky was temporarily jailed until police realized the entire thing was a setup.

"The story broke," he wrote. "Kenny said he had no idea what was going on. He was totally surprised. He said maybe it was one of his friends. The state of Alabama, the FBI and the NFL investigated. No one was charged or arrested. Curiously, there was no arrest report in Gulf Shores, even though I had been arrested and was going to get the maximum sentence.

"Apparently, the cocaine in the magnetic key case just magically adhered itself to my rental car. Maybe I was living an outtake from a Harry Potter movie. In a small town where you can hear someone sneeze, no one knew anything.

"I tried speaking to Snake at the beginning of the 1979 training camp. Walked up to him on the practice field at the now-gone El Rancho Tropicana in Santa Rosa and said hello.

"'Duck you,' said Kenny. Or something like that.

"I never enjoyed watching a quarterback more, and that includes the great Joe Montana or Peyton Manning or even Brett Favre, the closest I've seen to matching Stabler's charisma. It's a tossup for me who leads the offense 80 yards downfield with two minutes left, Joe or Kenny.

"What Kenny Stabler revealed to me was a truth I needed to know and I learned it 36 years ago: Athletes are human, like sports writers. They make mistakes, like the rest of us. They let ego trump common sense, like the rest of us. They are capable of exceptional examples of physical wonder. That's why we go to their games, to see possibly what has never been seen before, like the 'Sea of Hands' catch by Clarence Davis.

"If along the way they go sideways and make us scratch our heads, oh well. It's what us human beings do and have been doing for thousands of years. Such a conundrum can happen to the best of us or the least of us."

"I liked Kenny Stabler. And I will miss him."

The FBI, in a letter to me, says its files from that investigation were destroyed as part of their normal procedures. No one will ever know what the NFL's investigation discovered. Or the cops. Or the state of Alabama. No one seemed to know anything then, or anything now.

Did Snake do it? Did he set up an innocent man, forcing him to undergo a terrifying ordeal? My guess is no.

It's likely Snake wanted friends to prank Padecky and one of Snake's friends, or several of them, went too far. I actually believe Snake when he said, at that press conference, after the story became a national one, that he had nothing to do with the setup.

Padecky's words are worth reemphasizing. Snake was a man with extraordinary gifts, and not just the gift of playing football. He possessed the gifts of extreme intelligence and the ability to make every person around him feel special. But, yes, Snake had foibles, just like the rest of us.

———

Davis kept riding Snake in the press. Why? was the question. Maybe he was trying to get Snake to focus more on football in the off-season. Or maybe Davis was ready to move on from him, and this was his way of setting up that eventuality. Whatever it was, Davis was seriously irritating Snake, and Snake began doing the same to Davis. It would begin a decades-long freeze between the two men. Snake asked for a trade but Davis asked teams for two first-round picks and two players. No team was ever going to pay that for a thirty-three-year-old quarterback.

Because Snake was as competitive as Davis, if not more so, he felt the need to defend himself in the press. Journalist Lawrence Linderman did an interview with Snake, and asked him if he had spoken to Davis. "I wouldn't talk to him if he walked through the door right now. Davis wanted to talk to me when he came to the Blue-Gray game in Montgomery, Alabama, and he called my lawyer, Henry Pitts, to set up a meeting. He wanted to come up to Montgomery and meet with him to bury the hatchet. I'd like to bury the hatchet—right between Al Davis's shoulder blades."

Then Snake did something he'd never done before: he

criticized teammates. "[Offensive lineman] Henry Lawrence
didn't play very well, and sometimes when I went back to pass,
it felt like I was standing in the middle of a freeway. He got me
banged around a little, which also resulted in my throwing the
ball before I wanted to. And we had problems with our outside
receivers because another one of Al Davis's brilliant moves was
to bench Freddy Biletnikoff. 'The Genius' went to a youth movement and put Morris Bradshaw in there. Well, Morris doesn't
play very well, and Cliff Branch didn't play very well either last
year."

Snake's words predictably made news. Even in a world free
of social media, what he said became a massive story, from Oakland to the front of the sports pages in Pittsburgh. Snake would
eventually report to camp and make up with teammates, who
welcomed him with open arms. "Shhhh! All's Quiet in Oakland" read the August 6, 1979, *Sports Illustrated* headline. The
subheadline added: "Especially between Kenny Stabler and Al
Davis, who aren't speaking; but the Snake has silenced the dis-
cord created when he criticized several teammates."

"Kenny Stabler, scraggly bearded and feisty, finished a rap
session with the press one afternoon last week and strode onto
the field at the Oakland Raiders' training camp in Santa Rosa,
Calif.," said the story. "He took the snap from Center Dave
Dalby, dropped back and scanned the coverage. Finding Morris
Bradshaw free, he connected with him on a 50-yard scoring pass.
The play was vintage Stabler, and the members of the Raiders'
offense cheered, happily drinking it in.

"For all of the above, it was a whole new ball game. Snake Stabler had refused to talk to the press most of last season, preferring
not to discuss the fact that he rarely connected on any pass longer
than 30 yards—to someone wearing a Raider jersey, that is. As
recently as two weeks ago not many of Stabler's teammates were

of a mood to cheer anything he did. Indeed, not only had Stabler failed to report to camp on schedule with the other Raiders, not only had he demanded to be traded, but he also had ripped a number of his teammates in print—Receivers Bradshaw and Cliff Branch because they dropped too many of his passes last season, Offensive Linemen Henry Lawrence and Mickey Marvin because they hadn't blocked well enough for Stabler on pass plays."

"I always got along with the writers until last year," Snake was quoted as saying. "It was just that they were questioning my life-style. Hell, my life-style hasn't changed in 20 years. It was all right when we won the Super Bowl, but then we lost some games, and all of a sudden I'm a fat drunk, out of shape, overweight and all that.

"To be perfectly honest. I'm not going to change, because I don't know any other way. I'm going to live the way I want to live. I don't think it distracts me from doing what I want to do during the season. People say, 'You can't do those things as you get older.' Well, if I can't, and it hurts my game, I'll get out. But I'm not going to let football control my entire life. I play and I work as hard as I can, and in the off-season I do the things I like to do. That's not going to change.

"I think if you have a beef with a guy, you should call him into a room and sit down and look him in the eye and just tell him. I don't think it should be done with over-the-shoulder remarks to the media or stuff like comparing me to a baseball pitcher. He [Davis] says I get paid to take the criticism, but I don't think it has to be done in the press. Somewhere along the line they always ask for loyalty from the players. Why can't a player ask for some loyalty from management? When you win you hear how it always starts at the top—good team, good management, good organization. It's possible that losing starts there, too, but you never hear about that. I just think it could have been handled a little better.

But it won't affect the way I play the game. I have a great relationship with the players, and that's the only thing that's important. I don't have to have one with him."

Davis told the magazine, "It's disappointing, because I know down the road he's going to need help in life. He's a loner. He went through this same thing with Bear and made up. I've had this problem with him before, and we've made up. Right now I'm only interested in one thing—how he plays. Our only legacy is whether we win or lose. You can say we're glad he's here, and we hope he plays like the premier NFL quarterback he says he is."

Upshaw, as he often did, put everything in perspective. "I told him, I don't want to hear no more crap about being traded," Upshaw said. "We like him, he likes us, we're all in it together—and he knows that. There's no resentment about the things he said. They were things Kenny honestly felt, and he wouldn't be the competitor he is if he didn't react.

"I'll tell you, though. I'd like to be Al Davis' and Kenny Stabler's press agent. There's been nothing else in the papers for months. That's all you heard. I called my bank the other day and even they asked me about Kenny."

Despite the stories in the press that Snake's lifestyle was now a problem, he still lived it. That year, he drove to training camp in Oakland all the way from Alabama. One of his tires blew while en route and when a mechanic said it would take hours to replace, Snake went to a bar to hang out. What happened next was predictable. "I had tired of scotch a year or so ago and discovered a fondness for Jack Daniel's, which had a nice tang," he'd write in his biography. "Jack over ice was awful nice. I got into a bunch of Jack while shooting pool and hooked up with this girl who was playing the same Willie Nelson and Waylon Jennings songs I was on the jukebox. About 2 a.m. she took me home with her, which was a trailer a few blocks away. She fed me eggs and we flopped together till morning."

The most underrated football player of all time in a trailer, with a strange woman, drinking and eating eggs. It was perfect.

Snake drove that Porsche 911 eight hundred miles on his way to camp on a spare designed for only fifty miles. Later he traded it in for a $33,000 Porsche 928. The color of the Porsche was silver and black.

———

As Stabler's tenth season got under way, Davis continued to try to trade Snake. The Chicago Bears were the next team to decline a trade, saying they already had a good quarterback. On December 3, 1979, in New Orleans, the Raiders quarterback threw an interception, and while chasing down the Saints defender who picked it off, he was hit hard and his head bounced off the ground. In those days, the artificial turf in the dome was as hard as cement.

When Snake got up, he was dizzy. He had another concussion. Tom Flores was now the Raiders' coach, following the somewhat shocking departure of Madden. When Flores tried to talk to Snake following the hit, the quarterback didn't respond. The cobwebs in his head were still too thick.

In today's game, Snake would have likely been pulled and immediately examined. He might have missed several weeks as neurologists examined him. Snake went back into the game on the next series. Nothing was going to stop him from returning. That was simply his mental makeup.

When Flores tried to send in backup Jim Plunkett, who would later go on to his own lofty place in Raiders history, Snake waved Plunkett off. "I got us in this mess," he'd tell Upshaw, "and it's my job to get us out."

What happened next was both majestic and brutal. With forty years of medical hindsight, we now know that Snake staying in the game was absurdly dangerous. It was in those circumstances—

Snake's head already woozy, and him still getting knocked around—where the beauty of Snake was so gorgeous.

That interception return made it 35–14 Saints with eighteen minutes left in the contest. On his next drive, Snake completed five passes, which pulled the Raiders within two touchdowns. After that touchdown, Snake walked toward the sideline and shook his head in an effort to clear it. Upshaw asked if he was still shaken up. Stabler said he was but in typical Stabler form, he kept playing. It's likely this situation was like many others, all undocumented and largely ignored. It's likely the hit caused trauma to Stabler's brain.

On the next possession, Snake led another touchdown drive, the 150th of his career. The Raiders trailed by only 7. They'd get the ball back at their own 33-yard line with about four minutes left. Snake then found Branch, who got a block and sprinted 66 yards for the game-tying score.

The game was being broadcast on ABC's *Monday Night Football* and in the booth, the three-person team of Howard Cosell, Frank Gifford, and Don Meredith was in awe, praising Snake as courageous, reversing their words from the end of the first half, when Snake had struggled and the trio mocked him and the Raiders. When the Raiders took the lead with about two minutes to play, the announcers and everyone else watching couldn't believe it. They shouldn't have been shocked. The comeback (and eventual victory) was the kind of thing Snake had engineered his entire career.

"We've been there before," Snake told reporters after the game. "We've been in these so-called impossible situations in the past. We have a lot of experience at it."

———

The Raiders went 9-7 that season. Snake had retreated to Alabama following the mediocre record and the loss of a playoff spot. In the early winter, his phone rang. It was Davis. It was the first time they'd spoken in over a year.

"Do you still want to be traded?" Davis asked, not mincing words, or bothering to begin with some small talk.

"Yeah, Al," Snake responded, according to his biography. "I think that'll be best for everyone."

"You're sure that's really what you want?"

"That's it," Snake responded.

To assess Snake's time in Oakland, a good place to start is an editorial that ran in the *San Francisco Examiner* after Snake was traded to Houston for Dan Pastorini. Now an ex–Raiders head coach, John Madden wrote the particular *Examiner* column headlined "Nobody Can Replace Stabler."

"Ken has many special qualities," Madden wrote. "He is tough enough to stand under fire, he is a natural leader, he has a mind that absorbs knowledge easily, and he is one of the coolest people under pressure I have ever known. Oakland has been good to Ken Stabler, and Ken Stabler was good for Oakland."

When Snake led the NFL in passing, he completed 66.7 percent of his throws. It was the second best of all time. But like many aspects of his history, one part of it isn't as well known. That season, Snake also completed 9.4 yards per pass try. Think, for one moment, how difficult it is to complete so many deep passes, in an era when defensive backs could ring a receiver's neck, and a quarterback's as well. Only Kurt Warner in the year 2000 bettered Snake with 67.7 percent completion percentage at 9.9 yards an attempt. Warner did that when there were more rules inserted in football to protect receivers and pass throwers.

Snake went 96-49-1 in Oakland, won a Super Bowl, and earned seven postseason victories. That includes three playoff comeback games. He reached 100 wins faster than any other quarterback at the time, doing so in just 150 games, beating the 153 of Johnny Unitas. When Snake retired, his career winning percentage was .661; at the time, he was behind only Roger Staubach and Terry Bradshaw. As of 2016, that winning percentage, all these decades later, is still in the top ten (eighth). It's better than fifteen modern-era quarterbacks also in the Hall of Fame. Snake also won eleven consecutive Monday night games, more than Steve Young at ten and Joe Montana at nine.

He was one of only a handful of quarterbacks who could play in any era. Bradshaw made this point decades ago, in 1990, and it still applies today. "From one era to another," Bradshaw said, "the Sammy Baughs, the Otto Grahams, the Joe Namaths, they could play for any team. Roman Gabriel. John Brodie. A Ken Stabler or a Dan Fouts. They could do it all in any era. Time diminishes their importance because people don't remember them. You ask someone who Sammy Baugh was, and he can't tell you. But if Baugh were in his prime today, he'd still be able to throw it eighty yards. He'd still be just as great."

One of Snake's greatest assets in Oakland—really, throughout his career, including Foley and Alabama—was getting players to follow him. He did this not with words, but with his actions. His coolness was a type of fuel and his toughness made players not just respect him, but play harder for him. "Kenny lets you know that he'll do what it takes if you will," Upshaw once said. "If it's third and 20 and he's banged up, we know he's not going to throw some half-assed screen pass and wait for us to punt. If he needs extra time, he'll ask. And we'll bust ass to give it to him. Nobody wants to go back into that huddle knowing his guy nailed Kenny."

Stabler was profiled in a 1980 issue of *Inside Sports* magazine, which provided an accurate and fair description of Snake at a football camp he was hosting. "At his boys' summer football camp in Marion . . . Stabler was fast and glib with visitors who asked about the tales of his carousing. 'They're all true, unless you know some I haven't heard,'" Snake said in the Deadspin story by writer Pete Axthelm. "But moments later, he could be found in a huddle with Skeebo Whitcomb, the good old coach of the Selma High School Saints and the director of the camp. Skeebo wanted details about the patterns that freed tight end Dave Casper over the middle. Stabler explained in detail, then explained again to a couple of his campers. Then he ran some sweaty plays with the kids, oblivious to the fact that three of his favorite things—beer and air conditioning and a shapely young blonde—awaited a few hundred yards away.

"This is not meant to imply that beneath the fast-living image, there lurks the scholarly soul of a playbook librarian . . . But it is a reminder that there is more to Stabler than his own self-description of 'big pickup trucks, fat belt buckles and a few laughs.' He did not become perhaps the most accurate passer in history merely by standing grittily in a pocket and aiming in the general direction of Fred Biletnikoff's stickum-smothered body. He studies his business thoroughly.

". . . Can a master of his profession really be this childlike, this fun-loving, this free of deep or introspective concerns? The answer, as near as can be gleaned over several years in several places, is yes. Not that there is no contemplation. In particular, Stabler tends to reflect on his mortality as an athlete. But even that comes back to a justification of the onrushing lifestyle."

I once asked Upshaw what was Snake's legacy. His response was perfect. "He was a winner," said Upshaw, "who helped make us all winners."

I n one of his first practices with the Houston Oilers, Stabler once again was crisp. As in that practice leading up to the Raiders' Super Bowl against the Dolphins, few footballs hit the ground. The punishing Hall of Fame runner Earl Campbell remembers saying, "He's still got it."

———

Campbell would later tell me, referring to Snake, "He's one of the best people I've ever come across. He cared about you as a person."

The *Washington Post* profiled Snake in the summer of 1981. It captured the essence of who Snake was then as a player. Part of it read:

Stabler has long gray hair, like a hippie who grew old without noticing the world had turned. After an hour's football work in the sun, his hair is dark and wet and matted into mad dog strings. He sits on a rickety grandstand next to the Oilers' practice field. He blinks a lot to squeeze the sweat out of his eyes.

The Snake looks good. Not apple-cheeked, not after 20 years of goin' nowhere fast. Looks like a pirate who loves his work. The spotty beard is undecided between gray and brown and black. Sea-blue eyes squint through you. Looks real good. The flesh is holding up, he's tan, he's at the right weight, and if the crinkle-folds at his eyes say he has seen too much of too many nights, you can't tell it when he throws the football . . .

Taking a wild stab, a reporter asked, "Was Stabler one of the guys out to 4:30?"

"Er . . . ," Adams said. "I better not name names. But on every football team, at least 10 percent of them will be renegades, reprobates. If you don't discipline them, they'll take advantage of you."

Ladd Herzeg, the general manager, on the question of Stabler's presence at the Playboy Club: "I am supportive of our quarterback."

Ken Burrough, on the same subject: "If Kenny can party to 4:30 and throw four touchdown passes in the fourth quarter, I'll escort him to the party."

When somebody asked Kenny Stabler if he'd been to the Playboy Club until 4:30 the morning of the Jets' game, the Snake stared into the fellow's eyes and said one word only.

"No," he said.

Maybe he left at 4:28.

○────○

The Playboy Club. Snake was there. Of course he was there. And it was past four thirty.

The part of the *Washington Post* story about Snake hanging

with gamblers, which originally appeared in the *New York Times*, reflected whispers about Snake more than it did actual facts. In the end, the FBI cleared Snake of any wrongdoing. (A Freedom of Information Act request was made to the FBI for all of the agency's files on Stabler. The FBI said in a letter to the author that the files were destroyed by the bureau. The FBI said some files are routinely destroyed after a certain period of time. There was no further explanation.)

Snake wasn't the type to gamble on games, despite the fact he was beginning to have financial issues. The insinuation that his four interceptions against the Jets was possibly related to a bet he put on the game is even more ridiculous when you consider the actual reason for those errant throws. Which brings us back to the Playboy Club.

Before his days on the football fields of Foley, he was Kenny Stabler. Football transformed him into Snake. But as his body started to break down and he became more enamored with fatherhood than touchdowns, he began to morph back into Stabler.

Snake wasn't dead. Hardly. No number of nuclear megatons would ever kill Snake—and that's a good thing. Snake would live forever. Snake was still alive and well in Houston. But Stabler was the dominant personality now.

Stabler was ecstatic about the trade to the Oilers. Davis was happy as well. They'd both go on to the Hall of Fame and both would have more moments of greatness and more moments of pure insanity. Davis also had one frightening instance. When news of the Raiders' attempts to move from Oakland to Los Angeles became public, on January 18, 1980, at approximately 2:45 P.M., California time, the *Tribune* received a note in the mail. It read: "Maybe through the media we can get the word to Al Davis if he moves to Los Angeles he will not live to see the first game played there."

FBI internal memos show the threat was investigated and the envelope tested for clues, but none were found.

At the time, Stabler viewed his departure from the Raiders as setting him free of Davis's sharp elbows. In Houston he was welcomed as a hero, and Stabler rolled into the city driving a Ford Bronco, with a custom black paint job. On both doors was a small snake, coiled, and underneath it in tiny print: "The Snake."

It was 1980 and the city (as well as other parts of the country) was infatuated with the movie *Urban Cowboy*. Some men began dressing like the John Travolta character in the film. Part of wearing that gear was a natural for Stabler. He wore a massive cowboy hat and often sported alligator boots. It was slightly different from how he dressed in Oakland but it suited him.

Stabler liked to tell the story of when he met Houston coach Bum Phillips in his office just after he had signed with the Oilers. Stabler had spoken at his introductory presser and then he and Phillips went back to the coach's office. Phillips propped his ostrich-skin boots on the desk. The conversation would occasionally be interrupted by Phillips spitting tobacco juice into a soda can. Phillips was Stabler's kind of coach.

In one of Stabler's first meetings he said something that was then much discussed by the Houston media. "There have always been some people who thought my lifestyle would ruin me," he said. "I like to get out and get after it, always have. So what if I go out and drink, shoot pool, chase women, stay out late, don't come home. Everybody's system is different. Some people need six to eight hours of sleep a night. I can often get by on two hours just fine. Yeah, I carouse. I'm honest about it. I don't try to hide anything."

Stabler never hid who he was. This was one of his greatest assets. In his last days in Oakland, that part of his personality wasn't seen as a positive. In Texas, where people drank and partied in their sleep, Stabler's ability to do the first with the latter wasn't criticized, it was cherished. "Stabler is not afraid to reveal himself," wrote *Houston Post* columnist Herskowitz. "There seems to be absolutely no tension in him and no evasiveness. He is a refreshing change from other athletes."

He may have changed teams, but his friendliness, popularity, one-liners, and affinity for partying remained the same. As in Oakland, he was simultaneously defiant and charming. Not many players were able to pull that off. There was the time that Stabler mysteriously skipped practice. The next day, when Stabler did show up, reporters crowded around his locker. He sat there, naked, one leg crossed over the over, and was smoking a cigarette.

Why weren't you at practice? Stabler was asked.

"It was Veterans Day," he said, smiling, "and I'm a veteran, so I took the day off."

Stabler sat down for a 1984 interview with HBO's *Inside the NFL*. He wore a pink shirt, with a chain and medallion poking through the unbuttoned top, his graying hair neatly combed, and the oversize Super Bowl ring on his right hand. "I haven't changed much as far as me personally. . . . I feel pretty good about where I am and how I got here, from 1968 to now," he said. "I have a real good taste in my mouth about my career, what I've done, and how I did it. . . . I haven't really changed much at all. My appearance may change a little bit. More gray hair. A little older. A little more beat up."

Stabler explained why he stopped speaking to the Oakland press: "I had thirty interceptions [last year]," he said. "A lot of them my fault."

He stopped and interrupted himself. "All of them my fault," he continued. "Interception, interception. It doesn't matter who it bounces off of, or what happened, you take credit for them. That's just the way the game is. As a result, I had some writers that wanted to ask me about interceptions. Which would have entailed me being critical of my teammates and I refused to do that. So I just take the whole thing."

Stabler crafted additional chapters to his legend while with the Oilers. It was remarkable, actually, what he did there. He made the Oilers competitive and exciting, while still being Snake. Before those infamous games against Houston in New York and the Jets at Shea Stadium, it was Stabler who partied until early the next morning at the Playboy Club.

Oh, yes, back to that Playboy Club story.

But it didn't stop there. Stabler went to another club and a fan began talking about how Stabler could no longer throw the football longer than 30 yards. Stabler initially ignored him but when the man continued, Stabler did what many NFL players would have done: he punched the big talker in the face. Stabler was tossed out of the bar and went back to his hotel, where a teammate was having an argument with a woman over a fur coat. It was six in the morning. The game was just a few hours away.

In the game, Stabler threw four interceptions, including a pick-six, and at halftime Houston was losing to the Jets, 21–0. In the locker room at halftime, one player remembers hearing what sounded to him like someone throwing up. He went to look in the bathroom area and saw Stabler bending over a toilet. The partying from the night/morning before had caught up to him.

It seemed there was no way Stabler would finish the game, but he emerged from the bathroom wiping his face with a towel.

"You okay?" one of the players asked.

"Fuck yeah I'm okay," he said. "Let's go win this shit."

Perhaps because the alcohol had run its course through his system—or perhaps because it hadn't—the second half saw a different Stabler. In the fourth quarter, he threw four touchdown passes. The Oilers ended up tying the score but lost by three points.

In Stabler's biography he talks about that scene, and his feelings in its aftermath. "I knew I'd done a dumb thing," he wrote, "getting into the booze so deep I lost sight of time, of my responsibility, and ended up punching some pencilneck and staying out all night. Having often partied before games for years and been successful, it was almost as if I was afraid to change my routine. But this was one time I should have quit earlier because we should have beaten the hell out of that Jet team. One of my interceptions was returned for a touchdown and another gave the Jets a touchdown from the four.

"I thought about this on the bus ride to the airport, about the boozing, the scene in [the bar)]. 'All of that shit is part of me; it all goes into making me whatever the fuck I am,' I thought. The trouble is, I don't know who the fuck I am."

Stabler's stay in Houston ended soon, and while there would be another stint in the NFL, with another team—this time in New Orleans—his career ended quietly. It ended, in other words, the opposite of how it began.

Stabler was released by the Oilers in July 1982. He signed with the Saints the following month and as he had done in Houston, he entered training camp knowing almost every player's name on the roster. Because he had memorized them. Stabler would again play through intense pain, both in his knees and throwing shoulder. That didn't stop Stabler from leading an overtime victory over the Bears. After the game, Walter Payton walked into the Saints' locker room to shake Stabler's hand.

It wasn't long into his Saints career that Stabler decided—not easily, none of the greats ever do it easily—to retire. He phoned the New Orleans *Times-Picayune* to announce his retirement. The year was 1984.

I once asked Stabler if he had a single regret about playing in the NFL. He replied quickly. "It was how I left things with Al Davis," he said.

Stabler would elaborate on this in his 1986 book, one of the few public comments Stabler would ever make about Davis for decades. "Looking back now, from a little wiser perspective at age forty," he wrote, "I think I understand why I got so angry with Al Davis. I guess I always wanted more from Al, just as I wanted more from my father, than he could give or was interested in giving. It wasn't in either of them to give a lot of praise. I wanted my relationship with Al to be more like what I had with Coach Bryant and, even more so, with John Madden. I always did my best to try and make people like me, and I needed to know they did.

"I knew Al Davis respected me and my football abilities, but I never knew if he liked me because he never said it. Of course, I see now [that] wasn't his style. Hell, anyone who didn't like John Madden had a bunch of pages missing from his playbook, and I know Al liked him. But I'd be surprised if he ever told John that. I kept wishing Al would open up a bit with me, and that was naïve on my part. He wasn't going to change his style any more than my father was going to change his, any more than I was going to change mine. So be it."

But he was gone. No NFL player after Stabler would publicly live his life the way he did. There was never anyone like him. There never will be again. And there's something sad about that.

tabler's teammates say no one inspired them more than he did.
Dave Randolph/San Francisco Chronicle/*Polaris*

tabler with Raiders Hall of Fame coach John Madden. Stabler was often able to
alm Madden's frenetic personality.
Gary Fong/San Francisco Chronicle/*Polaris*

Stabler never let his troubled relationship with his father impact what was a close relationship with his daughters.
Kendra Stabler Moyes

A young Ken Stabler with his daughter Kendra Stabler Moyes.
Kendra Stabler Moyes

Among the least known parts of Stabler's life was his generosity toward children. He'd raise millions for, and give his personal time to, various charities.
Stephanie Maze/San Francisco Chronicle/*Polaris*

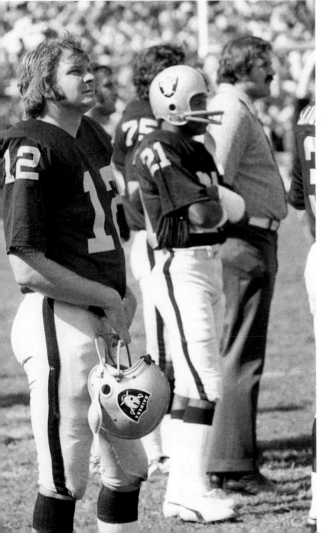

Off the field, Stabler partied. On it, he was constantly thinking and strategizing, looking for ways to attack defenses.
Jerry Telfer/San Francisco Chronicle/*Polaris*

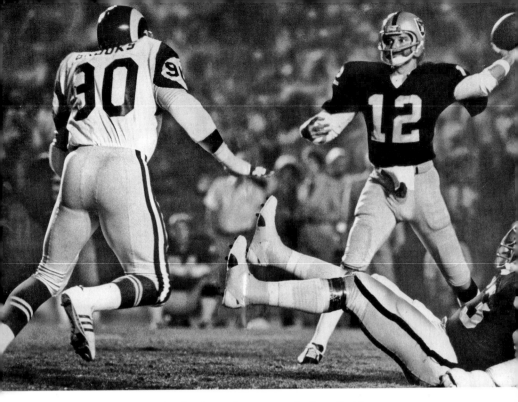

No player was cooler in the face of a pass rush than Stabler.
Bill Varie/Los Angeles Times/*Polaris*

Stabler would become one of the most cherished Raiders in franchise history.
Stephanie Maze/San Francisco Chronicle/*Polaris*

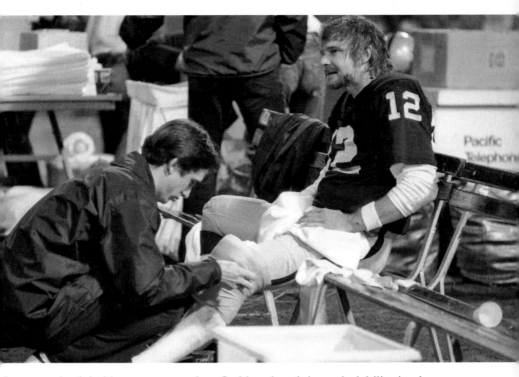

No quarterback in history was tougher. Stabler played through debilitating knee
pain and numerous concussions.
Terry Schmitt/San Francisco Chronicle/*Polaris*

Stabler would come to regret writing his autobiography but it remains one of the
more poignant sports stories ever written.
Michael Maloney/San Francisco Chronicle/*Polaris*

Stabler dancing with daughter Kendra at her wedding.
Kendra Stabler Moyes

The Stabler family with Stabler's longtime girlfriend, Kim Bush (third from right).
Kendra Stabler Moyes

Stabler remained close to the Alabama football program. Here he is with Kendra sporting the Crimson Tide gear.
Kendra Stabler Moyes

Stabler with Kendra. She is smart and generous like her father. She is also a fierce protector of the Stabler legacy.
Kendra Stabler Moyes

Stabler with daughters Alexa (left), Kendra (center), and Marissa (right).
Kendra Stabler Moyes

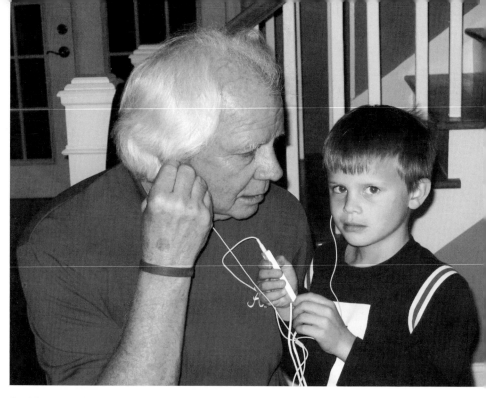

Stabler remained close to his grandkids until his death.
Kendra Stabler Moyes

Stabler with grandkids, Justin and Jack Moyes.
Kendra Stabler Moyes

CHAPTER THIRTEEN

Family

Some years before his death, Ken Stabler wanted to make something clear. It was a statement he would make, in one form or another, to many people close to him sometimes after his playing days.

"One of the things that happens when I speak to people now is that they always want me to tell them stories from the old days about the womanizing stuff," Stabler said. There were long pauses. He seemed to want to choose his words carefully.

"I made some questionable choices in my life and I'm not in a rush to relive them," he said. "I look back and I see that some of the things I did were selfish but I'm not that guy. I tell people who want to hear those stories, 'I'm not the guy you think I am.'"

Stabler acknowledged that a biography he coauthored decades ago, soon after his playing days, helped anchor in people's minds that he was an uber-partying womanizer. And he was. Stabler, back then, also didn't mind speaking about that time. Stabler was an enabler of the Stablerization of his life. After all, on the cover of that biography was a picture of a Raiders football helmet, with beer cans and a pair of woman's legs spilling out of it.

"We partied so much in our rooms, they became very popular with various female players," wrote Stabler. And by players, Stabler meant women willing to sleep with the Raiders. No, not a lot of subtlety here.

"At times we had to take reservations," Stabler continued. "We also began finding, the morning after, various bras and panties that women left behind. That gave us the idea to start a collection of women's undergarments. Kind of our trophies. We tacked the garments up on the walls, and watched the items multiply. Women readily contributed, with monogrammed panties being the choice donation of the elite. Those who wore bras also left them, though [one woman] apparently couldn't be without hers for too long without risking a backache."

Stabler also wrote: "Undergarment collecting became an annual rite of training camp. Someone called us the 'Fredericks of Santa Rosa.' In subsequent years, we tended to judge our preseason success not by how many tackles were made or how much yardage was gained. The bottom line was: How much lingerie did we collect?"

Was some of what Stabler wrote an exaggeration? No, not really. This was the life he lived then. It was a different time. For him, for society, for the Raiders.

A different Stabler would eventually emerge. "I've always taken responsibility for my actions," Stabler said, decades after that was written. "I'd say my biggest regret is that I wish I had done better in my marriages."

It's understandable why he'd feel this guilt. Stabler wrote in his 1986 biography: "I was married twice while a Raider, but I never felt like a husband. Perhaps because both of the women I married were more like sparring partners than wives. Obviously, the fault was not all theirs. But I was never deterred from the endless game of prowl-and-party."

His backup, David Humm, who lockered next to Stabler for five years, remembers the mail Stabler used to get from women. There were naked pictures, marriage proposals, and more naked pictures.

Humm remembers the stories, like how Stabler kept Wild Turkey and cartons of Marlboros in his locker, two offenses that would lead to a chastising from the commissioner in today's football. It also wasn't unusual for Stabler to take a practice break, go hit some of that bourbon, and then come back to practice and nail a perfect pass on a crossing route to one of the receivers. Yet every story of women and debauchery is followed by another of how much that person cared about Stabler and the lasting effect he had on them. When Humm once introduced Stabler to his family, Stabler remembered all of their names, despite the fact that Humm had only mentioned them once.

Another part of Stabler's book shows the levels Stabler and some Raiders went to when it came to chasing skirts. This section is long but instructive in that it illustrates where Stabler once was, and how far he later traveled, and transformed, to get away from that Stabler. "My roommates and I had a pact," he wrote. "We all took seats by the door at the 8 P.M. meeting and the moment it broke up—around 9:30—we sprinted to our rooms. We'd comb our hair, slap on face juice, and dash to the biggest car we had. . . . We only had ninety minutes to complete what we called 'The Circuit.' That consisted of hitting at least five bars before we had to be back for the 11 P.M. curfew. . . .

"Every year during the camp the women of Santa Rosa turned out in droves to greet the Raiders, many bearing dance cards that just had to be filled in. Some of the women were beautiful, a great many were attractive, and the balance ranged from plain to ugly as a mud fence. We tried to be selective. . . . We'd check out the women who appeared to be what we called 'players.' As we had to be in by curfew, all cars parked, dates would be set for eleven-thirty. The experienced female players knew the routine; others were quick learners. They would drive to El Rancho, pick you up, and haul you to their place or to another motel. Those players not familiar with the word 'shy' would join you in your room, uninhibited by the witnesses to the performance. There were a few tireless spirits who would attend to all five of us. They were known as '60-Minute Players,' or 'The OT Girls.'

"When one of the roomies came in real late with a girl, those of us who appeared to be (but were not quite) asleep would peak at the action. [One teammate] liked to crawl on the floor and get right up close. I bought a kid's plastic periscope to peek around the door frame into the inner room. But the damn thing didn't work unless all the lights in there were on."

Stabler described another scene where he was attempting to convince a woman to go to her home or a motel. They were leaning against a car when Stabler felt a hand on his shoulder. It was his second wife. "I hope she's worth it," she told Stabler.

Wrote Stabler: "She was. I had already been busted for a crime, so I figured I might as well go ahead and do the crime. Of course, I had to tell the girl that my wife and I were separated (which was true, as long as I was in camp and she stayed home) and going to get a divorce (in a year or so, but why be picky?). I had heard about a couple of other Raider wives who had driven the sixty miles from Oakland to search the bars of Santa Rosa for their husbands, but this was the first trip for my wife. I felt kind of bad that the very first time she had driven up she'd caught me. But then I said to myself, 'Almost any night she came she would have caught me.' I felt better."

Kendra Moyes says that her father always hated that biography and how it portrayed him (or how he portrayed himself).

It's understandable. In parts of the book, Stabler comes off as cocky and uncaring about the feelings of the women he married. That wasn't Stabler's intent. Part of Stabler's goal was to give true insight into what his life was like and, more important, what life in the NFL was truly like. He succeeded with both objectives. His book hit the *New York Times* bestseller list. Its success, and that of others like it that year, led to this October 1986 mention in the paper's book review section: "A GLANCE at yesterday's New York Times best-seller list shows that 7 of the top 15 nonfiction books were written by people best known for something other than writing. There are five autobiographies: 'Mayflower Madam,' by Sydney Biddle Barrows, with William Novak; 'Snake,' by Ken Stabler, the retired Oakland Raiders quarterback, and Berry Stainback; 'I, Tina,' by the singer Tina Turner, with Kurt Loder; 'McMahon!' by Jim McMahon, the quarterback for the Chicago Bears, with Bob Verdi; and 'And So It Goes,' by Linda Ellerbee, the television commentator. The other two books are less memoirs than meditations: Bill Cosby on being a parent ('Fatherhood') and the former Oakland Raiders coach John Madden (with Dave Anderson) on—what else?—football ('One Knee Equals Two Feet')."

Another motive for the book was hinted at in a rarely seen television interview Stabler gave to comedian David Brenner in 1986. Late in Stabler's career, as he got older, Stabler's partying and woman chasing was used against him by some in the media (and even Davis) as his statistics waned. This irked Stabler and the book almost served as a rebuttal as he detailed his various escapades and put them right next to his habit of playing remarkably. "You can go out," he said on the show, "and you can carouse and stay out and do whatever it is you're doing, and go out and play, and as long as you play well, as long as you do what you're supposed to do between those hash marks, then people don't really give a damn what you do off the field. . . . But as soon as you lose, or as soon as you start to age, or when you start playing with not as good a ballclub, or you have the knee operations . . . or you're not the athlete you used to be . . . then you don't get the job done, then it becomes ammunition for media people, sports writers, what have you. Now they'll say your off-the-field activities, your nightlife, or womanizing, or drinking too much, staying out too late, affects the way that you played. When the very same thing was glamorous a couple of years earlier."

(Stabler, as usual, also heaped praise on his teammates. His offensive line "kept him as clean as the board of health." His receivers "could catch anything.")

All of that anger—at Davis, the media, and others—was then. That was Snake. It bore no resemblance to the man his children and others would know decades later. What happens to most as they get older is they revisit their past. When Stabler looked back on those times, he felt disbelief. Stabler also said he felt embarrassment.

So Stabler made sure once he emerged from his playing days that, while the old Stabler would not be forgotten, it wouldn't be the engine that drove him in retirement, either. What would fuel him would be his daughters, and his determination to be the best possible father. In this he was highly successful, becoming as great a father—and later grandfather—as he was a quarterback.

It was tough for Stabler to leave the sport but it became increasingly obvious. "How do you know it's time to go?" he said. "When a receiver runs a 20 yard route and you throw it 15." Another sign came when he was in New Orleans, his last NFL team, and he was game-planning with Coach Bum Phillips, and Phillips turned to Stabler and said: "Have you ever thought about retirement?"

In retirement the satisfaction no longer came from football. It came from being a good dad, then a good grandfather. "One thing I told my daughters when they were growing up was that the dad they may read about or hear about is a different guy now," he said. "To them, I never wanted to be Snake. I wanted to be Dad."

⸺⸺⸺⸺⸺

There were always three Stablers.

There was Snake. Not *the* Snake. He always preferred simply: Snake. Snake was the partier, the signer of women's breasts. The man of many marriages. Snake embodied machismo, testosterone, and boldness. Alcohol and partying were to him what food and bowel movements are to mortal men. That Stabler, that persona, saw women as a new frontier, something to be won. Snake did what many men would do if they had his looks and charisma.

There was the Quarterback. One of the more confounding aspects of Stabler's personality is that off-the-field Stabler rarely interfered with the on-the-field one. There was always a vein of stability anchored inside the NFL's legendary partier. After all, this was a man who while at Alabama received a plaque that read: "The Neatest Room Award presented to Kenny Stabler 1965–66." It was a harbinger of neat-freak-ness to come.

"When I think of Ken Stabler, I think of a guy who was able to have so much fun," says Hall of Fame Cowboys quarterback Roger Staubach, "while also being so precise. I think of all the great quarterbacks from my era—Terry [Bradshaw], Fran [Tarkenton], Billy Kilmer, and several others. Kenny maybe had the most pure ability."

Added Staubach: "He was an artist out there."

Then there was the Dad. Stabler took to being a father (and later a grandfather) the way he did quarterbacking: with an almost unmatched relentlessness. It was this Stabler that almost no one outside of his family and close friends knew.

On the playground of Grayhawk Elementary School, nested in Scottsdale, Arizona, a man carrying lunch bags and some extra padding in the belly would sometimes make an appearance. It was Stabler, dropping by to see his grandsons, Justin and Jack, and play catch with them.

The grandkids always called him Poppa Snake. Justin and Jack beamed when seeing him. The other kids knew Stabler, all those decades after he played. Soon the tight spirals would start flying, as kids went out for passes, Stabler smiling as hard as he ever did when in the NFL. Stabler played with his grandkids despite knees that practically squeaked from multiple surgeries and numerous hits. Like other NFL players, particularly from that generation, the violence of the sport had wrecked Stabler's body. That still didn't stop Stabler from playing the role of quarterback granddad.

A kid would always ask about the rings. Stabler had two: his national championship ring, won at Alabama, and his Super Bowl ring, won with the Raiders. Stabler would present one or both, in overly dramatic form, and there would stand awed elementary school kids, glaring at the jewelry. Stabler would eventually give those rings to his grandsons. Jack would receive the Super Bowl ring and Justin the national title ring.

Stabler moved to Arizona to be close to his daughter and grandkids. In the years before his death, his life was filled with domestication. As Jack and Justin grew older, they did what Stabler had done, and turned to football. Elementary school playgrounds turned into high school practice fields, and there was Stabler, at most of their practices and all of their games. On Saturday mornings, after film study, a half-dozen kids would pile into a car, go to Stabler's house, and get his opinion on a play or series. Ken Stabler, one of the greatest quarterbacks of all time, was their scout.

———

Kendra is like her father—engaging, smart, and open-minded. She remembers the years with her father as dramatically different from the ones many know. Stabler didn't hide those years from Kendra. It's just that she saw all of Stabler, not just the quarterback who posed with a nude model for a magazine shoot, or collected women's undergarments. He wasn't Snake to her. He was Dadskers. As Stabler settled into post-football life, and then grandfathering, one of Stabler's favorite things to do was put on sweatpants and watch CNN. Stabler was usually awake before six and when he awoke Kendra and the other kids, he'd sing them a song. *Good morning to you. Good morning to you. We're all in our places with bright smiling faces. Good morning to you. Good morning to you.*

Kendra recalls moments with her father and when she does, there are tears, but there is always joy. There is a closeness the Stabler daughters have with him that hasn't waned; in fact, telling stories about their father only seems to strengthen what was a remarkable bond between Stabler and them. When the daughters describe Stabler, it sounds as if they are referring to an entirely different human being from the one NFL history has embraced.

Stabler had a craving for anything sweet and it hit him at all hours of the day and night. As a player, he'd be spotted at times carrying a box of donuts around the team facility early in the morning, and by later in the day, the box would be empty. Many times Stabler would share them, sometimes he wouldn't.

When he'd go to dinner with Kendra, the inevitable question would come. "You want dessert?" Stabler would ask.

"No thanks, Dadskers," Kendra would reply. "I'm stuffed."

Stabler would turn to the waiter: "We'll have one each."

Kendra's memories of her father consist of one wondrous piece of imagery after another. A blog posting she penned about Stabler after his death remains one of the most poignant things ever written about him. It had images of Stabler that seem so, well, non-Stabler. Like how Stabler enjoyed cooking but failed miserably at it. "He knew how to make very few things, and even those were, um . . . But we never had the heart to say anything," she remembered. Stabler would say: "I made some good soup." The nervous smiles of the family members would follow.

"His 'soup' usually consisted of boiled chicken, celery, onions, carrots, maybe a potato, and sometimes rice floating in an attempt at broth," Kendra wrote, "which was really just hot water with salt and pepper. Eventually he learned 1) how to brown meat and open a bottle of Ragu and 2) how to use JIFFY Mix. 'Spaghetti and Cornbread' became his signature dish."

Stabler was obsessed with neatness, keeping his house pristine. Closets and drawers were neatly organized, the kitchen spotless. He was a dog lover but unlike many NFL players, who like massive dogs with big teeth, Stabler liked smaller ones. Stabler called Kendra's Pomeranian—a tiny ball of hair and kisses—his "granddog."

He was a Facebook regular. He wasn't the grumpy old man who refused to use new technology. Stabler embraced it. Stabler's iPhone and iPad were always close.

Stabler was able to settle into his football afterlife minus the smothering confusion many players feel once their careers end. There is a sense of loss for many men in their post-NFL existence and players have difficulty finding what to do next. Stabler wasn't one of those ex-players. He was happy being a father. That was his next job. Not going into coaching. Just being Dadskers.

One of the things that cemented Stabler's relationship with his daughters was simply being there for them. Stabler's fractured relationships with the mothers of his girls never damaged his role with them. Stabler protected them, loved them, adored them, and chauffeured them. Said Kendra: "You have to remember he had all daughters. Movies, softball games, shopping trips, Spice Girls' concerts, he did it all. But he wasn't just Mr. Mom; he never wanted to miss a moment. When my parents separated, I was still living in Orange Beach, Alabama, and my dad was living in Mobile, about an hour's drive west. He would drive from Mobile every morning to take me to school and every afternoon to pick me up from school. He continued to do this every day until I turned sixteen and insisted on driving myself."

⌐⎯⎯⎯⎯⌐

There was possibly a fourth side to Stabler. As happy as he was in retirement, Stabler was at times also equally troubled.

Stabler was never good with money. It's possible he inherited that trait from his father, Leroy Stabler. Leroy bought the Stabler home on October 8, 1957. The foreclosure on the home was announced in the *Baldwin Times* in1963. It took place in May of that year.

As a Raiders player, Stabler didn't pay parking tickets. Despite being the highest-paid quarterback in football at the time, Stabler had his car repossessed. Not because he was broke, but because he just didn't feel like paying the monthly note. Once, with his first wife, Debbie Stabler, the couple left for a trip that lasted thirty-eight days. Rather than get a ride to the San Francisco airport, they drove, and parked their car there. Upon return, the bill was $109, about the same as paying almost $500 today. Stabler lived the high life, which he had earned, but along the way he failed to grasp the concept of paying the bills he accumulated.

Beginning in 1988, Ken would begin a dizzying odyssey of navigating financial judgments, lawsuits, and money issues that would continue for almost three decades, all the way until his death and, in some ways, even beyond. Many of those troubles would be battles against the Internal Revenue Service. Stabler's more serious financial troubles began in earnest in 1988 when he was successfully sued by AmSouth Bank and a default judgment was rendered against him for $77,057. Court records show that Stabler never contested the judgment. Three years later, Stabler's house was foreclosed, and he owed $122,500.

The tax liens would also begin that year, in 1991. A federal tax lien for the tax period ending in 1988 was for $40,405. There was another lien for the tax periods ending in 1989 and 1990 for unpaid balances of $29,388 and $15,599, according to IRS records. It wasn't until 1997 that Stabler paid off those taxes. The debts would get worse. The IRS fights would become so dire that Stabler was forced to sell his home. It sold for $680,000 but even after that there was little money left since $24,113 went to the realty company that helped sell the house, $1,425 was for property appraisal and liquidation by the IRS, $158,086 went to the first mortgage holder, $36,113 went to the second, half of the remainder went to the IRS for multiple years of unpaid taxes, and what was left went to his ex-wife, Rose Burch Stabler.

There is a picture of Stabler in court for one of his proceedings. He's wearing a dark suit and tie, and he's turned in his chair looking back at the courtroom behind him. Stabler has a look on his face that said: How in the hell did I get here?

The reason Stabler owed so much? "It just didn't get paid," said Stabler's attorney, Robert Galloway.

Stabler had simply decided not to pay the taxes. The reason why, some close to him explained, was that Stabler simply didn't have the money. Others felt strongly that Stabler was suffering from the debilitating effects of chronic traumatic encephalopathy (CTE), which can impair judgment and critical thinking. Some of those friends believe the disease hampered him for decades. They point to, among other things, the arrests.

The first came in 1995. Stabler was driving in Escambia County, Florida, and as he drove by a Florida Highway Patrol vehicle, he was unable to stay in one lane, the car weaving and dodging. When the officer approached the car and saw who was in it, he immediately knew this was no ordinary traffic stop.

Stabler agreed to have his blood-alcohol level tested. There were two tests. The first registered a .12 percent and the second

.125. At the time, the legal limit in Florida was .08. Stabler was legally drunk. He'd later plead no contest to driving under the influence.

The second arrest came six years later. Stabler was again driving, this time in Orange Beach, Alabama. He was again charged with driving under the influence but also in the car was a small container that held several dozen Vicodin pills. Stabler faced three separate charges: driving under the influence, reckless driving, and illegal possession of a prescription drug. He was offered a generous plea deal. If Stabler admitted to driving under the influence, the other charges would be dropped. Stabler took the deal.

The third arrest came seven years later. Stabler was sixty-two years old and this time police stopped him in Robertsdale, Alabama. It was his third DUI in thirteen years. When the officer asked Stabler to step out of his car, Stabler looked at him and simply said: "I'm sorry."

Something was becoming clear. Stabler believed he could handle his alcohol when it came to driving the way he had, when drinking and then going to play football. To Stabler, it was the same. He failed to realize this was a different era. It's unlikely these incidents were the first ones where Stabler consumed alcohol and then got behind the wheel. It's more likely Stabler had done this before, especially when he played, and simply wasn't caught.

Stabler spent that night in prison. His stark white hair, long and disheveled on the sides, clashed with his orange jumpsuit.

————

A sinister, brutal disease had choked Stabler's mind. He would be like hundreds of NFL players, and maybe thousands more both from Stabler's time and beyond, for whom football was an empowering engine that also damaged their very essence.

It's difficult to tell just how much CTE accounts for some of

Stabler's behavior, such as the drunk driving or not paying the IRS, though it likely did. One of the neurologists who discovered the disease, Benjamin Omalu, believes that O. J. Simpson, who won a Heisman Trophy and had a lengthy NFL career as a running back before being accused of murdering two people, suffers from CTE.

The certainty is that Stabler knew something was possibly wrong with him, so much so that Stabler became concerned about his grandkids playing the sport. "One year one of my boys wasn't sure he was going to play, and my dad was almost super-excited about it," Kendra told the *New York Times*. "He said: 'I think that's great. He can focus on his studies.' He loved that they played, he loved watching them, but he was so worried about concussions. He was worried about their brains."

Neurologists who study CTE say subconcussive hits—they are lesser than concussions but still cause the brain to rattle inside the skull—lead to a buildup of protein on the brain and affects the decision-making part of the mind. In effect, the movements of football that take place on virtually every down—blocking and tackling and running (then getting hit)—are CTE triggers. One work published in the journal *Study of Neurotrauma* tracked high school players in 2011 for four years. Across a fourteen-week season, quarterbacks sustained an average total of 467 hits to the head. This was in 2011—not the era when Stabler played and the games and practices were far tougher. Also, Stabler was a running quarterback, so he took more shots than most quarterbacks, who stayed in the comfort of the pocket. But using that number of 467 and extrapolating it to Stabler's four-year high school career, four-year college career, and sixteen-year NFL career, it's possible that Stabler endured some 12,000 hits to the head. Stabler began playing football, albeit sporadically at first, at the age of nine.

When Stabler was in the NFL, he wasn't smashed in those

practices the way he likely was in high school practices, but his mind was still being brutalized by the violence. Just how much would become clear on February 3, 2016. The news would come four days before the Super Bowl.

Stabler's family revealed publicly to the *New York Times* what many of Stabler's friends and family had suspected for some years: Stabler's brain was infested with CTE. The doctor who examined his brain, Ann McKee, said the CTE lesions in his brain were "quite established," meaning Stabler had CTE for some time, maybe decades. Stabler became the first Super Bowl–winning quarterback with the disease.

It is possible that CTE grabbed hold of Stabler at a young age, maybe even early in his NFL career, and affected how he lived for a significant portion of the rest of his life. This is my personal belief.

"I don't think you are off base," said Kendra. "One thing about my dad was he was so private. He never wanted anyone to worry about him. We know he struggled because we saw it towards the end but he did his best to hide it and not be a bother to anyone."

When Stabler died, his brain was sent to the Boston University experts who have studied the posthumous brains of dozens of NFL players. Stabler was diagnosed with high stage 3 CTE and thus Stabler would become one of the most famous NFL players to have been diagnosed with the disease. The list of players that died with CTE continues to lengthen, and includes some of the greatest players in history, including Frank Gifford, Junior Seau, and Mike Webster. The disease has been tracked to every position and almost every decade since the 1950s.

"He had moderately severe disease," said McKee, "pretty classic. It may be surprising since he was a quarterback, but certainly the lesions were widespread, and they were quite severe, affecting many regions of the brain."

Stabler's family and his longtime girlfriend Kim Bush knew there was something wrong with him. For some years, especially perhaps the last five or so, one of his daughters told me, Stabler wasn't himself. Bush says Stabler suffered from a constant ringing in his ears. The volume of music in the car, or on the television, had to be set low. This was the antithesis of Stabler. His music—hell, his life—was loud.

Stabler was a victim of a terrible conundrum. He had played with a graceful recklessness, going back to high school, where he sacrificed his body, holding the football an extra second in the face of the pass rush to complete that pass, or scramble to get that extra yard or first down. Stabler didn't care about the pounding he took because he knew other players were taking the same thing. So he went all out, all the time. The problem for Stabler was that that same selflessness led to an abundance of violent hits. Stabler wasn't your normal quarterback. He didn't avoid contact. He took on tacklers because he was fearless. But that fearlessness led to his taking numerous head shots and sub-concussive blows. So football created Snake and football partially destroyed Snake.

Stabler died of colon cancer. But along with what his foundation will do—the Stabler Foundation is dedicated to sports safety and reducing brain trauma in athletes—his name will carry on in the battle against football's biggest problem. Understanding CTE is the NFL's version of the moon landing: one of the most important endeavors it will ever undertake. Once, Stabler helped save a franchise. Now, even when he's gone, Stabler might one day help save lives.

CTE, as the *Washington Post*'s Sally Jenkins once wrote, is the black lung of the NFL. It is the league's greatest threat. There are many others—domestic violence, the NBA, arrogance—but none is bigger than CTE. One of the most underrated moments in recent league history, a time that will go down in football infamy, came in September 2014. That was when the NFL, after years of saying otherwise, stated in federal court documents that one-third of its retired players would develop long-term cognitive issues at much younger ages than the general population. *One-third.*

It's hard to imagine another business saying one-third of its retired employees will suffer from horrific brain diseases at notably younger ages than the general population.

This is why what Stabler did is so important, and selfless, and in many ways typical Stabler. For all of his robust living, he was actually the consummate team pro. The fact that Stabler, in his death, would also donate his brain to be examined so that others could possibly be helped is again typical Stabler. Stabler is another link in a long chain of trying to understand exactly what this disease does.

Amid all of the craziness and gloss leading up to Super Bowl 50, there was a beautiful moment involving Stabler. Future Hall of Fame quarterback Peyton Manning was asked about Stabler, who last played an NFL game in 1984, but all this time later remains an important part of the league's consciousness.

"Ken Stabler was a friend of my dad," said Manning, speaking of his father, Archie Manning, another longtime NFL quarterback. "I got to know him fairly well over the past years and the NFL quarterback fraternity lost a great one, lost a legend, when we lost 'The Snake.' I reached out to his family and told them they were in my thoughts and prayers. That is my reaction to that. I haven't had time to process the other information. What a prince of a guy. What a great leader. I have heard John Madden talk about him a number of times. He truly was one of a kind."

No, Stabler was not the man we thought he was. He was larger. More brilliant. Kinder, more progressive, more thoughtful. Perhaps more paternal. Perhaps more troubled. Definitely more troubled. His mind more injured, his brain more strangled from CTE than many knew. Perhaps more irresponsible. Taxes? Hell, I'll pay 'em when I pay 'em. Drink and drive, pills in the car? I do what I do. Pass the Wild Turkey.

Or, maybe, just maybe, Stabler was exactly who everyone thought he was. He was human, just more demonstrably so than the rest of us, in all of the ways that make us human. As a player, Stabler embraced his weaknesses by refusing to succumb to them, even when they tore apart his marriages. Then, later in his life, Stabler failed to control a different set of urges: drinking heavily and then getting into a car or ignoring the IRS. Whatever his intent, it didn't seem to matter, as Stabler always ended up in the same place, nestled between thoughtfulness and carelessness, sometimes in control, sometimes not even close.

Along the way came immense loyalty and dedication to Stabler, particularly from Raiders players and fans. This deep sense of love toward Stabler—really, that's the word—would begin almost the minute Stabler was traded to Houston for Dan Pastorini in what was basically a direct swap. It was the first time in NFL history a player was traded straight up for another player.

Pastorini was a physically tough and mentally sturdy quarterback who once played almost an entire season with broken ribs. He'd become the first quarterback (and maybe player) to wear a flak jacket to protect the midsection. Pastorini also experienced firsthand the Stabler cult that was to come, and there was no protection from that. "It was very difficult to win [Raiders fans] over," Pastorini said. "I kind of struggled a little bit." Part of it was that Raiders fans wanted Jim Plunkett, but another significant factor was no doubt resentment over Snake being gone. As a result, some took their irritation out on Pastorini.

"I always loved football," Stabler said. "Some of the best times of my life were spent in the NFL. The friendships I made there, and from when I played at Alabama, have lasted a lifetime. I wouldn't trade that for anything.

"What I will say, though, is I learned very early in my NFL career that players were expendable. I watched guys get discarded like they were trash. Guys you would see, who played before you, that weren't all that old and they couldn't walk straight. They couldn't remember things. It was always tough seeing guys like that. Guys in just their thirties and forties. Not that old at all. Sometimes younger."

Stabler remembered a scene in one of his last years with the Raiders, when he saw a friend who had retired just several years earlier. The friend was using a cane to walk due to a recent knee surgery, his third in five years. "He was in his early thirties," Stabler said. "He was probably going to walk with a limp for the rest of his life."

To Stabler, those men were like time machines. They showed him a possible future, where football was long over, but players were still constantly hobbled and ailing. Stabler was confident in his physical skills, even against the best athletes in the world in the NFL, but he was also reasonable and smart, much more than people knew. He saw those crippled men and made a decision.

"If I was going to be one of those guys," said Stabler, "I was going to enjoy myself along the way. I wasn't going to be a robot."

———

"The way I handled Kenny . . . it was one of my bigger regrets. I'll say that."

The man on the phone is Al Davis. I attempted to speak with Al for some years about Stabler. Davis had said no. And no. And no. And no again. Then, one day, Davis called. Why? He didn't want to answer that. Davis simply wanted to talk about "my boy Kenny." The conversation was extremely brief. The words were mighty.

You have to first understand who Al Davis was, to comprehend why what he said about Stabler is so important. If there were a Mount Rushmore for the NFL, to me, Davis would be on it. Davis hired the first woman team executive in NFL history in Amy Trask, the first Latino head coach in Tom Flores, and the first African-American head coach in the modern era in Art Shell. He was perhaps the most forward-thinking and intelligent owner in the history of sports. He scouted black colleges, something teams for years refused to do. He drafted the first black quarterback in the first round. Davis didn't care about your color. Your drinking. Your gambling. Practice smart, play hard on Sunday. That's all that mattered. And for much of his life as owner of the Raiders, that combination of progressive attitude and skill led to lots of winning. For two decades, between 1965 and 1986, Davis's teams did not have a losing record.

Yet for all of his greatness, he was also remarkably stubborn and in some cases—actually, many cases—he could be combative. It was this way between Davis and many in football, including his fellow owners and the commissioner. Davis battled commissioners Pete Rozelle and Paul Tagliabue bitterly and fiercely. The late Eagles owner Leonard Tose told how Davis and Rozelle were once supposed to meet and resolve their differences, avoiding what would become a series of legal actions that cost the NFL millions to fight. Instead, Rozelle refused to attend the peace conference. Davis stewed. "Get that motherfucker over here," Davis said. "We'll settle it on the front lawn. I'll beat the shit out of him."

Added Tose: "I could picture the two of them, the commissioner of the National Football League and former head of the defunct American Football League, duking it out like high school kids. But I knew it would never happen, even if Pete showed his face. Pete didn't have the balls to fight anyone, let alone a street tough like Al Davis, who probably *would* have killed him."

Despite Davis's occasional acidity, Stabler went out of his way to smooth things over with him. Often Stabler would publicly praise Davis. Stabler did this after the Super Bowl in 1977 by complimenting Davis and the Super Bowl rings Davis gave the team. "Al Davis is tough and it rubs off on the rest of us, all the way down the line," said Stabler. "But Al can be generous, too. Look at this Super Bowl ring—it's got to be the most expensive one any owner has ever given to his team."

The ring was stunning, with sixteen small diamonds representing each win that season, surrounding a large stone that symbolized the Super Bowl win. It was indeed a ring unmatched then for its expense.

In 1981, a *New York Times* story claimed Stabler was connected to a notorious gambler. There was nothing to the story, but it angered Stabler. Not solely because the story was garbage, but because he believed Davis had planted it, in an effort to embarrass both Stabler and the NFL office, an entity Davis constantly fought. "I'm caught in the middle of one of Al Davis's charades," Stabler told the *Washington Post*. "I don't want to dignify it by talking about it. If people can read that stuff and see what Davis is doing, using me like that. Well, I'm just going to let it die."

It seemed peace between Stabler and Davis would never come. "If I had to change anything in my career," Stabler said in a 1986 television interview, almost ten years after leaving the Raiders, "I'd have kept my mouth shut and stayed in Oakland. Play with a better ball club at the end of my career. Better offensive line, better receivers. Davis and I bumped heads and he traded me. . . ."

As recently as 2013, Stabler said, "I'm not that really close to the team." He told former Dallas Cowboy Drew Pearson in an interview that he watches the Raiders "like a fan. . . . I watch the Cowboys play. I watch the league as a fan. I don't watch the Raiders as a former player."

The coolness eventually ended with a meeting and hug. "When I let Kenny go, and he ended up [with Houston]," said Davis, in one of his rare interviews about his relationship with

Stabler, "I always wished he could have stayed with us. I was not always happy with Kenny and he wasn't always happy with me. But I loved Kenny. I loved him. I always appreciated what he did for us and I always wanted to tell him that and bury the hatchet with him."

That would happen in a secret gathering between the two men, not long before both passed away. "What I wanted to tell you was that Kenny was a Raider, and was always a Raider, and will always be a Raider," said Davis. It sounded on the phone as if he was weeping, and Davis was not the crying type.

The talk of Stabler, even during a short conversation like the one we had, even after decades had passed since Stabler and Davis were together on the Raiders, elicited great emotion. This is the effect Stabler had on almost everyone. Many who knew him felt an intense closeness to him. That closeness, in many cases, would last a lifetime. It did with Davis.

No, Stabler is not who we thought he was. He was so much more. So many people, so many lives affected in a positive way, so much history.

When I first met Stabler, and later began to speak with him when I'd see him at various events, signings, and other public outings, I barely recognized this man who had one of the wildest lifestyles of any professional athlete in history. I don't mean his face wasn't recognizable. His personality wasn't. Stabler was grounded. There wasn't a hint of the oversize persona I had read so much about. *I'm not the man you think I am.* An already great man, a great man with flaws, but still a great man, was even better than I knew.

———

Cam Newton is asked about Snake. Newton smiles. It is the smile of one great player acknowledging another.

"I went to Auburn and Alabama is our great rival obviously," said Newton. "Auburn fans hate Alabama and Alabama fans hate Auburn." After Newton's father was accused of soliciting payment from boosters to secure Newton's football services— Auburn would be cleared of any violations in his recruitment— Alabama fans got particularly nasty for the Iron Bowl game in Tuscaloosa. They called him Scam Newton and the school played the song "Take the Money and Run" by the Steve Miller Band over the stadium loudspeakers.

Despite that bit of nastiness, Newton is like other former and great Auburn and Alabama players, in that away from the field, there's respect between the two schools. There's also respect for historical players like Snake.

"The Snake to me was one of the originals," said Newton. "He was one of those quarterbacks that could beat you with the run or the pass. I think he led the way for guys like me."

How so? "What made him great was that he was such a good player on the field," Newton says, "and off the field, he lived his life how he wanted. He didn't care what people thought about him. The Snake was a great player and he brought fun to the game. I think what I liked about him the most. He really loved playing football."

———o———

Where Stabler was always almost perfect, where he rarely faltered, where he didn't make the catastrophic mistakes he did in marriage, was in being a father. That seems like a strange, even contradictory thing to declare about a man who had to be threatened with arrest to increase child support. As his daughters, like Kendra, began to grow, and the love between them and their father intensified, they became inseparable. When it came to fatherhood, few men were better. He stopped being Snake. He was Dadskers.

Fathers and daughters and love are an eternal and powerful mix. The Stabler family had the additional combustible element of fame. In some famous families, fame acts not to bond, but instead to split, creating a mushroom cloud. Not so with Stabler and his girls. They would come to protect their father and his legacy. There was no better example of this than an incident that happened in the spring of 2016.

In a Florida court on April 1, Rose Stabler, the third former wife, filed a class action lawsuit against the NFL alleging the league hid the effects of CTE from former players like Stabler. There was one problem with the lawsuit: it was bullshit.

The suit portrayed Stabler as someone who in his final years was in a dark, frightening place. But that's not how Stabler really was. Friends and family say the effects of CTE caused ringing in Stabler's ears, forgetfulness, and bad headaches, but that he was still humorous, sharp mentally, and coherent. My belief is the CTE impacted Stabler's decision making going back decades, maybe all the way to high school and his days at Alabama. There's no proof of this but that's my belief and it explains Stabler's occasional feelings of guilt over some of his behavior.

Stabler expressed to multiple people, including his daughters, that one of his only regrets was marrying Rose. The Stabler daughters, none of whom are related to her, came to despise Rose. This was particularly true of the eldest, Kendra, who has become a spokeswoman for the Stabler family. Kendra has the smarts and quick wit of her father. When Rose filed her action, it not only angered the Stabler daughters, it strengthened their tight bond despite being born to different Stabler wives.

Rose spoke about the lawsuit on the steps of the U.S. district courthouse where she filed the action. Soon the *Palm Beach Post*, which covered her court filing, was writing about Rose's background. Part of the *Post*'s story on her lawsuit read: "Rose Stabler also has a colorful past, one that includes telling one media outlet Ken threw her out of a moving car but telling another outlet on the same 1986 day that the couple was 'doing fine.' In

July, an arrest warrant was issued after she failed to appear for a hearing in Mobile, Ala. In 2011, she rolled up her sleeves for a newspaper photographer to show that her arms had no needle marks. She was rebutting a woman who said she saw her in a courthouse restroom with a needle in her arm. The *Press-Register* of Mobile reported that security secured the restroom and found Rose inside. A sheriff's spokesman said deputies thought she was under the influence of a substance but did not find a syringe, theorizing she might have flushed it down the toilet.

"Although Rose Stabler continues to assert she and Ken had physical confrontations, she said she could be the aggressor. She recounted a time, shortly after they were married, that they were in a grocery store in Louisiana. 'He had two black eyes, which I gave him,' she said. 'And this Cajun man came up to me—I love their accents—and he said, "I know you did that because if someone else did it, he'd have killed him or been in jail." ' "

Kim Bush, who had been Stabler's girlfriend since 1999, told the newspaper that Stabler tried to constantly distance himself from Rose but found it difficult. "In spite of restraining orders, [she] continued to harass him with literally hundreds of insane voice messages over the years," Bush wrote to the *Post*. "As a matter of fact, she continued to text his phone the week after his death knowing that it was sitting on my nightstand."

It wasn't long before Kendra countered Rose's claims that Stabler was seriously debilitated in his final years, and vehemently defended her father while also completely nuking Rose.

When the *Palm Beach Post* contacted Kendra, there was no holding back. "She's made-for-TV crazy," Kendra said. "You can't make this stuff up. I'm just frustrated and irritated because I want my dad to rest in peace and she needs to move on and stop riding on my dad's name, which she has done since the day she met him.

"He wasn't sitting in some dark, closed-curtain room, wasn't suicidal, he wasn't depressed," Kendra said. "He definitely had side effects. But up until the day he died, he was very coherent, very sweet, very loving."

Kendra remembers one of the first times she understood that her father was a star. She was six or seven and a huge fan of figure skater Dorothy Hamill, who won a gold medal in the 1976 Olympics. Hamill would begin a barnstorming tour with the Ice Capades after her Olympic victory. Stabler won the Super Bowl as Hamill started her Ice Capades stint. Hamill came to Oakland and Stabler took his daughter to see her. Before the show began, an announcement was made that Stabler was present. There was a loud ovation and Stabler stood to acknowledge the crowd.

"After then he sat down and every dad that had taken their daughter to see Dorothy was now lined up to get an autograph," Kendra remembered. "I watched in amazement as he once again didn't turn anyone away and it clicked that he was kind of a big deal."

Yet despite the fame, Stabler never changed. He remained a grounded father, especially on the issues of race. In the last years and months of his life, Kendra and Snake used to take long walks. She noticed her father opening up more about almost everything, including his views on race, which were pretty simple, despite growing up among the brutal complexities of Jim Crow.

"That is what I love most about my dad," Kendra said. "He didn't see color. Everyone was equal to him and he was like that at a very young age. It is so crazy to think of the racism he grew up around. Alabama in the sixties doesn't get much worse yet he never let anyone's views sway him. Black, white, brown, or purple, everyone was the same. I am not sure if his father or mother instilled that in him. He didn't talk about it because being of a different race was never a topic in our family. We had many long talks over the years and last year they grew deeper, almost as if he knew he was running out of time."

But there would be lots of time with her father, and lots of memories. "There are so many stories," she said. "Later in my life after high school I would travel with my dad a lot. Speaking engagements, commentating, TV deals, etc., and I would listen to him talk and was just hanging on every word like anyone else. He had a way of storytelling. He was so fun to listen to. He was funny and just so quick with his wit. He was an even better papa. He would visit my boys' elementary school and have lunch with them in the lunchroom, sharing stories with the young boys, taking his rings off and letting them pass them around and try them on. He would follow them all to recess after lunch and throw the ball over and over to about twelve boys that couldn't get enough of Jack and Justin's Papa Snake. He always made sure we all met up at fun events he was doing and we never missed his Celebrity Golf Tournament in Point Clear, Alabama, raising monies for CF [cystic fibrosis], Ronald McDonald House of Mobile, Children's Hospital, and the list goes on.

"My favorite stories are not filled with the glitz and glamour of having a famous athlete for a dad. My favorite stories are not exciting. My favorite stories are of just simple days spent with him, watching CNN or NASCAR, watching him throw the ball with his grandsons. He was so doting. Always wanting us to eat something he had made. Soup was a favorite of his. Pretty much everything in the fridge thrown in a pot. We did the Disneyland trips, the championship Alabama games, the TV tapings and book signings, and those were great, but my favorite stories are the ones with just family, laughing, playing games, etc. My dad was a neat freak. He would make hotel beds the second one of your feet hit the floor. His closet was [organized] by color, short to long sleeve. He actually has an award for neatest room in college. I have it and cherish that more than his Super Bowl trophy."

———

On Christmas Day in 2015 on the Sports Xchange site, writer Tom LaMarre, who covered Stabler, told a story about Stabler few people know: LaMarre wrote a book with Stabler in 1975, and while they were working on it at LaMarre's house, as the Sports Xchange account notes, the writer's two sons, then seven and four, told their friends Stabler was going to be at their home.

Initially, when a number of kids arrived, Stabler said he would see about visiting them after he did his work with LaMarre. "When Snake walked out of the house a little after 4, the street was full of neighborhood kids waiting to see him," the story said. "He borrowed a football . . . and played catch with the kids until the sun disappeared."

What also isn't known is that Stabler, almost by himself, is responsible for massive donations to numerous charities. He contributed $450,000 to the World Health Education Foundation. There was $100,000 for the Boys and Girls Club. Stabler also helped teammates, such as Hall of Famer Biletnikoff, who runs a foundation that fights domestic violence. "Kenny was always here for whatever we needed and he was awesome with people," Biletnikoff told the Sports Xchange. "Even when he had troubles in his own life, Kenny dropped everything to come out and help. He had a way with people, made everybody feel like a friend. His mere presence was sometimes worth thousands and thousands of dollars for us and, hell, he could barely afford the plane trip himself."

———

Stabler found love in the last years of his life. It helped buoy him for the fight to come. William Browning wrote an excellent story for SB Nation about those final days.

"Kenny Stabler learned he had colon cancer in February [2015]," Browning began. "He was in Phoenix, Arizona, where he had been renting a home since the fall of 2014 so he could watch his two grandsons play football for Chaparral High School. One is a receiver. One is a defensive back. Stabler called them his 'grandsnakes.' In January, he had called Kim Bush, his partner for the last 16 years of his life, and told her of a consistent pain in his stomach.

"She now suspects it had bothered him for months. Bush, who works in Mississippi, told Stabler to go to the doctor, something he avoided. She had made him numerous doctors' appointments through the years. 'And he would always cancel them,' Bush said, not so much with sadness, but with the annoyed tone women can take when discussing stubborn men in their lives. This time, Stabler went to the doctor. Scans were done. Bush flew to Arizona to go with him to get the results. It was cancer, Stage 4. Stabler was told he had two years. . . .

"In early March, Stabler and Bush went home to Gulfport, Mississippi, where they had lived together about six years. There, about three miles from the Gulf of Mexico, Stabler dug in for the fight of his life. 'We knew we were facing an uphill battle,' Bush said. Every other week, Stabler would sit in his favorite leather chair for the chemotherapy. It sapped his energy. His appetite was not much. He would need three days to recover from a session before feeling like himself again. Bush said he never complained.

"One afternoon Bush got home from work. In the foyer were several cardboard boxes that had been opened and strewn about. On each one was the word 'Everlast.' Puzzled, she called out to Stabler.

"'What's all this?'

"'I'm going to start working out,' he responded.

"He had bought some boxing equipment—a speedbag and a heavy bag—and he set them up in the garage, beside a stationary bicycle. For the next four months, when he had the energy, Stabler walked alone into the garage and threw punches until he couldn't throw anymore. Faced with his own mortality at 69, that is how he responded. By balling up his fists and swinging.

"In his mind," Bush said, "he was going to beat the hell out of cancer."

⁙

Perhaps the best way to end a book about Ken Stabler is to again show the positive effect he had on people. This was, after all, one of his greatest traits.

When Stabler died, John Madden took part in a conference call with a handful of journalists. Madden was emotional and delivered a gorgeous summation of Stabler's life.

"You think of the good times and the memories," Madden said. "All the games and all the practices and all the meetings. No matter what you threw in front of him, he enjoyed it. He always had a twinkle in his eye and a smile. He was one of the greatest competitors ever. When you think of the Raiders in the seventies, Ken Stabler has to be right on top."

At Stabler's Hall of Fame ceremony, his grandsons both unveiled Stabler's Hall of Fame bust. Justin gently kissed his grandfather's likeness on the forehead. The moment was perhaps the most emotional in the ceremony's history.

Among those deeply moved by Stabler was one of the best actors of all time. Soon after Stabler's death he sent two of Stabler's daughters a note:

Dear Kendra and Alexa,

Beyond the heroics on the field and, say, a Super Bowl victory, why a young fan takes to any one football player is a mystery. A personal attraction.

In Oakland, the capitol of Raider Nation, the years I was a kid there we had everyone from the Black Panthers, the Hell's Angels, the Zodiac Killer, and Charley O. Finley. And, we had the Raiders. . . .

Your father, with his left-handedness and those two bad knees, displayed a permanent smile of bemusement that said—win or lose—"ain't this fun?" I really did see in him the honor to be found in playing the game, of using one's god given talent, of taking pleasure in the effort.

That Ken Stabler came from the likes of Alabama yet played right there in my home town helped me understand the variety found in the USA. Using a pair of pliers to change the channel on my busted kids TV (it had a few knobs missing) I would tune in San Diego to see your Dad play, or Shea Stadium to see him take on the Jets—learning that if you were good enough you could do your thing anywhere you wanted.

I'm honored to wear the fine bit of Stablerwear you sent along and will continue to offer up to anyone who comes my way, and maybe asks how I ended up where I am, that you just have to throw deep, baby. . . .

It was signed by Tom Hanks.

Author's Note and Acknowledgments

Forty years after Stabler inspired his Raider teammates on the football field, he was still inspiring them.

In 2016, three former Raiders who played with Stabler—George Atkinson, George Buehler, and Art Thoms—told the *San Jose Mercury News* they pledged their brains to the Boston-based Concussion Legacy Foundation. That group studies the effects of CTE.

The three men said they were making the pledge as a show of solidarity for Stabler.

"When you see your teammate deteriorate a lot through the end of his life, to see him go out like that, it brings us together," said Thoms, a defensive tackle who played for the Raiders from 1969 to 1976.

So, as he had so long ago, he was inspiring the Raiders. This is what Stabler did. In many ways, this is what he will always do.

———

I have said this many times: one of the nicest human beings I have ever known was Ken Stabler. I have never met another person (outside of my family) who was more sincere, open, honest, decent, kind, and compelling. I always felt, even now, Stabler is the most underappreciated player in NFL history. Not one of. Not maybe. Definitely.

He was also genuinely funny. The first time we met it was the early 1990s. He shook my hand. "Well, you're not very handsome," he said. Stabler initially said it with a straight face and then laughed.

I would go on to interview Stabler dozens of times—sometimes for stories, sometimes just for conversation, always with the intent of one day doing either a long-form story or a book.

This book is a biography but also, truthfully, it is part appreciation. Mostly an appreciation of Stabler but also for that era of football. We know now just how brutal it was and what it did to the bodies, and particularly the minds, of the men who played it. The game is less brutal now. It's not safe, by any stretch, but it is less physically nasty.

The game now is also grossly corporate and homogenized. It has less violence, which is good, but it also has less soul. Less character. Today's players make more money but there is far less, well, fun.

Stabler hated the biography he wrote. The older Ken Stabler was uncomfortable seeing in print the decisions of the younger Ken Stabler. Yet I believe that book is one of the best sports biographies ever written because it *is* so honest. It's greatly underrated, like Stabler himself. In football, there's never been another book like it. There probably never will be.

That book was one of three that helped shape this one. There were two others. One was *Badasses* by Peter Richmond. It's not a coincidence that Stabler's book and Richmond's are two of the best football books of all time. That's because they chronicle those Raiders. Richmond did so with excellent reporting and beautiful writing.

The third was *Madden*, by the late Bryan Burwell, who was a friend and a mentor. He always hated when I called him a mentor but he was one of the best journalists I've ever known.

There are several people I really want to thank. First, my wife, Kelly. She has done nothing but show me love, even during the tough times. I will always be grateful.

My editor, Matthew Daddona, showed great skill and patience in editing this book. He's a true gem. Thank you also to Katie Steinberg, the senior publicist at William Morrow and Dey Street Books. Gail Sideman of PUBLISIDE Personal Publicity was also invaluable.

I also want to thank my agent, Andrew Stuart of the Stuart Agency. He's creative and hardworking. He also fights for his clients. You can't ask for much more.

Jennifer O'Neill is the best fact-checker in the history of the world. She always saves my ass. Thank you.

The Stabler family background was provided by Nedra Dickman Brill, Certified Genealogist, from Genealogists.com. She's a true professional.

Also, Kendra Stabler Moyes was kind and gracious to me. This is not a shock. Her father was the same way. The apple doesn't fall far from the silver and black tree.

Sources

Associated Press. "Castoff Turns It for NFC." *Oakland Tribune*, January 21, 1975: 33.

———. "Franco's on Rampage." *Oakland Tribune*, January 1, 1976: 25.

———. "Miami Decided to Forget About Finesse." *Oakland Tribune*, December 31, 1973: 7.

———. "Ralston Numb with Schock." *Oakland Tribune*, November 3, 1975: 39.

———. "Yepremian Survives Pro Bowl Pressure." *Oakland Tribune*, January 21, 1974: 30.

Atkinson, Rick. *The Day of Battle: The War in Sicily and Italy, 1943–1944*. New York: Henry Holt, 2007.

"Atmore Toppled by Foley 14–0." *Foley Onlooker*, October 24, 1963: 9.

"Baby Tiders Beat Auburn Freshmen." *Anniston Star*, November 22, 1964: 16.

"Backfield Power Will Be Feature of All-Star Tilt." *Anniston Star*, July 19, 1964: 15.

"Bama-Bound Stabler Wrecks North All-Stars, 34 to 7." *Anniston Star*, August 15, 1964: 8.

"Bama Frosh Beat Billow." *New Orleans States-Item*, October 24, 1964: 12.

Barra, Allen. *The Last Coach: A Life of Paul "Bear" Bryant*. New York: Norton, 2006.

"Baseball." *Foley Onlooker*, April 20, 1961: 8.

"Baseball Season Opens for Foley Lions March 31." *Foley Onlooker*, March 12, 1964: 12.

"Basketball Games Set for County High Schools." *Foley Onlooker*, January 5, 1961: 1.

Belson, Ken. "Brain Trauma to Affect One in Three Players, NFL Agrees." *New York Times*, September 12, 2014. http://www.nytimes.com/2014/09/13/sports/football/actuarial-reports-in-nfl-concussion-deal-are-released.html?_r=0.

Bergman, Ron. *Oakland Tribune*, December 12, 1977: 25.

———. *Oakland Tribune*, November 14, 1977: 23.

———. *Oakland Tribune*, December 19, 1977: 23.

———. *Oakland Tribune*, November 29, 1977: 21.

———. "Accent on Sports." *Oakland Tribune*, November 15, 1976: 21.

———. "Accent on Sports." *Oakland Tribune*, September 19, 1977: 23.

———. "No Jolly Afternoon for Jolley." *Oakland Tribune*, December 3, 1973: 35.

"Bitterness Forgotten on 'Starr' Day." *Anniston Star*, February 14, 1968: 10–12A.

Briley, John David. *Career in Crisis: Paul "Bear" Bryant and the 1971 Season of Change*. Macon, GA: Mercer University Press, 2006.

"Broncos Steal Raider Script." *Oakland Tribune*, November 14, 1977: 24.

Bryant, Paul, and John Underwood. *Bear: The Hard Life and Good Times of Alabama's Coach Bryant*. Chicago: Triumph Books, 2007.

"Bryant Checks Negro Hopefuls." *Tuscaloosa News*, April 6, 1967.

Burwell, Bryan. *Madden: A Biography*. Chicago: Triumph Books, 2011.

Clark, Peter. "Raiders Hit in Pittsburgh." *Oakland Tribune*, December 7, 1976: 33.

Crewdson, John. "Pro Football's Ken Stabler Is Linked to a Gambler." *New York Times*, August 30, 1981. http://www.ny times.com/1981/08/30/sports/pro-football-s-ken-stabler-is -linked-to-a-gambler.html.

"Defense Comes of Age." *Oakland Tribune*, November 1, 1976: 35.

"Dodging Storms, Remembering an Old Pal." *Anniston Star*, March 30, 1975.

The Drew Pearson Show. Fox Sports Southwest, November 8, 2013. https://youtu.be/xFRVUlm6sT8.

"11 Stars Are Tiders." *Anniston Star*, July 19, 1964: 14.

Fainaru, Steve. "Latest Studies: Brain Disease from Contact Sports More Common." *ESPN*, March 16, 2016. http://espn .go.com/espn/otl/story/_/id/14982032/nfl-admission-foot ball-lead-brain-disease-came-amid-new-science-suggest ing-sports-related-trauma-becoming-more-common.

"Foley Blanks Tigers 3–0." *Foley Onlooker*, April 25, 1963: 16.

"Foley Eagers Win One, Lose One." *Foley Onlooker*, January 30, 1964: 9.

"Foley-Fairhope Game Here Friday." *Foley Onlooker*, November 14, 1963: 9.

"Foley Fans See Vigor Nudge Lions Out 20–14." *Foley Onlooker*, September 12, 1963: 8.

"Foley High Lions Will Meet Theodore in Season's First Game Friday Night." *Foley Onlooker*, September 14, 1961: 1.

"Foley High School Basketball Scores." *Foley Onlooker*, December 8, 1960: 8.

"Foley High Wins County A and B Hoop Titles." *Foley Onlooker*, February 13, 1964: 1.

"Foley Lions." *Foley Onlooker*, September 26, 1963: 9.

"Foley Lions Baseball Team." *Foley Onlooker*, May 7, 1964: 19.

"The Foley Lions First Home Game Friday." *Foley Onlooker*, September 14, 1961: 10.

"Foley Lions Have 30 Out for Football." *Foley Onlooker*, August 27, 1961: 8.

"Foley Lions 1963 Football Schedules Includes Vigor and WS Neal Teams." *Foley Onlooker*, February 21, 1963: 16.

"Foley Lions Overwhelm Bay Minette Tigers 41–0." *Foley Onlooker*, October 26, 1961: 18.

"Foley Lions Play Thursday Night." *Foley Onlooker*, October 3, 1963: 9.

"The Foley Lions Play Vigor Friday." *Foley Onlooker*, August 29, 1963: 16.

"Foley Lions Roll Past Fairhope." *Foley Onlooker*, January 23, 1964: 9.

"Foley Lions Start Baseball April 4." *Foley Onlooker*, March 28, 1963: 8.

"Foley Lions Third in AA Tournament." *Foley Onlooker*, March 7, 1963: 16.

"Foley Lions Win One Lose One This Week." *Foley Onlooker*, May 7, 1964: 19.

"Foley Lions Win 21–14 over Cadets." *Foley Onlooker*, November 14, 1963: 9.

"Foley Lions Win 27–0 over Bears." *Foley Onlooker*, October 17, 1963: 9.

"Foley Lions Win Two; Play Fairhope Friday." *Foley Onlooker*, January 16, 1964: 9.

Foley Onlooker, August 27, 1970: 8.

Foley Onlooker, October 4, 1962. http://www.gulfcoastnewstoday.com/the_foley_onlooker/sports/article_ffebc572-26df-11e3-94e6-0019bb2963f4.html.

"Foley-Robertsdale to Play Thursday." *Foley Onlooker*, April 27, 1961: 8.

"Foley Throttles Catholic 33–0." *Foley Onlooker*, October 10, 1963: 9.

"Foley Wins Again: Whips Baker 52–0 in Eight Victory." *Foley Onlooker*, November 9, 1961: 16.

"Foley Wins County Championship with Win over Fairhope." *Foley Onlooker*, May 2, 1963: 15.

"From the Stablers' Kitchen." *Oakland Tribune*, October 13, 1976: 53.

"George Smith Sports Editor, The Star." *Anniston Star*, August 16, 1964: 10.

"George Smith Sports Editor, The Star." *Anniston Star*, November 19, 1964: 23.

"A Great Bunch of Kids Who Wanted to Play." *Foley Onlooker*, November 23, 1961: 16.

High Command of the Armed Forces. "Fuehrer Directives 1942–1945." January 28, 1944, pp. 121–22. http://der-fuehrer.org/reden/english/wardirectives/52.html.

"High School Baseball Season Opens Saturday." *Foley Onlooker*, March 30, 1961: 8.

"Homecoming Queen Picked." *Anniston Star*, October 31, 1967: 5.

"The Hurricane of 1752." *South Carolina Gazette*, September 13, 1752.

"Impossible Dream a Reality." *Oakland Tribune*, November 19, 1973: 41.

Jenkins, Sally. "NFL Must Pay for Its Handling of Concussion Issues—or Congress Should Intervene." *Washington Post,* October 1, 2014. https://www.washingtonpost.com/sports/red skins/nfl-must-pay-for-its-handling-of-concussion-issues -or-congress-should-intervene/2014/10/01/8e0cc6ae-4984 -11e4-b72e-d60a9229cc10_story.html.

"Johnson, Fans Agree Defense Had Its Day." *Oakland Tribune,* December 17, 1973: 33.

Jones, Robert. "Gettin' Nowhere Fast." *Sports Illustrated.* September 19, 1977. http://www.si.com/vault/1977/09/19/621980 /gettin-nowhere-fast.

"Ken Stabler." *Foley Onlooker,* July 30, 1964: 20.

"Ken Stabler Loses Father." *Cullman Times,* August 23, 1970: 12.

"Ken the 'Snake' Has Pro Problems." *Anniston Star,* January 28, 1968: 26.

Kindred, Dave. "Stabler and Oilers See Hand of Al Davis' in Dudich Link." *Washington Post,* September 3, 1981. https:// www.washingtonpost.com/archive/sports/1981/09/03/stabler -and-oilers-see-hand-of-al-davis-in-dudich-link/53309462 -bed4-4dc1-a7a0-95581b46c296/.

Knowland, Joseph. "Tribune Editorial." *Oakland Tribune,* January 10, 1977: 1.

LaMarre, Tom. "Battered Raiders Walking Tall." *Oakland Tribune,* September 27, 1976: 31.

———. "Big Raider Loss: Cline." *Oakland Tribune,* September 17, 1974: 33.

———. "Blanda Toehold in Football History." *Oakland Tribune,* December 22, 1975: 39.

———. "Branch Rewrites Wells' Script." *Oakland Tribune,* November 8, 1976: 31.

———. "Catch Up Season for Raiders." *Oakland Tribune,* November 6, 1972: 47.

————. "Conservative Raiders in Control." *Oakland Tribune*, October 18, 1976: 31.

————. "Defensive Sparkle Saves Raider Record." *Oakland Tribune*, October 6, 1975: 31.

————. "Formalities Over for 13-1 Raiders." *Oakland Tribune*, December 13, 1976: 19.

————. "Franco Freaks the Raiders." *Oakland Tribune*, December 24, 1972: 15.

————. "Giants Ground Under." *Oakland Tribune*, November 5, 1973: 33.

————. "Giveaway Day for Raiders." *Oakland Tribune*, November 12, 1973: 29.

————. "How Hendricks Did It." *Oakland Tribune*, November 22, 1976: 39.

————. "Injured Cline Out of Playoffs?" *Oakland Tribune*, December 22, 1975: 37.

————. "'Just Two to Go,' Winning Raiders Yell." *Oakland Tribune*, December 23, 1973: 29.

————. "Korver Lost, Marv Out 6 Weeks." *Oakland Tribune*, September 23, 1975: 37.

————. "Like Old Days for Raiders." *Oakland Tribune*, October 15, 1973: 33.

————. "A Mulligan Saves Raiders." *Oakland Tribune*, November 24, 1975: 43.

————. "New Miracle." *Oakland Tribune*, September 13, 1976: 23.

————. "New Orleans Er, San Diego—Via Detroit." *Oakland Tribune*, November 11, 1974: 29.

————. "No Denying the Raiders." *Oakland Tribune*, December 27, 1976: 35.

————. "No Miracle for Raiders." *Oakland Tribune*, October 23, 1972: 39.

————. "Now Raiders Can Do It All Themselves." *Oakland Tribune*, November 26, 1973: 29.

————. "Ol' George to the Rescue—Twice." *Oakland Tribune*, December 1, 1975: 35.

————. "One TD Obliterates Raiders." *Oakland Tribune*, November 19, 1973: 41.

————. "Philyaw Finds a Home." *Oakland Tribune*, September 27, 1976: 33.

————. "Pittsburgh's Big D Stops the Raiders." *Oakland Tribune*, December 30, 1974: 29.

————. "Raider Dreams in Deep Freeze." *Oakland Tribune*, January 5, 1976: 35.

————. "A Raider Explosion." *Oakland Tribune*, November 15, 1971: 37.

————. "Raiders Grab Reins." *Oakland Tribune*, October 11, 1976: 19.

————. "Raider Rally Beats Broncs." *Oakland Tribune*, October 11, 1971: 29.

————. "Raider Runaway on His Best Day." *Oakland Tribune*, November 17, 1975: 29.

————. "Raider Sacks Put Title in Bag." *Oakland Tribune*, November 1, 1976: 33.

————. "Raiders Bludgeon the Chiefs." *Oakland Tribune*, September 23, 1974: 29.

————. "The Raiders Buy Home Insurance." *Oakland Tribune*, November 15, 1976: 21.

————. "Raiders End Dolphins' Dynasty, Outdo Heidi." *Oakland Tribune*, December 22, 1974: 31.

————. "Raiders Fall Off of the Cliff." *Oakland Tribune*, December 31, 1973: 5.

————. "Raiders Fatten on Home Cookin'." *Oakland Tribune*, November 10, 1975: 35.

————. "Raiders Find End Zone." *Oakland Tribune*, October 8, 1973: 33.

———. "Raiders Find Losing a Lousy Experience." *Oakland Tribune*, December 15, 1975: 33.

———. "Raiders Ground Gilliam." *Oakland Tribune*, September 30, 1974: 29.

———. "Raiders Let Win Slip Away." *Oakland Tribune*, October 23, 1973: 33.

———. "Raiders Like Playoff Pairing." *Oakland Tribune*, December 19, 1972: 35.

———. "Raiders Nail Down Toughest Title Yet." *Oakland Tribune*, December 17, 1973: 33.

———. "Raiders Not Pushing Panic Button." *Oakland Tribune*, October 20, 1975: 31.

———. "Raiders Put Bomb Back in Offense." *Oakland Tribune*, October 27, 1975: 31.

———. "Raiders Put Pats on Brink of Elimination." *Oakland Tribune*, December 2, 1974: 31.

———. "Raiders Rewrite Comeback Script." *Oakland Tribune*, September 29, 1975: 31.

———. "Raiders See Hope Among the Ruins." *Oakland Tribune*, October 4, 1976: 19.

———. "Raiders, Steelers in New Showdown." *Oakland Tribune*, December 29, 1975: 39.

———. "Raiders Stir Avalanche in Rockies." *Oakland Tribune*, November 3, 1975: 37.

———. "Raiders Survive Another Dogfight." *Oakland Tribune*, October 28, 1974: 29.

———. "Raiders Take Defeat with No Excuses." *Oakland Tribune*, November 25, 1974: 41.

———. "Raiders Use Heidi Script on Bengals." *Oakland Tribune*, October 21, 1974: 29.

———. "Raiders Walking Narrow Line." *Oakland Tribune*, October 25, 1976: 29.

———. "Raiders Win in Last 10 Seconds: Even Stabler Calls Finish 'Unbelievable.'" *Oakland Tribune*, December 19, 1976: 39.

———. "Raiders Win the Biggest One of All." *Oakland Tribune*, January 10, 1977: 19.

———. "Raiders Wreck Chiefs, Think Broncos." *Oakland Tribune*, December 9, 1973: 55.

———. "Raiders' Defense Does It." *Oakland Tribune*, October 10, 1972: 37.

———. "Raiders' Offense Emerges." *Oakland Tribune*, October 7, 1974: 27.

———. "Raiders' Plan Falls into Place." *Oakland Tribune*, December 9, 1974: 31.

———. "Raiders' Torture Ends With a Smile." *Oakland Tribune*, December 3, 1973: 33.

———. "Rams Routed 45 to 17." *Oakland Tribune*, October 30, 1972: 33.

———. "Snake Silent This Week on Steelers." *Oakland Tribune*, January 1, 1976: 25.

———. "Stabler Engineers a Victory." *Oakland Tribune*, October 29, 1973: 33.

———. "Stabler OK—In Every Way." *Oakland Tribune*, September 21, 1976: 31.

———. "Stabler Salutes His Miracle Receivers." *Oakland Tribune*, December 22, 1974: 33.

———. "Stabler's Passes Crush Bengals: Raiders Eliminate All Doubts." *Oakland Tribune*, December 7, 1976: 31.

———. "Stabler's Super Bowl Game Plan." *Oakland Tribune*, November 29, 1976: 19.

———. "Steelers Stymie Raiders." *Oakland Tribune*, September 18, 1972: 35.

———. "Surprise! Raiders Are 1-0, Not 0-1." *Oakland Tribune*, September 23, 1975: 35.

————. "Tatum's Theft Saves a Long Day for Raiders." *Oakland Tribune*, October 14, 1974: 27.

————. "Title Old Hat." *Oakland Tribune*, November 22, 1976: 37.

————. "A Verbal Aftermath Stirs Feud." *Oakland Tribune*, November 24, 1975: 45.

————. "When Will It Be in the Cards for the Raiders?" *Oakland Tribune*, December 30, 1974: 31.

————. "Where's Oakland's Offense." *Oakland Tribune*, October 1, 1973: 29.

Levitt, Ed. *Oakland Tribune*, December 15, 1975: 33.

————. "Accent on Sports." *Oakland Tribune*, November 1, 1976: 33.

————. "Accent on Sports." *Oakland Tribune*, January 10, 1977: 19.

————. "Accent on Sports." *Oakland Tribune*, October 11, 1976: 19.

————. "Accent on Sports." *Oakland Tribune*, September 13, 1976: 23.

————. "Accent on Sports." *Oakland Tribune*, November 22, 1976: 27.

————. "Accent on Sports." *Oakland Tribune*, October 25, 1976: 29.

————. "Accent on Sports." *Oakland Tribune*, December 27, 1976: 35.

————. "Accent on Sports." *Oakland Tribune*, October 4, 1976: 19.

————. "Accent on Sports." *Oakland Tribune*, December 7, 1976: 31.

————. "Accent on Sports." *Oakland Tribune*, November 8, 1976: 31.

————. "Bay Area a Winner." *Oakland Tribune*, September 27, 1971: 33.

———. "Blanda's Buddy." *Oakland Tribune*, October 29, 1973: 33.

———. "Brandos & Madden." *Oakland Tribune*, October 8, 1973: 33.

———. "Can Browns Make It 10?" *Oakland Tribune*, November 17, 1975: 29.

———. "Dan and His Dad." *Oakland Tribune*, November 15, 1971: 37.

———. "Day of Dramas." *Oakland Tribune*, December 24, 1972: 15.

———. "Dee-fense! Dee-fense!" *Oakland Tribune*, September 30, 1974: 29.

———. "Even Winners Moan." *Oakland Tribune*, December 9, 1975: 35.

———. "Everyone Played 1,000 Countdown." *Oakland Tribune*, December 13, 1976: 19.

———. "Harris' Golden Goof." *Oakland Tribune*, December 24, 1972: 15.

———. "It's Not Over Yet." *Oakland Tribune*, November 6, 1972: 47.

———. "Jim's Mom Cheered and Cried." *Oakland Tribune*, December 2, 1974: 31.

———. "Key to the Super Bowl." *Oakland Tribune*, December 29, 1975: 39.

———. "Kisses for TD." *Oakland Tribune*, October 1, 1973: 29.

———. "Koufax in Kneepads." *Oakland Tribune*, November 11, 1974: 29.

———. "Losing at Big Ben's." *Oakland Tribune*, September 18, 1972: 35.

———. "Love Scenes for George?" *Oakland Tribune*, December 1, 1975: 35.

———. "Madden Zonked." *Oakland Tribune*, December 31, 1973: 5.

———. "NY's All Shook Up." *Oakland Tribune*, November 5, 1973: 33.

———. "Old Wrinkle for Playoffs." *Oakland Tribune*, December 22, 1975: 37.

———. "Paper Champs." *Oakland Tribune*, November 19, 1973: 41.

———. "Raiders Bury a Rival." *Oakland Tribune*, September 23, 1974: 29.

———. "The Real Al Davis." *Oakland Tribune*, October 18, 1971: 33.

———. "Reggie Helps Raiders." *Oakland Tribune*, October 21, 1974: 29.

———. "The Ryan Express." *Oakland Tribune*, January 21, 1975: 30.

———. "Shula vs. Davis." *Oakland Tribune*, December 9, 1974: 31.

———. "The Smell Lingers." *Oakland Tribune*, September 20, 1971: 33.

———. "Steelers Bad News." *Oakland Tribune*, November 12, 1973: 29.

———. "Steelers Will Lose." *Oakland Tribune*, December 17, 1973: 33.

———. "Three to Go." *Oakland Tribune*, November 26, 1973: 29.

———. "Thriller in the Capital." *Oakland Tribune*, November 24, 1975: 43.

———. "Tough Act to Follow." *Oakland Tribune*, October 28, 1974: 29.

———. "A True Test of What." *Oakland Tribune*, January 5, 1976: 35.

———. "Why Raiders Never Make It." *Oakland Tribune*, December 30, 1974: 29.

———. "Why They Never Let Up." *Oakland Tribune*, October 27, 1975: 31.

"Lions Are Number One in Class AA State Poll." *Foley Onlooker*, November 30, 1961: 16.

"Lions Get Token of Appreciation." *Foley Onlooker*, March 14, 1963: 16.

"Lions Lose 68–65 to UMS Cadets." *Foley Onlooker*, February 28, 1963: 16.

"Lions Rip Bears." *Foley Onlooker*, February 14, 1963: 16.

"Lions Win GCCC Fourth Consecutive Season." *Foley Onlooker*, November 21, 1963: 9.

"Lions Won One, Lost One So Far." *Foley Onlooker*, January 9, 1964: 7.

"Locker Room Comments." *Oakland Tribune*, December 19, 1976: 42.

"Locker Room Quotes." *Oakland Tribune*, October 31, 1977: 23.

"Locker Room Viewpoints." *Oakland Tribune*, September 13, 1976: 27.

"Madden Wants to Win 'Em All." *Oakland Tribune*, November 22, 1976: 39.

Mobile Register, October 7, 1998.

Newhouse, Dave. "Aching Snake Bites Bills." *Oakland Tribune*, November 29, 1977: 21.

———. "Big Play Finish Saves Raiders." *Oakland Tribune*, November 14, 1977: 23.

———. "Blue Cross Raiders in Playoffs." *Oakland Tribune*, December 12, 1977: 25.

———. "49ers Celebrate Quietly." *Oakland Tribune*, December 21, 1970: 45.

———. "49ers Give It Away." *Oakland Tribune*, November 1, 1976: 33.

———. "Holding Sour Grapes." *Oakland Tribune*, October 11, 1976: 21.

———. "A Nose out of Shape." *Oakland Tribune*, December 19, 1976: 42.

———. "One Tough Raider Angel." *Oakland Tribune*, December 19, 1977: 23.

———. "Owen Earns Praise from the Opposition." *Oakland Tribune*, October 28, 1974: 29.

———. "A Prime-Time Raider Thriller." *Oakland Tribune*, October 4, 1977: 23.

———. "A Raider Sledgehammer." *Oakland Tribune*, September 19, 1977: 23.

———. "Raiders Crush the Broncos." *Oakland Tribune*, October 31, 1977: 21.

———. "Raiders Expect Stabler to Start." *Oakland Tribune*, November 28, 1977: 23.

———. "Raiders Like Baltimore's Style." *Oakland Tribune*, December 19, 1977: 23.

———. "Roughing Passer Call: Pats Blast Refs." *Oakland Tribune*, December 19, 1976: 39.

———. "Steeler Gamble Flops." *Oakland Tribune*, December 27, 1976: 35.

———. "Swann Admission: Hardnosed but Clean." *Oakland Tribune*, December 27, 1976: 37.

———. "'We'll Be Back' Vikings Accept It." *Oakland Tribune*, January 10, 1977: 19.

———. "Wild Card Only Raider Hope." *Oakland Tribune*, December 5, 1977: 23.

Newnham, Blaine. "Emotion Was Lacking." *Oakland Tribune*, December 21, 1970: 46.

———. "49ers Upstage the Raiders, 38–7." *Oakland Tribune*, December 21, 1970: 45.

"News About Our Boys in the Service." *Foley Onlooker*, November 2, 1944: 1.

"Picture Spread of Stabler and Doda Sells Out." *Lodi News-Sentinel*, November 1, 1979. https://news.google.com/news papers?nid=2245&dat=19791101&id=IHszAAAAIBAJ&s jid=tjIHAAAAIBAJ&pg=3646,89688&hl=en.

Porter, John. "Rookie Thumps 49ers: Raider Preview." *Oakland Tribune*, December 5, 1977: 23.

"Raider-Brown Quotes." *Daily Review* [Towanda, PA], October 10, 1977: 22.

"Raider-Charger Quotes." *Daily Review* [Towanda, PA], November 21, 1977: 28.

"Raider, Jet Quotes." *Daily Review* [Towanda, PA]. October 24, 1977: 23.

"Raider Loss Buoys Broncos." *Oakland Tribune*, December 5, 1977: 25.

"Raider-Seahawk Quotes." *Daily Review* [Towanda, PA], November 7, 1977: 23.

"Raider-Steeler Quotes." *Daily Review* [Towanda, PA], September 26, 1977: 22.

"Raiders Post-Game Chatter." *Oakland Tribune*, December 27, 1976: 37.

"Raiders Wallow, Swallow Broncs." *Oakland Tribune*, December 9, 1975: 35.

"Reactions of Raiders, Bears." *Oakland Tribune*, November 8, 1976: 33.

"Rebels to Throw in Search of Victory." *Anniston Star*, August 14, 1964: 7.

Richardson, Ken. "Raiders Just Had a Bad Day." *Daily Review* [Towanda, PA], October 17, 1977: 21.

Richmond, Peter. *Badasses: The Legend of Snake, Foo, Dr. Death, and John Madden's Oakland Raiders*. New York: Harper-Collins, 2010.

Ross, George. "Bills Create New Race in Grid East." *Oakland Tribune*, September 17, 1974: 35.

———. "Chiefs Wonder Where Raiders Went." *Oakland Tribune*, November 6, 1972: 49.

———. "Custer Had It Just as Bad." *Oakland Tribune*, October 10, 1972: 39.

———. "Daryle's Plan? Loosen 'Em Up." *Oakland Tribune*, October 18, 1971: 35.

———. "The Defense Rests." *Oakland Tribune*, September 18, 1972: 37.

———. "Elmendorf's Wry Tribute." *Oakland Tribune*, October 30, 1972: 35.

———. "Go You Bengals." *Oakland Tribune*, December 23, 1973: 29.

———. "Hank Intended to Open It Up." *Oakland Tribune*, October 1, 1973: 31.

———. "Hubbard Praises the Chiefs." *Oakland Tribune*, December 9, 1974: 33.

———. "It's Uphill for Sistrunk." *Oakland Tribune*, October 28, 1974: 31.

———. "John: Never a Doubt." *Oakland Tribune*, October 21, 1974: 29.

———. "Monte Johnson's Debut." *Oakland Tribune*, September 23, 1974: 31.

———. *Oakland Tribune*, November 15, 1971: 39.

———. "Pete and Hank Light a Fuse." *Oakland Tribune*, December 9, 1973: 55.

———. "Plunkett's Everyday Play Crossed Up Raiders." *Oakland Tribune*, September 20, 1971: 36.

———. "Post-Game Game Plan." *Oakland Tribune*, December 21, 1970: 46.

———. "Precision Pros Ad Lib." *Oakland Tribune*, December 2, 1974: 32.

———. "Raiders Reaction—Disbelief." *Oakland Tribune*, December 31, 1973: 5.

———. "Ralston's Simple Blueprint: Run Right at 'Em." *Oakland Tribune*, November 25, 1974: 43.

———. "Steelers Fought a Myth." *Oakland Tribune*, September 30, 1974: 30.

———. "Tatum's Save Turned Game Around." *Oakland Tribune*, October 11, 1971: 26.

———. "To Stuff a Lion." *Oakland Tribune*, November 11, 1974: 29.

"Sex Stars: Our Naked Celebrity Hall of Fame." *Partner Sex Stars*, 1981.

"60-Second Sports." *Oakland Tribune*, December 28, 1974: 8.

Smilgis, Martha. "The Super Bowl Was 'a Meat Market'— No, Not the Game, the Women After Ken Stabler." *People*, November 14, 1977. http://www.people.com/people/archive/article/0,20069536,00.html.

"Snake Betrayed by Mates' Errors." *Oakland Tribune*, October 23, 1973: 33.

Soliday, Bill. "Blanda of Old Ignites Raiders 27–23 Triumph." *Daily Review* [Towanda, PA], December 15, 1974: 31.

———. "Chiefs at Best, Raiders at Worst." *Daily Review* [Towanda, PA], October 13, 1975: 17.

———. "Interceptions Bring Raider Streak to End." *Daily Review* [Towanda, PA], October 17, 1977: 19.

———. "Lip Treatment Fails: Raiders Silence Cleveland." *Daily Review* [Towanda, PA], October 10, 1977: 19.

———. "Olander: The Giant Killer." *Daily Review* [Towanda, PA], November 21, 1977: 28.

———. "Raider Scoring Barrage Ends Seattle's Squawking." *Daily Review* [Towanda, PA], November 7, 1977: 19.

———. "Raiders Happy with 'Extras' in Win." *Daily Review* [Towanda, PA], December 18, 1972: 17.

———. "Raiders Play Keep Away from Broadway Richard." *Daily Review* [Towanda, PA], October 24, 1977: 19.

————. "Raiders' Victory Over Steelers Costly." *Daily Review* [Towanda, PA], September 26, 1977: 19.

————. "Rhubarb Corner." *Daily Review* [Towanda, PA], December 18, 1972: 17.

————. "Spoilsport Chargers Knee Raiders." *Daily Review* [Towanda, PA], November 21, 1977: 23.

"Sports News." *Foley Onlooker*, February 7, 1963: 16.

"Sports Spotlight." *Foley Onlooker*, December 21, 1961: 24.

"Sportswriter Predicts Baldwin Grid Stars Will Go to Alabama." *Foley Onlooker*, November 28, 1963: 8.

"Sportswriters Praise Stabler's Performance." *Foley Onlooker*, August 20, 1964: 1.

"Spring Football Game Will Be Played on March 24." *Foley Onlooker*, March 16, 1961: 8.

"Stabler, Johns Named Captains." *Anniston Star*, January 28, 1968: 27.

Stabler, Ken, and Berry Stainback. *Snake: The Candid Autobiography of Football's Most Outrageous Renegade*. Garden City, NY: Doubleday, 1986.

"Stabler Owes IRS $280,000." *Athens News Courier*, September 16, 2003: 3.

"Stabler Plans Return to Pro Football." *Anniston Star*, November 19, 1969: 7–9.

"Stabler Quits Team Because of Attitude." *Anniston Star*, July 30, 1969: 15.

Stephenson, Creg, and Kirk McNair. *Always a Crimson Tide*. Chicago: Triumph Books, 2011.

"Super Bowl Quotes." *Oakland Tribune*, January 10, 1977: 30.

"Tatum, Atkinson on Spot." *Oakland Tribune*, October 4, 1977: 21.

"Tatum's Tackle Saves the Day." *Oakland Tribune*, November 15, 1976: 23.

"Tide." *Anniston Star*, December 8, 1963: 16.

"Tigers' Spud Davis Named on All-South." *Anniston Star*, December 22, 1963: 35.

"Top Schools Claim Stars." *Anniston Star*, August 5, 1964: 18.

"Two from Baldwin to Play August 14 in All-Star Game." *Foley Onlooker*, July 24, 1964: 16.

"Two Home Basketball Games Are Scheduled for the Foley Lions." *Foley Onlooker*, January 24, 1963: 13.

"U. of A Homecoming Queen." *Cullman Times*, November 2, 1967: 11.

"Valentine's Day Massacre." *Oakland Tribune*, February 14, 1975: 19.

Valli, Bob. "Another One Right Out of Fantasyland." *Oakland Tribune*, December 19, 1976: 41.

———. "Blanda's Boots Haunt Bart Anew." *Oakland Tribune*, December 1, 1975: 37.

———. "Book on the Raiders Makes Keating Hero." *Oakland Tribune*, November 12, 1973: 29.

———. "Branch's Rare Game as Decoy." *Oakland Tribune*, November 15, 1976: 23.

———. "Brodie Didn't Forget 1957." *Oakland Tribune*, December 21, 1970: 47.

———. "Butterfingers Betray Vikes." *Oakland Tribune*, December 12, 1977: 37.

———. "The Call That Nailed the Steelers to the Wall." *Oakland Tribune*, December 23, 1973: 31.

———. "CD on Wrong Side of Field." *Oakland Tribune*, October 27, 1975: 33.

———. "Day of Joy for Team, Fans." *Oakland Tribune*, January 10, 1977: 1.

———. "Denver's Big Tight Ends Exploit Raider Coverage." *Oakland Tribune*, October 23, 1972: 39.

————. "Eight Reasons the Bears Lost." *Oakland Tribune*, November 8, 1976: 33.

————. "53,039 Shares of Raider Game Ball." *Oakland Tribune*, December 29, 1975: 39.

————. "How the Oilers Pick a Winner." *Oakland Tribune*, December 15, 1975: 33.

————. "Loss Not the End for Miller." *Oakland Tribune*, October 31, 1977: 23.

————. "Madden Finds Plusses in Second Loss." *Oakland Tribune*, October 20, 1975: 33.

————. "Madden's Answers." *Oakland Tribune*, December 30, 1974: 29.

————. "Miracle to Forget Franco By." *Oakland Tribune*, December 22, 1974: 31.

————. "Never Been Beaten So Badly, Says Hank." *Oakland Tribune*, December 9, 1973: 55.

————. "A New Breed of Angries." *Oakland Tribune*, November 1, 1976: 35.

————. "No Dirty Play: Villains Bowl a Bust." *Oakland Tribune*, December 27, 1976: 37.

————. *Oakland Tribune*, December 13, 1976: 21.

————. *Oakland Tribune*, October 31, 1977: 21.

————. "An Official Brouhaha." *Oakland Tribune*, October 18, 1976: 33.

————. "Phillips Wasn't Surprised." *Oakland Tribune*, October 4, 1977: 21.

————. "Prothro Wound Up Over Clock." *Oakland Tribune*, September 19, 1977: 23.

————. "Raiders Go Belly Up; Licked by a Rookie." *Oakland Tribune*, September 20, 1971: 33.

————. "Raiders Sniffed Ralston's Rose Bowl Gadget." *Oakland Tribune*, December 17, 1973: 39.

———. "Raiders' Playoff Foe Format." *Oakland Tribune*, December 12, 1977: 25.

———. "Rallying Raiders Crush Eagles." *Oakland Tribune*, October 18, 1971: 33.

———. "Rodgers Railroaded." *Oakland Tribune*, September 19, 1977: 25.

———. "Rotor-Raiders Rip Chargers; Front Four Plus Three." *Oakland Tribune*, September 27, 1971: 33.

———. "Steeler's Plan: Run, Run, Run." *Oakland Tribune*, December 30, 1974: 30.

———. "Super Bowl Ticket Race On." *Oakland Tribune*, December 27, 1976: 1.

———. "Super Stopper No. 7." *Oakland Tribune*, January 5, 1976: 35.

———. "Swann Fears for His Life." *Oakland Tribune*, September 13, 1976: 23.

———. "'They Undressed Us,' Says Forzano." *Oakland Tribune*, November 11, 1974: 31.

———. "A Tough Adjustment for Moore." *Oakland Tribune*, November 29, 1976: 21.

———. "Tucker Calls Giants a Bunch of Quitters." *Oakland Tribune*, November 5, 1973: 33.

———. "Uppy Fit to Be Tied." *Oakland Tribune*, October 25, 1976: 29.

———. "Upshaw: Now We Can Lay Down—in Bed." *Oakland Tribune*, December 7, 1976: 33.

———. "Wright Blames Official for Bronco Loss." *Oakland Tribune*, December 9, 1975: 33.

"Vigor Edges Foley 2–1." *Foley Onlooker*, April 18, 1963: 16.

Walsh, John A. "Fear and Loathing at the Super Bowl." *Rolling Stone*, December 21, 1973. http://www.rollingstone.com /sports/features/fear-and-loathing-at-the-super-bowl-1974 0228?page=15.

"What Raiders, Chargers Said." *Oakland Tribune*, September 19, 1977: 25.

"What Raiders, Patriots Said." *Oakland Tribune*, October 4, 1977: 21.

"Who Will It Be This Year." *Anniston Star*, August 12, 1964: 13.

"Who's That Quarterback I Saw with You." *Fremont Argus*, December 7, 1975: 8–9.

"Who's That Quarterback I Saw with You." *Hayward Daily Review*, December 7, 1975: 8–9.

Williams, Pat, and Tommy Ford. *Bear Bryant on Leadership: Life Lessons from a Six-Time National Championship Coach.* Charleston, SC: Ford Advantage Media Group, 2010.

United States. Department of Commerce, Bureau of the Census. "Fifteenth Census of the United States: 1930." Alabama: 1930. 16B.

———. "Sixteenth Census of the United States: 1940." Alabama: 1940. 16B.

About the Author

Mike Freeman is a football columnist for Bleacher Report. He has previously been a writer for the *New York Times*, the *Washington Post*, the *Boston Globe*, the *Dallas Morning News*, CBSSports .com, and the *Florida Times-Union*. He is the author of eight books, including *Two Minute Warning: How Concussions, Crime, and Controversy Could Kill the NFL (and What the League Can Do to Survive)* and *Clemente: The True Legacy of an Undying Hero*.